ANGLICANISM AND THE BIBLE

The Anglican Studies Series

Theodore Alan McConnell
General Editor

What is Anglicanism?
by Urban T. Holmes III

The Spirit of Anglicanism
by William J. Wolf, John E. Booty & Owen C. Thomas

Anglican Spirituality
William J. Wolf, editor

The Anglican Moral Choice
Paul Elmen, editor

Anglicanism and the Bible
Frederick Houk Borsch, editor

Theology in Anglicanism
Arthur A. Vogel, editor

Anglican Theology and Pastoral Care
James E. Griffiss, editor

Anglicanism and the Bible

Frederick Houk Borsch, editor

Morehouse Barlow
Wilton

Morehouse Barlow Co., Inc.
78 Danbury Road
Wilton, Connecticut 06897

ISBN 0-8192-1337-3

Library of Congress Catalog Card Number 83-62717

Composition by The Publishing Nexus Incorporated,
1200 Boston Post Road, Guilford, Connecticut 06437
Printed in the United States of America

Contents

Introduction

Official statements of the Anglican and Episcopal Churches stress this Communion's faith that "The Holy Scriptures of the Old and New Testaments [are] the revealed Word of God."[1] Inspired by God the Bible is authoritative for the Church as "the ultimate criterion of its teaching and the chief source of guidance for its life."[2] "Holy Scripture containeth all things necessary to salvation"[3] and is "the rule and ultimate standard of faith."[4] These statements are echoed and expanded upon in other official documents and by various Anglican writers, frequently with reference to Hooker's formulation of the basis of Anglican belief and prctice being the three-cornered stool of Scripture, reason and tradition.[5] Often noted is the role which biblical language is given in the liturgies of Anglicanism and the central place of the reading and hearing of Scripture in worship. In Church discussions and debates on a variety of issues the Bible is regularly cited and sometimes expounded.

That the Bible has a central and unique position in Anglican life is clear, yet there has never been any easy agreement regarding the precise character and function of its authority. Anglicanism is far from alone in experiencing uncertainty about Scripture's role, but there are particular historical reasons which have fashioned special tensions in this Church's use of the Bible. The insistence of many of the reformers that the Bible must be the sole guide to Christian faith and practice was taken very seriously by a Church which yet valued and gave credence to a number of traditions which had developed during the early centuries of Christianity and had been subsequently interpreted in the ongoing life of the Church. Reformation Anglicanism could maintain that the Apostles', Nicene and Athanasian Creeds "may be proved by most certian warrants of Holy Scripture"[6] and that the Church has "power to decree Rites and Ceremonies, and authority in controversies of Faith" as long as it does not "ordain anything that is contrary to God's Word written."[7] Perceptive theologians like Hooker realized, however, that this acceptance of tradition introduced a measure of qualification of the *sola scriptura* of the more rigorous advocates of the reformation for, while Scripture might be said to dictate the development of creeds and certain Church practices, it was inevitable that they should also influence how Scripture itself was read. Nor could human reason, guided by the Holy Spirit, be excluded from this process. And is then "all things necessary to salvation" to be heard in a positive and inclusive manner, emphasizing the fullness of scriptural revelation for Christian living, or is it to be understood in a more minimalist fashion, excluding as authoritative any teaching which cannot clearly be based in Holy Scripture? If the former, the Bible might be used to dictate much of the conduct of public and private life. If, however, heard in minimalist terms, the Bible might allow for the development of new practices and understandings as long as they were neither contrary to Scripture nor taught as themselves necessary to salvation.

Subsequent generations tell the story of these tensions, sometimes felt more acutely, sometimes less so within the Churches of the Anglican Communion. Often the fact that those who held disparate views could yet agree that Scripture was the centerpiece of their argument disguised issues regarding the interpretation of Scripture and biblical authority. The challenges of the new scientific and historical consciousness, however, together with the new awareness of the claims of other religions, brought questions about scriptural authority and interpretation very much to the fore. Some Anglicans sought to restate the role of Scripture so that not only its unique place but its supremacy would be secured against the challenges of historical study, science and relativism. Over time others seemed so to yield the Bible's position that it became not the sole test or even the main test but *a* testimony about Christian faith. Most others sought intermediate ground and variations on the understanding of the primacy of Scripture for Christian living and belief. How the Bible could be said to be inspired also came to be a problematic issue for many Christians.

The six essays of this volume are not a comprehensive treatment of the history of the use of Scripture in Anglicanism, but they do highlight and explore essential themes and developments. William Haugaard's foundational chapter tells the story of the translation of the Bible into its English versions, during the course of which he describes many of the social, political and theological factors which fashioned the Anglican reformation and settlement. He examines how the Bible helped form the understandings of that time and how the translation, interpretation and use of Scripture were in turn shaped by the currents which flowed so strongly together through this period. In fascinating detail Marion Hatchett illustrates the controlling and pervasive role that the Scriptures were then given in Anglican worship, a role which has continued and developed through modern liturgical reforms. How Scripture has been read, how it has been prayed in liturgical language, and how it has been sung are the subjects of his comprehensive study of Anglican lectionaries, liturgies and use of the Bible in Church music.

By the early eighteenth century, however, the attitudes of deists and rationalists had begun to undermine the place of the Bible as the cornerstone of faith. Through John Booty's contribution we hear the voices of the reformers and missionaries of the eighteenth and early nineteenth centuries who were determined to restore the Bible to supremacy. We learn how the Bible was also given a primary role by the Tractarians within their understanding of Church and tradition.

But, as Booty notes at the end of his essay, the most serious forces of erosion were now gathering strength. The rising historical consciousness and the new historical-critical interpretations of the Bible seemed to a number of people to endanger the very possibility that the Bible could be regarded as inspired by God. The canons of historical research, although offering numerous new and valuable insights into the biblical writings, seemed also to make them into purely human compositions. Meanwhile the revolution in scientific understanding appeared to threaten many cherished Christian beliefs linked to the biblical worldview.

Reginald Fuller tells the story of how historical criticism was resisted, accepted and developed within the Anglican tradition, often causing uncertainty and pain, but bringing new directions for faith as well. Taylor Stevenson, writing as a contemporary Anglican theologian, takes a hard analytical look at the conflict between science and the Bible and finds it instead to be a conflict between the imperialistic and misguided claims of scientism and the biblical view of life as God's creation. The true spirit of science may be seen to arise from the biblical worldview and, while presenting myriad new understandings about the physical world, it is far from incompatible with biblical faith.

The final chapter presents a candid view of the present place of the Bible in Anglican faith and practice and concludes with a positive assessment. There are certainly causes for concern and criticisms to be made. Yet, while for some the Bible may seem to have lost its place of primacy in the life of the Church, it can be maintained that the Bible may today play an essential role in these Christian communities which is, in fact, nearer to its original place in Christian belief and living.

Throughout all the chapters there is a concern with what is sometimes called the Anglican *genius*; that is, a special ethos or character of Anglican tradition and life. Can it be seen in the role that Scripture is given in the Anglican Churches? Does a special Anglican character influence this Communion's ways of using and interpreting the Bible? Or does the central role of the Bible help shape the Anglican *genius*? Or, in the historical periods here under review and in the issues and themes examined, can we perceive a more complex interaction between the two?

1

The Bible in the Anglican Reformation

by William P. Haugaard

Practicing Anglicans outside England, who far outnumber worshiping members of the Church of England, share in the heritage of the English reformation. Yet they share ambiguously, for the political establishment of the Church that loomed so large in reformation life and thought and that still exists in a highly diluted form in England, no longer prevails in other churches of the Anglican Communion. As throughout sixteenth-century Europe, English politics and religion were intimately and formally interrelated, and sovereign and parliamentarians played major roles in the changes that took place in church life. Today, in those parts of the Commonwealth where overtones of a former legal establishment remain, Anglicans in those nations often regard them as more of a liability than an asset. On the other hand, Anglicans the world over, whether in Eastern or Western hemispheres, whether black, white, or oriental, whether using Prayer Books in English, Japanese, or Swahili, all have inherited a tradition that has been partly shaped by the events that took place in sixteenth-century England. Anglicanism emerged from sixteenth-century England as a particular way of understanding and practicing the Christian religion, and in spite of the many new developments and changes in the Church of England and her varied daughters, the period of its distinctive reformation remains crucial to an understanding of its character. Most Anglican theologians would insist that *no* period from the second century to the present can be regarded as a normative standard against which teaching and community life must be judged, but they would also agree that any accurate perception of the Anglican Christianity today or of its life in the intervening centuries requires an appreciative acquaintance with the sixteenth-century English church.

A Reformation Heritage: the Bible in English Religious Life

The role of the Bible in the Reformation Church of England provides one of the essential keys to an appreciation of a nascent Anglicanism. Illustrative of the change wrought by the Reformation in English attitudes toward the Bible are two works written a century apart by Thomas More and Francis Bacon. Both were men of letters who became Lord Chancellors, one under Henry VIII in whose reign the ties of authority between England and Rome were severed, the other under James I who succeeded to the throne after the Reformation had run its course. Each writer described an imaginary ideal human society across the seas: More in his *Utopia* of 1516, set in the "New World" and Bacon in his *New Atlantis* of 1627, set in an island somewhere off the Pacific coast of Peru. Citizens of Utopia already lived by a morality similar to that of Christianity; many embraced the new faith when More's narrator and his companions told them of "the name of Christ, His teaching, His character, His miracles, and the no less wonderful constancy of many martyrs whose blood freely shed had drawn so many nations far and wide into their fellowship." The narrator mentioned only one problem that faced the newly converted Utopians in establishing their church; they debated "whether, without the dispatch of a Christian bishop, one chosen out of their own number might receive the sacerdotal character." More did not try to resolve that problem of theology and church polity, but merely reported that, when the visitors left the island, although the Utopians had not yet chosen a candidate, it seemed that they would do so.[1]

In Bacon's tale, the official who welcomed the English travelers to New Atlantis described himself as a Christian priest by vocation, for his people had been Christians for centuries. Christianity had reached the distant island not through the preaching of a missionary, but rather by a "small ark or chest of cedar" which the apostle Bartholomew had committed to the seas at the direction of an angel and which had been borne to New Atlantis under a cross of light surmounting a great pillar. When the amazed islanders had opened the chest they found, along with a letter from the apostle Bartholomew, a book containing "all the canonical books of the Old and New Testaments."[2] Reading had converted them to the Christian faith, and they presumably had organized their church on the basis of what they read. The Bible, with no human interlocutor, provided all that they needed.

The contrast in these two manners of evangelization strikingly points up the change in attitudes toward the Bible in the English Church from 1516 to 1627. Not that the Bible was unimportant to More who welcomed Erasmus' Greek New Testament, approved its translation under authority, and continually quoted and alluded to holy Scripture. Yet it would never have occurred to More, as it did to Bacon, that the Bible and the receptivity of its readers were sufficient of themselves to create authentic Christian faith and practice with no further historical bonds to the larger community of Christians. By the end of the sixteenth-century reformation, the Bible as a *book* had assumed a role in the religious life of the English people which their forebears had never known—despite the many witnesses to a genuine reverence given to holy Scriptures throughout the centuries.

Quite apart from Anglicanism, the history of modern England requires attention to the role of the Bible in English life, for the social and political history of the nation, at least through the nineteenth century, is intimately bound up with the changing and often conflicting religious convictions of English men and women. In spite of the significant, but relatively small Roman Catholic segment of the English population in earlier times, national identity became increasingly defined in response to the pressures of international politics which nurtured English suspicion of continental Roman Catholic powers and their sporadic intrigues with English sympathizers. The nation became "Protestant England" in the minds of her citizens and foreigners alike. Regardless of the substantial differences between the Church of England and both dissenters at home and Lutheran and Reformed churches abroad, their usual common front, with its pervasive political implications, against papal Rome provided a far more decisive division in the minds of Roman Catholics and Protestants alike than the differences of these latter with one another. Roman Catholics claimed that the continuing magesterium of the Church, finding its focus in the papal office, expressed and defined authentic Christian teaching and practice. The other bodies of the sundered western church countered with their claim that the Bible, as each group understood and interpreted it, provided a far more certain test of an orthodox faith and catholic community life. English churchmen expressed a judgment common among these Protestants in the preface in the King James' Bible of 1611 that the Bible was

> a fountain of most pure water springing up unto everlasting life. And what marvaile? The originall thereof being from heaven, not from earth; the authour being God, not man; the enditer [composer], the holy spirit, not the wit of the Apostles or Prophets; the Pen-men such as were sanctified from the wombe, and endewed with a principall portion of Gods spirit; the matter, veritie, pietie, puritie, uprightnesse; the forme, Gods word, Gods testimonie, Gods oracles, the word of trueth, the word of salvation, &c. the effects, light of understanding, stablenesse of perswasion, repentance from dead workes, newnesse of life, holinesse, peace, joy in the holy Ghost; lastly, the end and reward of the studie thereof, fellowship with the Saints, participation of the heavenly nature, fruition of an inheritance immortall, undefiled, and that never shall fade away.[3]

Such fulsome recommendation of the Bible is not the exclusive property of heirs of the sixteenth-century reformation, and the author of this preface drew heavily from church fathers for examples of exaltation of the Scriptures. Nonetheless, it strikes an emphasis in Christian faith and devotion that was central to the English Church and other Protestants who pitted the Holy Writ against the Holy See of Rome.

Gutenberg Ingenuity and Renaissance Learning

In the first printed English Bible of 1535, the translator and editor Miles Coverdale had written in his prologue:

> Methink we have great occasion to give thanks unto God, that he hath opened unto his church the gift of interpretation and of printing, and that there are now at this time so many, which with such diligence and faithfulness interpret the scripture, to the honour of God and edifying of his people.[4]

With enthusiastic rejoicing, Coverdale welcomed the printing press and the literary accomplishments of Renaissance humanists. Inventive technology and academic intellectual curiosity had forged the two tools that enabled the words of the Bible to become forceful instruments of change. The Scriptures of the Old and New Testaments captured the minds and hearts of many with such might that they questioned established ways of thinking about God and his Church. Words proved to be, as always, dangerous in the eyes of established interests, for changes in thought led to changes in time-honored patterns of religious, political, and economic life.

Printing by movable type revolutionized the use of language 'n two ways: it provided standardized texts—impossible when manuscripts had to be copied one by one—and it enabled ideas to be disseminated with a rapidity that the western world had never known.[5] The texts of the Scriptures themselves, in the original Hebrew and Greek, in the international language of learning and liturgy, Latin, and in the various spoken languages of western Christendom could be made available to the growing number of competent readers. Contemporary interpreters of the Bible could spread their understandings abroad in books and pamphlets that reached from Poland to Scotland and from Sweden to Italy.

The learning of the humanists complemented the technology of printing. Literary scholars explored the range of meanings in the common European and in the three classical tongues. A widening circle of western students mastered Greek and a more exclusive fraternity, Hebrew. Latin had ceased to belong primarily to the clergy and religious as increasing numbers of the nobility and the middle classes found the mastery of Latin both useful for politics and business and a rewarding skill for diversions. The proportion of people who could read even their own spoken language constituted a minority of the total, but it was a growing minority. These literate citizens, with their varying linguistic skills, included those whose decisions determined the future course of European societies. Increasingly rare in the sixteenth century was the illiterate political leader who maintained his rule solely by military prowess. With this quickening of linguistic pursuits, skills in translation had been honed to a sharpness unknown for centuries. Religious reformers were nurtured on the linguistic fruits of the humanists. Luther urged civic officials to support schools that might produce scholars

> who can dig into Scripture, expound it, and carry on disputations. A saintly life and right doctrine are not enough.... Languages are absolutely and altogether necessary in the Christian church.[6]

English reformers were not less indebted to humanistic studies. When Coverdale wrote "interpret" or "interpretation," the words carried with them the older sense of "translation" as well as that of exposition or explanation. He declared that God had provided his Church with the gifts of "interpretation" and of "printing" which made possible a Bible in English.

The Bible in the Middle Ages

The Reformation did not suddenly introduce the Bible as a book unknown to the people of England. Religious life and culture of the Middle Ages, in England as in the rest of Europe, was steeped in the lore of the Bible. One scholar has gone so far as to say that "medieval culture was essentially biblical culture."[7] The rhythm of the calendar responded to the church year, and the celebrations of Christmas, Epiphany, Easter, and Pentecost, together with the solemn observances during holy week, were all important community events, closely intertwined with liturgical observances that called to mind the biblical events which were commemorated. The Epistle and Gospel were read in the Latin Mass regularly attended by most men and women and daily celebrated in most parish churches and religious houses of monks and nuns. Sermons were preached which drew on these liturgical propers or other parts of Scripture. Drama in the later Middle Ages emerged in religious dress, and some cycles of mystery plays, based on biblical stories and usually performed in churches, depicted the whole course of salvation history from creation to the last judgment. Scenes, colorfully painted on the walls and shining through stained glass windows in cathedrals and many parish churches depicted popular stories of the Bible. The crucifix set on the rood screen between nave and choir, usually flanked by statues of Mary and John, proclaimed the climactic events of the four gospels. In a pre-Gutenberg world people were attuned to such visual presentations to a degree that is difficult for us to appreciate; they were able to absorb the contents as a child who listens intently to an oft-repeated and well-loved bedtime story. When the conservative bishop, Stephen Gardiner, a few months after Henry VIII died, protested the destruction of images by the reforming authorities, he pointed to the value of images, described a few years earlier in regulations for their use as "the books of unlearned men." Gardiner, so much closer to the Middle Ages than we, drew a parallel that our word-conscious age can only partially appreciate:

He that cannot rede the scripture written about the Kinges great seale, . . . yet he can rede Sainct Georg on horsback on the one side, and the Kinge sitting in his majestie on the other side; and readeth so much written in those images as, if he be an honest man, he wil put of[f] his cap.[8]

So much of the social and cultural lives of the people in medieval times was centered in the Church that, inevitably, they were exposed to extensive portions of the scriptural saga.

Those with special church vocations were, of course, more deeply immersed in biblical literature. In the religious houses, the sevenfold daily office brought the men and women of monastic communities to their chapels to offer God praise in forms largely built on the psalter, by intention to be recited in its entirety in the course of a week. If the biblical lessons at Matins were arbitrarily arranged, and lessons in other offices limited to invariable fragments, sections of the Bible were often read in course during mealtime. The small proportion of clergy who studied theology in the universities after their education in the arts concentrated on the dual poles of the Bible and systematic theology as it was summarized in the *Sentences* of Peter Lombard. Even though a thirteenth-century scholar such as the Franciscan Roger Bacon could complain that "the reading of holy scripture itself is of small account compared to the study of [the] *Sentences*," nonetheless graduates in theology were expected to be able to discern the various levels of scriptural interpretation: the literal meaning, its tropological implications for Christian morality, the allegorical significance of particular passages for God's acts in creation and redemption, and the anagogical meanings pointing toward the finalities of heaven and hell.[9] Matthew Tyndale, the pioneer of sixteenth-century English biblical translators, was typical of Protestant critics of medieval biblical criticism when he insisted that the senses tropological and anagogical were "altogether unnecessary" since "this word allegory comprehendeth them both, and is enough."[10] Yet whatever the limitations and frequent artificiality of the fourfold system, it provided a flexible instrument which allowed for a variety of imaginative interpretation. The more able medieval biblical interpreters always had understood Tyndale's point that a large part of the interpretive task is found in the interface between what seems to be the literal sense of the words and their farther-reaching spiritual implications.[11]

In spite of the wealth of biblical materials which enriched

medieval life, the liturgical public readings of scripture were in a language that most people could not understand, vernacular translations were almost non-existent, and the laity were dependent upon the teaching of their parish clergy. In a 1530 proclamation prohibiting for the time being English translations of the Bible, Henry VIII summarized the situation when he declared that

> it shall nowe be more convenient that the... people have the holy scripture expoun[d]ed to them, by preachers in their sermons, accordynge as it hath ben of olde tyme accustomed before this tyme.[12]

Unfortunately, the majority of parish priests did not possess the learning that graced most of the preachers of the chapels royal or other pulpits from which the king heard scriptural expositions. Not only were most parish clergy not university graduates; many could not read Latin freely and some could not translate it at all. From time to time, concerned bishops and synods issued regulations affirming the responsibilities of parish clergy to instruct their people, usually advising them to build such instruction about the articles of the creed, the ten commandments, the Lord's Prayer, the sevenfold groups of sacraments, sins, virtues, and works of mercy. All of these implied scriptural teaching, but did not direct attention to the Bible. None of the manuals intended to guide parish priests in the care of their people urged them to study the Bible themselves or to encourage their people to do so, nor to translate the eucharistic lections in their sermons. Margaret Deansely has summarized the situation of the medieval clergy in a description that aptly applies right up to the time of the Reformation:

> However hard working and zealous [the parish clergy] might have been, their proper work was always regarded as the administration of the sacraments, the teaching of the elements of the faith, and the exhortation to lives of virtue; it did not include personal study of the Bible, or much preaching on the biblical text to their parishioners.[13]

Vernacular translations of the Bible were rare indeed in the Middle Ages. Portions appeared in occasional conflations of the Gospels in unified lives of Christ, such as that of St. Bonaventure, meditations on the passion of Jesus, the popular *Golden Legend*, largely, but not entirely consisting of the lives of post-biblical saints, and summary versifications of salvation history in which biblical stories mingle with apocryphal materials. Vernacular Bibles tended to be associated with dissident groups whom church authorities regarded as heretics. In England the Oxford scholar John Wyclif, as part of his theological program for the renovation of church and society, initiated and encouraged the translation of the Bible into English, so that, as he judged, clergy and people might clearly understand how far the church had strayed from its biblical roots. A quarter century after his death the Archbishop of Canterbury wrote the Pope that "this pestilent and wretched...son of the old serpent...endeavoured by every means to attack" sacred doctrine, devising "the expedient of a new translation of the scriptures into the mother tongue."[14] As part of the response to the Lollard followers of Wyclif, a provincial synod held at Oxford in 1408 ordered that, except with the approval of the synod or the diocesan bishop, no translation of the Bible was to be allowed, nor, under penalty of excommunication, was anyone to read the present or future Wycliffite versions in circulation.[15] These Oxford constitutions were at least partially responsible for the failure of English printers to publish any vernacular Bibles before the Reformation. The Lollard movement, however, did not die, and, illegal though they were, a sufficient number of manuscripts have survived to demonstrate that small coteries of sectarian believers scattered in the towns of the nation eagerly copied and preserved the texts of the Wyclif Bibles. The consistent efforts of ecclesiastical authorities to stamp out Lollardy throughout the fifteenth and early sixteenth centuries were not entirely successful, but they ensured that the supporters of "orthodoxy" would view an English Bible with the most profound suspicion. Even such a staunch humanist and friend of Erasmus as Thomas More wanted diocesan bishops, not only to oversee and authorize translations, but to determine which persons in his diocese would be permitted to own portions of the Bible that he judged appropriate for them. More feared that

> who so wyll not unto the study of scrypture take the poyntes of the catholyke faythe as a rule of interpretacyon, but ... study to seke in scrypture whyther the fayth of the chyrche be trewe or not, he can not fayle to fall in worse errours and farre more jeoperdous than any man can do by phylosophy wherof the reasons and argumentes in matters of our fayth have nothynge in lyke authoryte.[16]

The Bible truly permeated medieval culture and religious life, but many of the changes that took place in England in the century after More's martyrdom can be directly related to the accessibility of the Bible to More's country men and women that followed close upon the separation of the English Church from Rome—a separation which More had protested with his death.

Continental Convictions:
Humanist, Lutheran, Reformed, and Roman Catholic

The Anglican Reformation of the sixteenth century can only be understood in relation to the larger pattern of events on the continent of Europe. Culturally and religiously, England belonged to western Christendom, and perhaps no aspect of the English Reformation more fully reflects this than the course of biblical translation and interpretation. English scholars, theologians, and prelates carried on their work among, and in response to, their counterparts among the interlocking humanist, Lutheran, Reformed, and Roman Catholic communities on the European continent.

Although literature, language, and the visual arts have provided historians with the first evidences of that humanist movement labeled "renaissance," religion was inevitably deeply involved from the beginning. The renaissance created both scholarly tools and a climate of opinion that underlay many changes in religious attitudes and understandings. The same intellectually exhilerating cry *"ad fontes"*—to the sources—that accompanied revivified interest in Homer and Cicero, led theologically inclined scholars first to the fathers of early Christian centuries and then, moving beyond the Latin text of the Vulgate Bible, to the texts of the Old and New Testaments in their original Hebrew and Greek.

Jewish communities in northern Italy, with newly fashioned Hebrew type, produced the first printed Old Testament in 1488. The peripatetic German Hebraist Johannes Reuchlin and scholars at the Spanish University of Alcala, more than any others, stimulated and facilitated Old Testament study among Christians. Reuchlin, whose travels took him throughout Germany, France, and Italy, produced a grammar and lexicon in 1506 which opened the door to the study of Hebrew in western Europe. He later clashed with a coterie of obscurantist Dominicans bent on destroying all Hebrew manuscripts on account of their heretical content. Not only did Reuchlin succeed in halting destruction of irreplaceable documents, but the ensuing furor called further attention to the importance of Hebrew studies. At the turn of the century, the Archbishop of Toledo, Ximenez de Cisneros, had founded the University of Alcala ("Complutum" in Latin) as a center of humanistic learning. In spite of the recent expulsion of the Jews from Spain, the nation, long a center of Jewish-Christian encounter, retained the resources for Hebrew linguistics. The polyglot Complutensian Bible, printed by 1517, authorized by the pope in 1520, and issued in 1522, included the Vulgate text of the Old Testament flanked by parallel columns of the Hebrew text and the Greek Septuagint version with its own interlinear Latin translation. At this same time, a Bible with rabbinical commentaries appeared under Christian auspices in Venice, and within two decades the Dominican Santi Pagnini in Lyons and Sebastian Munster in Protestant Basle had each produced literal Latin translations that enabled those who had not mastered the language to grasp the distinctive characteristics of the Hebrew text.[17]

Although the revival of Greek among western scholars was earlier and far more pervasive than the recovery of Hebrew, the Greek New Testament took longer to make its appearance than its antecedent which enjoyed Jewish interest and patronage. The New Testament was printed in the second decade of the sixteenth century, not in Italy where Greek studies were first renewed, but in those other two principal centers of renaissance scholarship: Spain and the upper Rhineland. In Alcala the sheets of the Complutensian polyglot New Testament, printed in 1514, waited for eight years to be published. In the meantime, the towering figure of the Christian Renaissance, Erasmus of Rotterdam, had published two editions of his New Testament text in Basle. When exemplars of the polyglot finally appeared, five times as many copies of Erasmus' New Testaments were already in circulation. His accompanying Latin renderings of the Greek departed from the authoritative Vulgate and evoked outraged protests from defenders of the prevailing orthodoxy.[18] They well knew that the biblical texts in the original languages provided an opportunity for the fresh interpretations that were beginning to challenge the accepted teaching of the church. Martin Luther posted his ninety-five theses in 1517. With the arrival of the Hebrew and Greek texts of the holy Scriptures into the center of western Christendom's arena of theological discussion and debate, the players found that they no longer shared a common understanding of the rules of the game to which they were so passionately committed.

The humanists not only provided the texts—they also insisted that the Bible could not be rightly interpreted unless its books were first understood as literary entities rather than simply as a collection of divine oracles. The skills of the grammarian who had developed tools better to understand a Homer or a Cicero could be effectively employed in biblical interpretation as well. Erasmus wrote in a letter to a friend:

> Mere knowledge of grammar does not make a theologian; still less does ignorance of it; and certainly some scholarship conduces to a knowledge of theology, while the want of it impedes such knowledge.[19]

The new tools of the humanists, emphasizing historical and

literary contexts made possible new perspectives on the well-worn literal and analogical interpretations of biblical texts.

Erasmus was committed to putting the text of scriptures into the hands of any who could read their vernacular tongue:

> I would desire all women should read the gospel and Paul's epistles.... I would to God that the ploughman would sing a text of the scripture at his plough-beam; and that the weaver at his loom with this would drive away the tediousness of time.... We cannot call any man a Platonist, unless he have read the works of Plato. Yet call we them Christian, yea and divines, which never have read the scriptures of Christ.[20]

The Rotterdam humanist never wavered from this conviction. Even after he took up the cudgel to attack Luther's teaching, he ridiculed a cliché of the age:

> "If the people be allowed to treat of the holy scriptures, there is a danger that, coming into places of little respectability, they will be handled by hands anointed with leather and grease." O weighty reasons! As if holy scriptures are not considered worthy of common use if they are not amidst silken garments and are not to be handled by hands unless they have been anointed with balsam.[21]

Christian humanism represented by Erasmus laid the foundation for an understanding and use of the Bible within the Christian community: scholarly acquaintance with the text in the original tongues, developed linguistic and literary skills for their interpretation, and a concern for translations into the common languages so that those literate, at least in the tongue they spoke, might read for themselves the account of God's acts of revelation and redemption.

The continental reformers of the sixteenth century discovered in the pages of scripture teachings which they judged to be ignored or even contradicted by current church teachings and practices. Ulrich Zwingli in Zurich described his own experience:

> When I was younger, I gave myself overmuch to human teaching.... But eventually I came to the point where led by the Scriptures and Word of God I saw the need to set aside all these things and to learn the doctrine of God direct from his own Word.[22]

In commenting on Psalm 111:20, "The fear of the Lord is the beginning of wisdom," Martin Luther wrote that to become wise, "one must regard [wisdom] to be God's word; then everything can be learned easily." People who do so regard Scriptures determine to "listen with seriousness and awe, as one ought to listen to a God...[and he] can teach such people anything through his word."[23] John Calvin wrote that "no one can get even the slightest taste of right and sound doctrine unless he be a pupil of Scripture."[24] Zwingli and Calvin, the best known of the founders of the theological tradition of the Reformed family of churches, were at one with Martin Luther in stressing both the primary doctrinal authority of the Bible and the need for baptized Christians to become directly acquainted with its teachings.

These reformers were staunch churchmen and, in urging individual Christians to read the Bible, they, in no sense, intended that they should interpret Scriptures for themselves. Martin Luther did not challenge current church teaching as a private Christian, but as a professor of Scripture to whom the Church had granted the doctorate precisely in order to authorize him to interpret Scripture:

> I was forced and driven into this position in the first place, when I had become a Doctor of Holy Scripture against my will. Then, as a Doctor in a general free university, I began, at the command of pope and emperor, to do what such a doctor is sworn to do, expounding the Holy Scriptures for all the world and teaching everybody. Once in this position, I have had to stay in it, and I cannot give it up or leave it yet with a good conscience, even though both pope and emperor were to put me under the ban for not doing so. For what I began as a Doctor, made and called at their command, I must truly confess to the end of my life.[25]

Luther criticized the curriculum which ordered that the Bible be taught at the bachelor's level and Peter Lombard's textbook, the *Sentences*, at the doctoral level.[26] Biblical interpretation must be at the apex of the theological enterprise which enables the Christian community to understand the scriptural message. Calvin claimed New Testament precedent for making "doctors" one of the four permanent offices of ministry. In describing the teaching responsibilities of a pastor in a particular cure, Calvin allows that they may be "assigned the name of doctors, but only if we recognize a distinct class of doctors who have charge of both the formation of pastors and the instruction of the whole church."[27] The continental reformers labored diligently so that individual Christians might hear and read the words of the Bible, but they were to be guided by the authoritative teaching of those learned in the Scriptures.

Lutherans and Reformed disagreed in their understanding of the application of biblical norms to church life in their own day. In general, the Lutherans judged that the Church might use anything proper and expedient which was not expressly prohibited by the Bible; the Reformed required a specific biblical sanction for establishing practices and structures in the worship and organization of the Church. Luther declared that he was not "of the opinion that the gospel should destroy and blight all the arts, as some of the pseudo-religious claim"; rather, he "would like to see all the arts . . . used in the service of Him who gave and made them."[28] The Reformed attempted to follow Calvin's principle by which he approved "only those constitutions which are founded upon God's authority, drawn from Scripture, and, therefore, wholly divine."[29]

Lutheran and Reformed also differed in their attitudes toward the deutero-canonical or apocryphal books of the Old Testament which were not in Hebrew Bibles, but were in the Septuagint which early Christians took over from Greek-speaking synagogues. Luther included these books in his German Bible, which became a national theological and literary classic, but he commented that they were to be read for edification, not for the determination of doctrine, substantially reflecting the stance that Jerome had taken when he had translated the

Vulgate. For Luther, the Word was always primarily God's deed, and the undoubtedly canonical books of the written "Word of God" varied in their capacity to convey that primary deed of revelation. A sharp distinction between canonical books and the Apocrypha was less important a tool for theological discrimination than a right understanding of the meaning of law and gospel. The Reformed, deeply influenced by the humanists' dedication to the literary text, regarded the authority of Scripture to be more equally distributed throughout the biblical books, and, therefore, they insisted that the limits of canonical authority be clearly defined. Reformed translators continued generally to include the Old Testament Apocrypha, but Reformed churches carefully avoided any use, such as liturgical readings of these books, which might imply that they carried the same authority as the divinely inspired canon.

The reformers' appeals to biblical authority convinced those in the western church who remained loyal to the papacy that popular use of the Scriptures could only lead to heresy. When the Council of Trent opened discussion on the Bible in 1546, voices from France and Spain urged a flat prohibition of vernacular Scriptures, but the council refused to go so far. Trent declared the Latin Vulgate to be the authentic text for "public lectures, disputations, sermons, and expositions," and required ecclesiastical approval for the text and notes of any published edition of the Vulgate or translation. The council included the Old Testament apocryphal books among those "of which God is the author," and they were listed in the traditional order which scattered them among the other Old Testament writings. In its most controversial decision concerning the Bible, the council declared that "all saving truth and rules of conduct... are contained in the written books and the unwritten traditions" from Christ and the apostles.[30] Although some twentieth-century Roman Catholic theologians insist that the decree means that the unwritten traditions must be tested against the written Scriptures, generally opponents and supporters at the time understood that the decree placed tradition alongside the Bible as an equally valid source of teaching authority. The climate of the Roman Catholic Church in the sixteenth century discouraged priests and people from taking advantage of the opportunities for the use of the Bible in devotion and study which humanist scholarship and Gutenberg's press had made possible.

The English Church reflected the interaction of humanist, Lutheran, Reformed, and Roman Catholic theologians and ecclesiastics in the larger European scene to which they belonged. English attitudes and policies toward the Bible and its interpretation developed as the English people responded to, and participated in, the conflicts of the reformation.

The Struggle for an English Bible

Continental influences from reformers and humanists merged with the native Wycliffite stream in England to produce pressures for the production of a vernacular English Bible. The resistance, however, was fierce. The strictures on vernacular Bibles in the Oxford constitutions were still observed and willingly supported by most church officials who wanted no part of the disturbances in Germany. Henry VIII had been introduced to a level of humanist and theological learning unusual for royalty, but he was constitutionally a conservative in religion—as might be suggested by the title "Defender of the Faith" given him by Pope Leo X for his anti-Lutheran treatise *Assertio Septum Sacramentorum*.[31] In the sea of conflicting currents regarding an English Bible at the time of the formal break between Luther and the papacy, it would have been difficult to predict that a vernacular translation would have been produced and authorized within twenty years. A few English clerics, however, acting on their own initiative and their commitment to reform, single-mindedly pursued the goal of providing the holy Scriptures in their mother tongue. When the swirl of political events in court and parliament provided opportunities for advancing the cause of the English Bible, the reformers were ready.

By the time that the Lutheran movement emerged at the beginning of the third decade of the sixteenth century, humanism had already secured an influential place in English religion and scholarship. Although reformation England did not contribute to the fundamental ground-work of humanistic learning as it was to do in later centuries, its intellectual life was as profoundly influenced by renaissance currents as any nation in Europe.[32] Corpus Christi and Cardinal (later Christ Church) colleges at Oxford and Christ's and St. John's at Cambridge were all founded in the early sixteenth century as centers of humanistic scholarhip. John Colet, Thomas More, and Erasmus himself all witness to the penetration of renaissance thought in English religion on the eve of the reformation. Colet, one of stream of Englishmen who imbibed the heady new learning in late fifteenth-century Italy, became Dean of St. Paul's as the new century began. He had brought back a knowledge of Greek, an understanding of historical perspective in literary analysis, and a zeal for biblical studies. When he preached on the letters of St. Paul, he dealt not with isolated texts, but with the larger context of the writing as a whole and with the human situation and circumstances to which it was addressed. He preached a course of sermons on a gospel book so that his congregation might perceive Jesus as the writer had portrayed him. Erasmus, who had visited England at the turn of the century, returned at the invitation of the youthful Henry VIII to spend seven years in London and Cambridge where he completed his work on the New Testament. Colet nourished Erasmus' own bent for treating biblical writings as literary entities rather than collections of isolated dicta, and, with the younger Thomas More, they encouraged one another's enthusiasm for scriptural learning. The universities, the capital city of London, and the court of the Renaissance King Henry all were centers where scholars and students, statesmen and dilettantes discussed and debated the fruits and issues of the Christian humanism which, inevitably, directed attention to the holy Scriptures. When the storm of the reformation broke, the stream of English humanists, like those on the continent, divided between those who, like Erasmus and More, read in their Bibles the message of Christian unity and opposed the sundering of the western church and those who found in it teachings demanding reform of doctrine and practice whatever might be the cost to western unity. These latter could all echo Coverdale's thanks to God that the humanists' "gift of interpretation," along with printing and scholarly dedication, eventually made possible the English Bible.

Lutheran publications had already appeared in England by 1520, the year in which the pope excommunicated Luther and the reformer, in turn, burned the bull of excommunication, together with a book of canon law, symbolically repudiating papal authority. In centers of trade and scholarship, there were the curious and the devout who read the reformers' contraband literature with increasing commitment. English and foreign merchants of London and of East Anglia included numbers of lay persons whose attraction to the new articulation of Christian teaching was at least partly aroused by its emphasis on scriptural authority. Some could read the Latin Vulgate, and a few had access to vernacular Lollard manuscripts of the Bible. Many more lay folk gained a new sense of a revelation which they could grasp for themselves as they heard biblical words read aloud or as they studied quotations in popular pamphlets. The new ideas from across the North Sea whetted appetites for an English Bible.

Oxford and Cambridge were inevitable battlegrounds for the new ideas. Some younger scholars were, as in every generation, susceptible to new ideas that challenged established orthodoxies. Although evidence suggests that both universities harbored their Lutheran sympathizers, Cambridge provided the larger proportion of reformers. Its location in East Anglia and the recent residence of Erasmus at the university both contributed to the growth of the Cambridge concern for reform. Among the reformers at Cambridge in the late teens and early twenties of the century were Augustinians Robert Barnes, the prior of the Oxford community, and Miles Coverdale, Observant Franciscan friar William Roy, and the secular priests William Tyndale, who came with his two Oxford degrees to study at Cambridge, George Joye, and two future archbishops of Canterbury, Thomas Cranmer and Matthew Parker. These were all to play significant roles in the promotion of an English Bible.[33]

Whatever may have been the indirect influence of the Wycliffite biblical manuscripts circulating in England in the early sixteenth century, the initial work for the translation and printing of the modern English Bible was done, not in Britain, but across the North Sea on the continent. The arrival of Lutheran ideas and literature on English shores had reinforced the natural inclination of conservative administrators to withhold the approval required by the Oxford constitutions before anyone might "translate any text of Holy Scripture into the English or other language, by way of a book, pamphlet, or tract."[34] Accordingly, when William Tyndale, the pioneering translator of the modern English Bible, sought the patronage of the learned and humanist Bishop of London, Cuthbert Tunstall, he was flatly turned down. Crossing to the continent in 1524 to accomplish his chosen task, he began translating the New Testament, and before he was executed as a heretic a dozen years later, Tyndale had published English versions of all the books of the New Testament, six books and scattered passages of the Old, and he had nine more Old Testament books in manuscript. At home in England, the ecclesiastical ties with Rome now severed, an authorized vernacular Bible was about to appear. Tyndale was closer to his goal than he could have known when, as the martyrologist John Foxe reported, he cried "at the stake with a fervent zeal and a loud voice, 'Lord! open the king of England's eyes.'"[35]

Tyndale combined humanist skills in language with the fervor of one who had gained through the Gospel unleashed by Luther a new vision of the meaning of human life. Comparative analyses have established the fact the Wycliffite versions influenced Tyndale, if at all, only through repeated and remembered phrases.[36] Tyndale had thoroughly mastered Greek and gained sufficient grasp of Hebrew to make effective use of the text. He worked on the New Testament from Erasmus' Greek text with the aid of Luther's German translation and two Latin versions, the Vulgate and that of Erasmus. His proficiency in German enabled him to find in Luther's words and phrasing suggestions for English equivalents of Anglo-Saxon origin that more forcefully rendered the Greek. In translating the Old

Testament, Tyndale's ability to make use of available grammars and lexicons enabled him to use the Hebrew along with the familiar Latin vulgate and the Greek Septuagint versions. Tyndale was not the type of humanist whose immersion in classical languages dulled his affection for his mother-tongue; rather he sifted the words and crafted the sentences of English with such discrimination that much of his work has remained a permanent part of our literary heritage. Over one-third of the wording of the New Testament in the King James Version maintains his wording and so much of the rest his structural frame that ninety percent has been identified as bearing the stamp of the powerful simplicity and engaging rhythm of his style. Subsequent English versions of the Old Testament owe only a slightly smaller debt to Tyndale.

Tyndale's own debts to Erasmus and to Luther were profound. The English cleric honed his linguistic skills in the workshop of humanistic enthusiasm to which Erasmus had so largely contributed, and he employed the New Testament text that Erasmus had provided. Erasmus was Tyndale's tutor in religion as well as in scholarship. Between his residence in Cambridge and his unsuccessful attempt to secure Tunstall's support, Tyndale took a post as tutor to the children of a country gentleman. There, he translated for the spiritual nurture of the parents a book which he himself valued: Erasmus' *Enchiridion*, or *Manual of a Christian Soldier*. This popular early work of the Rotterdam humanist provided a practical guide for Christian devotion and life that evidently had appealed to Tyndale's religious instincts. In typical Erasmian fashion, the work directs the reader to the Bible:

> It is a common practice of the Holy Spirit to use water as a symbol of knowledge of God's law ... The frequent references in sacred writings to wells, fountains, and rivers suggests nothing less than a diligent scrutiny of the secret meanings of Scripture. For what is water hidden in the heart of the earth but mysterious truth hidden under the literal sense? And what is this same bubbling up as a spring but that mystery opened up and illuminated? And when this is amplified in both length and breadth, why should it

not be called a river? Therefore, if you will devote yourself to the study of the Scripture, if you will ponder the law of the Lord both day and night, you will have no fear...but be disciplined and trained against every onslaught of the adversary.[37]

After Tyndale had determined, as he later wrote, that not only "was no room in my lord of London's palace to translate the new Testament, but also that there was no place to do it in all England," his continental exile soon took him to Luther's Wittenberg where he probably completed his translation of the New Testament.[38] When the first edition was published in Germany in 1526, its arrangement, introductions, and explanatory notes all bore the marks of Luther's German work, a similarity not likely to commend it to authorities in England where Luther's writings had been solemnly burned by Cardinal Wolsey and theologically refuted by the king himself.[39] In the same year Tyndale published an introduction to Romans which was almost a paraphrase of Luther's preface to the book in his New Testament. By this time Erasmus had publicly attacked Luther's teaching, and Tyndale, like many other humanists, had clearly chosen to follow the German reformer rather than the Dutch humanist in his ecclesiastical loyalties. To the end of his life, Tyndale was not unjustly identified as a "Lutheran." Yet the Englishman read his Bible through a lens of increasingly different focus from that of Luther, a focus that he seems to have developed independently from that of the reformed theologians which it resembles. A modern historian has suggested that Tyndale was the leading theologian of a group of early English Protestants whose

interest ran more to morality than to theology....Whereas for Luther faith and justification primarily denoted the humble posture of forgiven sinners in the presence of a compassionate God, the Englishmen construed justification by faith as initiating a morally blameless life characterized by observing God's law in one's daily deeds.[40]

Tyndale owed much to both Erasmus and Luther, as he chose

and implemented his goal to make the holy Scriptures available to his countrymen and women in their own tongue. Neither of these honored teachers, however, wholly determined the message that Tyndale read and interpreted as he pondered the biblical texts.

Tyndale's New Testament received a warm welcome from English who sympathized with continental reformers and a fiery repudiation by ecclesiastical authorities. Before 1526 was out, Bishop Tunstall, who had refused to patronize Tyndale's project, preached at a burning of the New Testament at Paul's Cross in London. Archbishop Warham of Canterbury devised a scheme to buy up all the copies of the book to prevent their illegal distribution. Although the scheme proved successful to a large degree in securing most of the initial editions, Tyndale and his colleagues simply used the profit to finance the continuation of their work. Antwerp, with its supply of printers, its proximity to England, and its colony of English merchants became the center from which reforming publications issued and were smuggled across the North Sea.

None other than the humanist Thomas More stood in the forefront of the opposition to the English New Testament. An increasingly prominent member of Henry's council and an uncompromising opponent of what he judged to be heresy, More took pen in hand in 1529 to try to stem the growing Lutheran threat in England in his *Dialogue concerning Heresies.* The English New Testament was a prime target in the lengthy work, and More accused Tyndale of choosing words that distorted the meaning of the biblical text in order to further Lutheran heresies:

> The confederacye betwene Luther and [Tyndale] is a thynge well knowen.... The cause why he chaunged the name of charyte and of the churche and of presthed is no very grete dyffyculte to perceyve. For syth Luther and his felowes ... [teach]that all our salvacyon standeth in faythe alone, and towarde our salvacyon nothynge force of good workes, therefore it semeth that he laboureth of purpose to mynysshe the reverent mynde that men bore to charyte, and therefore he chaungeth that name of holy vertuous

affeccyon in to the bare name of love, comen to the ver-
tuous love that man bereth to god and to the lewde love that
is bytwene [man and wife]. And for bycause that Luther
utterly denyeth the very catholyke chyrche in erth and
saythe that the chyrche of Cryste is but an unknowne
congregacyon of some folke, . . . [Tyndale] . . . tourneth it in
to the name of congregacyon. . . . Luther and his adher-
entys holde this heresy, that all holy order is noth-
yng. . . . [Tyndale] doth . . . therefore, . . . after his maysters
heresye, put awaye the name of prest in his translacyon as
thoughe presthed were no thynge.[41]

Tyndale wrote a lengthy reply to More, who, in the troublesome
final months before his resignation as Lord Chancellor, prepared his *Confutation of Tyndale's Answer*. More, who consistently defended the propriety of a properly authorized and
controlled vernacular translation, clearly stated the reason for
his opposition to Tyndale's New Testament. Responding to
Tyndale's accusation that More had never criticized his "dar-
ling" Erasmus when, in his Latin testament, he had used the
word the *congregatio* instead of the Vulgate's *ecclesia*, More
explained:

I have not contended wyth Erasmus my derlynge, bycause
I found no suche malycyouse entent wyth Erasmus my
derlynge as I fynde with Tyndale. . . . Erasmus . . . detesteth
and abhorreth the errours and heresyes that Tyndale
playnely techeth and abydyth by and . . . shall be my dere
derlyng styll. . . . Now for hys translacyon of *ecclesia* by *congregatio* hys dede is nothynge like Tyndals. For the laten
tonge had no laten word byfore used for the chyrche, but
the greke word *ecclesia*; therfor Erasmus in hys new translacyon gave it a laten worde. But we had in englysshe a
proper englysshe word [church]. . . . Erasmus also ment
none hereseye therein as appereth by hys writinge
agaunste heretykes, but Tyndale entended no thynge ellys
thereby as appereth by the heresyes that hym selfe techeth
and abydeth by.[42]

It was Tyndale's Lutheranism, not a linguistic error, that drew
More's polemical fire. Reformers and authorities alike viewed
the printed English testament an integral part of the Lutheran

program and campaign. After Henry consulted with the bishops and his council in 1530, he ordered that all persons with copies of "the newe testament or the olde translated into englisshe, beinge in printe" turn them in to their bishops or parish priests. At the same time, however, he declared that, once his people had abandoned "all perverse, erronious, and sedicious opinyons," and all heretical biblical translations and other books

> be clerely extermynate and exiled out of this realme of Englande for ever: his highnes entendeth to provyde, that the holy scripture shalbe by great, lerned, and catholyke persones translated in to the englisshe tonge, if it shall then seme to his grace convenient so to be.[43]

The references in Henry's proclamation to the Old Testament may refer to Tyndale's translation of the Pentateuch (Genesis to Deuteronomy) which had appeared in print five months earlier. Tyndale published the book of Jonah in 1531, and to a 1534 revision of the New Testament he appended the Old Testament passages that were used as liturgical epistles at mass on some days in the church calendar.[44] Whatever may have been his judgment about the faults in the form and understanding of the eucharist in the Latin rite, he intended to provide an aid by which lay persons might relate their scripturally based faith to the public worship at which they assisted. In Tyndale's 1530 Pentateuch, he wrote introductions and notes that struck much harder at ecclesiastical corruption and asserted more forcefully Lutheran teaching, modified by his increasing emphasis on obedience to scriptural law as a necessary fruit of faith. Yet in his revision of Genesis alone in 1534, he reduced the strident tone of these notes, and his final 1535 revision of the New Testament appeared unglossed. Apparently he felt that the Bible could speak its own message and that such editions might have a better chance of securing an accepted place in English society.

Various Englishmen were associated with Tyndale's translations during his self-imposed exile. The Observant Franciscan

William Roye joined him at Wittenberg and the two men together saw the initial New Testament through its printings at Cologne and Worms.[45] Tyndale described the strained personal relationship between the two men as he took advantage of Roye's proffered and needed assistance:

> As long as [Roye] had no money, somewhat I could rule him; but as soon as he had gotten him money, he became like himself again. Nevertheless, I suffered all things till that was ended, which I could not do alone without one, both to write, and to help me to compare the texts together. When that was ended, I took my leave, and bade him farewell for our two lives, and (as men say) a day longer.[46]

Although Thomas More and Cardinal Wolsey continued to link Tyndale and Roye in a common continental campaign of heretical propaganda aimed at English orthodoxy, the two men had clearly gone their separate ways. Three other Englishmen, however, were important to Tyndale's continued work on the Bible: George Joye, whose relationship with Tyndale was equally stormy, if more substantial than that with Roye, Miles Coverdale whose quieter involvement in Tyndale's work abroad was to establish his own principal vocational direction, and John Rogers who crossed to Antwerp in 1532 as chaplain to the English merchants and was close to Tyndale in his final years of work and imprisonment.

Joye, from his crossing to Antwerp in 1529, was in frequent and often acrimonious contact with Tyndale until returning to England in 1535. During this time he produced a series of biblical translations of his own. In his pioneering vernacular *Primer*, a lay devotional manual patterned after the medieval Latin books of hours, he included, along with other devotional and instructional materials, more than thirty psalms, an account of Christ's passion conflated from the four gospels, some prayers embedded in Scripture, and a few other scattered biblical passages.[47] At the beginning of 1530, Joy brought out an English translation of the Psalter, largely made from a Latin edition that the reformer Martin Bucer had just published in Strasbourg. Joye continued to translate parts of the Old Testament from such new Latin versions that were based on fresh studies of the Hebrew text: the books of Isaiah and Jeremiah and a second version of the Psalter, all from the Zurich reformer Ulrich Zwingli's translation, Proverbs from the Lutheran Philip Melanchthon's work, and Ecclesiastes from an as yet unidentified source.[48] Whether Tyndale and Joye ever collaborated in a plan to produce a full Old Testament remains an open question. Joye likely chose the Psalms for their devotional popularity; his choices of other Old Testament books suggests that, if he was not collaborating, he at least sought to avoid duplicating Tyndale's work. The two men exchanged bitter verbal jabs after Joye agreed to correct Tyndale's New Testament for an Antwerp printer who had published three editions full of errors. Joye not only corrected obvious errors which the Dutch typesetters made in English, but also sought to "improve" the translation, most glaringly substituting "life after this" for Tyndale's "resurrection" in a number of passages. Tyndale wrote that Joye "had not used the office of an honest man, seeing he knew that I was correcting it myself," but Joye insisted he took on the work because Tyndale "prolonged and differred so necessary a thing." Tyndale especially resented Joye's failure to acknowledge his own responsibility for the changes he introduced:

> I beseech George Joye, and all others, to translate themselves, whether from the Greek, Latin or Hebrew, or else (if they will) to take my translation and alter it, and publish the work under their own names, but not to play bo peep after Joye's manner.[49]

When Joye put out a second revised edition of the New Testament, he added the liturgical epistles from the Old Testament that Tyndale had included in his own revision which had been published between Joye's editions. Some of Joye's corrections found their way into these epistles in Tyndale's final revision of the New Testament.[50] Although partnership may be too strong a word to describe the joint efforts of the two English exiles to produce an English Bible, the minor contributions of

Joye did complement the major accomplishments of Tyndale. Even if Joye did not work from the Hebrew text, he translated from those who had taken advantage of contemporary Hebraic studies. Since Joye's *Psalter* appeared in print one day before Tyndale's *Genesis*, to him belongs the honor of producing the first complete Old Testament book in modern English.[51]

Miles Coverdale, according to John Foxe, met Tyndale by previous arrangement at Hamburg where he "helped him in the translating of the whole five books of Moses, from Easter till December, . . . 1529."[52] In the prefatory address to the reader of his 1535 English Bible, Coverdale acknowledges his own lack of learning in the biblical tongues in a tone that suggests that his expressions of humility reflected an attempt at honest self-appraisal rather than literary artifice:

> Considering how excellent knowledge and learning an interpreter of scripture ought to have in the tongues, and pondering also mine own insufficiency therein, and how weak I am to perform the office of a translator, I was the more loath to meddle with this work. . . . And to help me herein, I have had sundry translations, not only in Latin, but also of the Dutch [German] interpreters, whom, because of their singular gifts and special diligence in the Bible, I have been the more glad to follow.[53]

Lack of pretensions may have made Coverdale a far more congenial associate to Tyndale than either Roye or Joye had proven to be; in any case, no suggestion of personal conflict has left its mark on the historical record.

Coverdale assembled, translated, and edited the various sections of the English Bible in the succeeding years abroad. The first edition was printed in Cologne at the expense of a Dutch merchant in Antwerp, but the sheets were assembled and bound in England, and were being sold by early 1536.[54] The English ecclesiastical scene had changed radically since 1529. Henry VIII and his lords and commons in Parliament had promulgated a series of statutory laws repudiating papal authority, effectively establishing the juridical independence of the Church in England. The national need for a male heir to the throne and Henry's passion for Anne Boleyn combined to help convince the king that the papal dispensation for his marriage to his brother's widow, Catherine of Aragon, was invalid, contravening, as it did, a clear prohibition in the book of Leviticus. The theologically conservative Henry found himself aligned with the reformers on the crucial issue of scriptural versus papal authority. Parliament followed the king's lead, partially motivated by subservience to royal wishes and partially by more reasoned concerns: solicitude for orderly succession on Henry's death, recognition of widespread anticlerical sentiments, and a measure of genuine religious convictions about reform. Thomas Cromwell, who succeeded Cardinal Wolsey and Thomas More as Henry's chief minister, favored the reformers. At Canterbury, Thomas Cranmer, who had succeeded Archbishop Warham, brought not only his exposure to reforming ideas at Cambridge, but also firsthand experience of Lutheran reforms in Germany. The Convocations, consisting of the bishops and other clerical representatives, had formally repudiated papal authority. Even as the sheets of the Bible were on their way from Cologne to Southwark, Thomas More was beheaded for his refusal to endorse the king's new policies.

Coverdale judged the political hour ripe for his project and dedicated the Bible to Henry, pointing out in words calculated to win royal appreciation:

> The only word of God, I say, is the cause of all felicity: it bringeth all goodness with it, it bringeth learning, it genereth understanding, it causeth good works, it maketh children of obedience; briefly, it teacheth all estates their office and duty. ... it lighteneth all darknesses, ... letteth no prince be disobeyed, permitteth no heresy to be preached; but reformeth all things, amendeth that is amiss, and setteth everything in order.

Coverdale left his biographers a clue to his manner of working when he declared to the king, undoubtedly with More's strictures on Tyndale in mind, that with God to record his conscience,

I have neither wrested nor altered so much as one word for the maintenance of any manner of sect, but have with a clear conscience purely and faithfully translated this out of five sundry interpreters, having only the manifest truth of the scripture before mine eyes.[55]

Two Latin and two German Bibles have been clearly identified as four of these five sources: the Vulgate and the literal Old Testament translation of Santi Pagnini together with Luther's Bible and the Zurich Bible, the latter a collaborative effort of the Swiss reformers which had attained its standard textual form in 1531.[56] If Coverdale intended to indicate an Englishman as his fifth "interpreter," he could be none other than Tyndale from whose translations Coverdale drew heavily in the Pentateuch, Jonah, and the whole New Testament.[57] Joye's work finds only an occasional echo in Coverdale as, for example, when he once picks up Joye's coined word "backslider" which was to find later popularity with King James' translators.[58] Coverdale lacked competency in Hebrew and Greek, but in his ability to appropriate from German English equivalents with Anglo-Saxon roots and in his general mastery of the English language, he was the equal of Tyndale. As a modern commentator has observed,

Coverdale was no servile imitator; he had his own sense of what was suitable in expression, and even in those parts of his work that were based on Tyndale, he shows considerable independence of judgment in his literary style.[59]

Taking account of the legislation that declared Henry "chief head of the church of England," Coverdale declared that he thought it his duty, not only to dedicate the work to the king,

but wholly to commit it unto the same; to the intent, that, if anything therein be translated amiss, . . . it may stand in your grace's hand to correct it, to amend it, to improve it, yea, and clean to reject it, if your godly wisdom shall think it necessary.[60]

When Coverdale wrote these words, he had some knowledge of

pressures at court seeking to win Henry's approval of an English Bible. A petition at the end of 1534 from the bishops, abbots, and priors in the upper house of the Convocation of Canterbury asked the king to take measures to confiscate heretical literature, forbid lay arguments over doctrine, and to make better provision for the care of the poor. Among these conservatively unexceptional requests, they also asked that the Scriptures "be translated into the vulgar English tongue by certain upright and learned men to be named" by the king and be "delivered to the people for their instruction."[61] In effect they were asking Henry to implement the possibility he himself had suggested in his proclamation four years earlier. Cromwell had indicated sufficient personal interest in the project for the English distributor of Coverdale's Bible to write the royal official in August 1535 a letter accompanying copies of the dedication and of the sheets of Scripture which had already arrived in England:

> As your goodnes ever and only hath put forth your fote for the preferremente of goddes worde: even so that your mastership wyll now sett to your helpynge handes that the holye byble may come forth.[62]

Anne Boleyn, whose personal fortunes were firmly tied to anti-papal policy, provided another voice at court for the vernacular Bible. Matthew Parker, later Elizabethan archbishop of Canterbury, was her chaplain at the time, and he later described the court struggle in which conservative bishop Stephen Gardiner opposed the project which came to a temporary stall as Anne lost both Henry's favor and her head:

> By the favour and intercession of [Anne] permission was at last obtained from the king that the holy bible be printed in English and placed in every church in a place where the people might be able to read it. But this concession of the king did not yet take effect because his famous queen was soon afterwards beheaded.[63]

The following order was included in the initial version of

Henry's first set of royal injunctions, issued in his name by Thomas Cromwell in 1536, but it was subsequently withdrawn:

> Every parson ... shall ... provide a book of the whole Bible, both in Latin and also in English, and lay the same in the choir, for every man that will to look and read, ... and shall discourage no man [from reading, but rather] ... admonish every man to read the same, ... whereby they may the better know their duties to God, to their sovereign, ... and their neighbor: ... exhorting them that ... they do in no wise stiffly or eagerly contend ... but refer the declaration of those places that be in controversy to the judgement of them that be better learned.[64]

Had this injunction been promulgated and enforced, Coverdale's Bible, the only full vernacular edition in existence, would have fulfilled all the hopes with which its editor had sent it forth. As it was, Coverdale's work remained another year in the legal limbo of tolerated illegality.

The advocates of the Bible at court continued to press toward their goal. In summer of the following year Cranmer wrote Cromwell a note accompanying a new version of the English Bible:

> So farre as I have redde, ... I like it better than any other translacion hertofore made.... I pray you my Lorde, that you woll exhibite the boke unto the kinges highnes; and to obteign of his Grace, if you can, a license that the same may be sold and redde of every person ... untill such tyme that we, the Bishops shall set forth a better translacion, which I thinke will not be till a day after domesday.[65]

This is the Bible which bears the name "Thomas Matthew." The editor's real name, however, as contemporaries and most modern historians have judged, was John Rogers, resident chaplain to the English merchants in Antwerp during the last four years of Tyndale's life. The edition was printed in Antwerp, but bound and issued by English publishers.

Rogers based his Bible on the work of Tyndale and Coverdale. With access to Tyndale's manuscript translation of the historical books from Joshua through Chronicles, Rogers put these into print for the first time, and Tyndale's published books provided his basic text for the Pentateuch and the New Testament. Coverdale was his guide for all the rest with the exception of the Prayer of Manasses in the Apocrypha, which Coverdale had ignored. Rogers translated this brief book, relying principally on the 1535 French Bible of Calvin's cousin, Pierre Olivetan. The Frenchman also was the most important of the various continental authorities on whose work Rogers depended for the minor changes he introduced into the existing English texts. In contrast to Coverdale's unglossed Bible, Rogers included more than two thousand notes and various introductions and tables which he drew from both Tyndale and a cluster of continental humanist, Lutheran, and Reformed commentators.[66] Although Rogers does not reproduce the more militantly protestant notes of Tyndale's Pentateuch, he does include such material as Tyndale's paraphrase of Luther's introduction to Romans. Interpretative apparatus of this stripe was not calculated to endear the volume to conservative ecclesiastics. Nonetheless, royal permission was granted for Matthew's Bible to be sold in England. When Coverdale's version was reprinted this same year, 1537, in a folio and a smaller quarto edition, the latter explicitly testified to its legal status by royal license.

Although Tyndale did not quite live to see the day, in less than a dozen years after his New Testament had been solemnly burned by English authorities, vernacular English Bibles, to which he had so handsomely contributed, were publicly bought and read. Tyndale and his associates in the work of translation, in alliance with officials at church and court favoring reform, had gained their initial objective.

The Great Bible and the Use of Authorized Scriptures

The change in English attitudes toward the Bible had only just begun in 1537. Even among the theologically literate, attitudes still resembled those of Thomas More far more closely than those which Francis Bacon was to reflect nine decades later. A small nucleus of reformers, however, were determined to make Holy Scripture an integral and lively part of religious devotion and practice among congregations throughout the land. Their progress, culminating in the King James Bible in 1611, was to leave an indelible mark on English society.

In the years from 1536 to mid-1539 the reformers had good reason to hope that the legalized vernacular Bible would play an increasingly prominent role in the religious life of the nation. If they had lost a friend at court with the fall of Anne Boleyn, members of Jane Seymour's family were known to sympathize with their cause. Henry was sending and receiving political and ecclesiastical envoys to and from Lutheran Germany. Following the leadership of Archbishop Cranmer of Canterbury and of the king's Vicar-General in affairs ecclesiastical, Thomas Cromwell, the bishops and other clergy in and out of Convocations were promulgating mildly reforming doctrinal standards and encouraging pastoral and devotional reforms, which, if they fell far short of gospel norms as perceived by continental protestants, nonetheless boded well for the future.

Although the proposed 1536 order for a Bible to be set up in every church had been withheld, some authorities nonetheless enjoined the use of English Scriptures. The reform-minded Bishop Hugh Latimer of Worcester issued injunctions for a monastery in his see city noting the "ignorance and negligence" of many monks who indulged in "idolatry and many kinds of superstitions and other enormities." Considering that the king, "for some part of the remedy of the same, hath granted by his more gracious license, that the Scripture of God may be read in English of all his obedient subjects," Latimer ordered: "a whole Bible in English to be laid fast chained" in church or cloister; each monk to procure, "at the least, a New Testament in English," lectures on scripture, and, in the refectories of both community and prior, one chapter in turn, "from the beginning of Scripture to the end," to be read at meals. In the diocese at large Latimer ordered all with pastoral cure to have "of your own a whole Bible . . . or at the least a New Testament, both in

Latin and English," and to "read over and study every day one chapter."[67]

The Primer, which had been pioneered by Joye, appeared in a number of editions, published both at Rouen in France and at London, some in English and others with English and Latin in parallel columns.[68] With these primers, those who were literate could use devotionally a major portion of the Psalms and snippets from other biblical books in the vernacular. Editions of the liturgical epistles and gospels in English, sometimes bound with the primers, also were sold as early as 1537.[69] The small quarto edition of Coverdale's Bible of the same year contained a table of the epistles and gospels for Sundays and for Wednesdays and Fridays in Lent, and marginal crosses indicated the beginning of the passages in the text. Those who brought such volumes with them to church could participate devotionally in the mass in a new way, following the lections in English while the celebrant whispered the Latin words.

The initial intent of the draft of the 1536 royal injunctions was implemented in the set that appeared two years later requiring all clergy with pastoral cures to procure "one book of the whole Bible of the largest volume in English," to be "set up in some convenient place" in the church where "parishioners may most commodiously resort to the same and read it." Parsons were to "provoke, stir, and exhort every person" to read

> the very lively word of God, that every Christian man is bound to embrace, believe and follow if he look to be saved; admonishing them nevertheless to avoid all contention, altercation therein, and to use an honest sobriety in the inquisition of the true sense of the same, and refer the explanation of obscure places to men of higher judgement in Scripture.[70]

Circumstantial evidence and subsequent events establish the intention of Cromwell to provide a new revision supervised by Coverdale to fulfill the requirement of the injunction for a "Bible of the largest volume." Although churches were supposed to secure the Bible by Easter 1539, copies were not available until November, thirteen months after the injunction had been issued. Coverdale and one of the English publishers had gone to Paris where the Bible was to have been printed. After part of the work had been completed, French authorities seized the printing on grounds of possible heresy and threatened the English engaged in the project. Extensive diplomatic negotiations failed to secure the printed sheets, but the French released the rest of the materials, including the type, and the printing was completed on English soil. Coverdale continued to edit, and the second revised edition appeared in April of 1540, to be followed by five more editions with only minor further changes before the end of 1541.[71] The Church of England now possessed a fully authorized and promulgated version of the Holy Scriptures in English known to contemporaries and subsequent generations as the "Great Bible."

As Coverdale prepared the new version for the press, the indefatigable and self-effacing scholar took the text of Matthew's Bible rather than that of his own 1535 edition. Thus Tyndale's translation provided the foundation for the books from Joshua through Chronicles, as it had for the Pentateuch and the New Testament in Coverdale's own edition. Most of the further changes which Coverdale introduced into the Great Bible were based on two authorities: Sebastian Munster's Latin Old Testament of 1535 and Erasmus' Latin New Testament, perhaps in its most recent revision of 1536. The literalism of Munster's version made it far superior to the Zurich Latin Old Testament on which Coverdale had previously depended. Coverdale made two chief concessions to conservative critics of the Matthew Bible. First, the notes and tables that gave a strong reformation flavor to the translation did not reappear in the Great Bible; this was only partly Coverdale's doing. In December, 1538, Coverdale wrote Cromwell from Paris asking to know his sponsor's "pleasure concerning the annotations of this bible, whether [to] proceed therein or no." He already had placed the figure of a pointing forefinger to indicate places in the text for which he intended to supply such notes. Promising utterly to avoid "any private opinion or contentious words," which presumably would include a number of those in Matthew's Bible, Coverdale offered to submit proposed notes to the judgment of Edward Seymour, the Earl of Hereford, who was conveying already printed pages to Cromwell for his perusal.[72] Since the Great Bible appeared with Coverdale's pointers, but without notes, clearly his proposal for even inoffensive explanatory annotation met with Cromwell's opposition, an opposition which the king's disapproval may have fired or even, just possibly, which may have been engendered by the politic wisdom of the cautious Archbishop of Canterbury. The second concession is found in the distinguishable smaller type which translated phrases and clauses of the Latin Vulgate for which there were no counterparts in the Hebrew and Greek. Otherwise, the changes which Coverdale introduced reflected his concern to achieve greater fidelity to the original texts and increased clarity of English expression. As for the choice of words that More had identified as code words of Lutheran heresy, Coverdale largely followed Tyndale's judgment and ignored conservative unhappiness with the loss of more traditional English equivalents. The worth of the Great Bible is rooted in Coverdale's healthy respect for the competence of his various sources and in a justified confidence in his own ability to judge amongst them and to frame his own appropriate English style.

Archbishop Cranmer's personal commitment to the English Scriptures, as well as his caution, is reflected in the letter he wrote to Cromwell in the month that the first edition of the Great Bible appeared. He asked about Henry's pleasure "concerning the preface of the bible which I sent you to oversee," requesting Cromwell if it be approved, to send it on to the printer, "trusting that it shall both encourage many slow readers, and also stay the rash judgments of them that read therein."[73] Appearing in the second edition of April 1540, the prominence of the preface has resulted in the common description of the Great Bible as "Cranmer's Bible." In the opening paragraph, Cranmer set the theme which he had already suggested in his letter to Cromwell, the concern for some "too slow [that] need the spur" and others "too quick [that] need more of the bridle":

In the former sort be all they that refuse to read, or to hear read the scripture in the vulgar tongues; much worse they that also let or discourage the other from the reading or hearing thereof. In the latter sort be they, which by their inordinate reading, undiscreet speaking, contentious disputing, or otherwise by their licentious living, slander and hinder the word of God most of all other.... These two sorts ... both deserve in effect like reproach.

The bulk of the rest of the preface consists of a loose translation from John Chrysostom that "it is convenient and good the scripture be read of all sorts and kinds of people" and another from two works of Gregory Nazianzus against "idle babblers and talkers" who show no "increase of virtue or example of good living."[74] The first edition had reflected this same note of caution in its explanation of the omission of the notes corresponding to the pointing hands scattered throughout the text, advising the reader that

> when thou commest at soch a place where a hande doth stande (or any other where in the Byble) and thou canst not attayne to the meanynge and true knowledge of that sentence, then do not rashly presume to make any pryvate interpretacyon therof: but submytte they selfe to the judgement of those that are learned.[75]

The fall of Thomas Cromwell from power coincided with the publication of the Great Bible, and without his consistently measured policy of reform, Henry's ventures in ecclesiastical affairs zigzagged during the remaining seven years of his reign between one affirming the increased use of the vernacular Scriptures, as Cranmer would have it, and one which heeded the warning of Stephen Gardiner that the Apostles' Creed contained "knowledge sufficient" for "rude and unlearned wits" while "discussion of the Scriptures requireth Goddes further giftes of erudicion and lernynge."[76] As the king's policies lurched in one direction and then in another, so did the conflicting orders from parliament, convocation, and bishops. Immediately after the 1538 royal injunctions, both the conservative Archbishop Lee of York and the reform-minded Bishop Shaxton of Salisbury, who was to resign the following year in the wake of the conservative resurgence, issued regulations that in parishes on holy days shall be read "the Gospel and the Epistle of that day out of the English Bible, plainly and distinctly."[77] Recognizing that English was not the vernacular of all his diocese, Bishop Voysey of Exeter called for clergy on Sundays "to declare," a word which implied *expound* as well as *read*, "in the English tongue, or in the Cornish tongue . . . all or part of the Epistle, or Gospel of that day," or else the Lord's Prayer, Hail Mary, Creed, or Ten Commandments.[78] Bishop Bonner of London, later to be known as the "bloody butcher" for his persecution of protestants under Queen Mary, in 1542 ordered preachers to begin their sermons with the epistle or gospel readings of the day "which they shall recite and declare to the people plainly, distinctly and sincerely."[79] It is difficult to know how extensively in these dioceses, or in others in which similar directions may have been given, vernacular lections were read at principal masses in parishes in the remaining years of the reign. In a 1541 proclamation Henry forbade lay persons to expound the Bible, to dispute over its interpretation, or to disturb mass by reading aloud. The main thrust of the proclamation, however, was to demand that parishes which had not yet done so "provyde Bybles . . . set and fyxed . . . accordying to the . . . former Injunctions."[80] In 1543 the Convocation of Canterbury ordered the reading of a chapter of the Bible in course on Sundays and holy days at Matins and Vespers.[81] In cathedrals these offices would be sung, and in many parishes parsons would read the two principal monastic offices at stated times. Some of the more devout would attend, usually saying their own prayers while the priest sang or quietly whispered the psalms, canticles and prayers in Latin. With this directive from Convocation and the tentative episcopal injunctions, the two types of vernacular Bible readings in church services characteristic of the continental reformation had made their initial bows in the Church of England: course-reading and liturgical lections at mass. Close to the end of the reign in 1545, Henry authorized an official Primer, a revision of the primers of the late thirties, containing vernacular psalms and other bits of

Scripture that were intended to provide a staple of personal devotional life.[82]

At the same time that these steps were taken to promote the use of the English Bible, conservatives, checking the official drift toward the teaching and practices of the continental reformation, were able to impose some limits on the use of Scripture. About the same time that Shaxton and Latimer resigned their sees, both Coverdale and Joye returned to the more favorably protestant climate on the continent where John Rogers had remained, and the work of translation and revision of the English Scriptures ceased for a decade and a half.[83] Bishops dissatisfied, as Thomas More had been, with the choice of words in translation that reflected protestant teachings, pressed in the 1542 Convocation for a revision that would have brought the English Bible into greater conformity with the Latin Vulgate. Bishop Gardiner, in a letter to Cranmer a few years later, described how Henry in a dinner conversation had supported a revision of the Bible, offering to bear "the cost to have it printed again." In Gardiner's opinion the faults were "in a marvellous number and very daungerous," God's truth being so contaminated "with the malice of the translatour, as may appere where the words and sense be evidently changed, sometyme by ignorance, and sometyme by negligence." Cranmer managed to secure an order from Henry to refer the matter to the universities where the project died.[84]

The conservative bishops and their allies were, however, more successful the next year in Parliament when Tyndale's "crafty, false, and untrue translation" was prohibited and prefaces and notes ordered to be removed from any other English Bibles.[85] The act did not touch the legal Great Bible, the greater part of which reflected Tyndale's "crafty" words, but another portion of the act forbade the lower classes from reading the English Scriptures at all, and enjoined noble and gentle women, merchants and other commoners above the level of artisans from reading the Bible aloud. Noble and gentle men might read it to their households where relatives and servants would gather to listen. The rationale for this partial frustration of the goals, not

only of protestant reformers, but of Erasmian-minded humanists as well, is clearly set forth in the preface to the "King's Book"
of this same year, a doctrinal treatise which carried the
authority of both king and convocation:

> For the instruction of [that] part of the church, whose
> office is to teach other [that is, the clergy], the having,
> reading, and studying of holy scripture . . . is not only con-
> venient, but also necessary: but for the other part of the
> church, ordained to be taught, it ought to be deemed
> certainly, that the reading of the Old and New Tesatment is
> not so necessary for all those folks, that of duty they ought
> and be bound to read it, but as the prince and the policy of
> the realm shall think convenient, so to be tolerated or
> taken from it. Consonant whereunto the politic law of our
> realm hath now restrained it from a great many, esteeming
> it sufficient for those so restrained to hear and truly bear
> away the doctrine of scripture taught by the preachers, that
> they may observe and keep them inwardly in their heart.[86]

In a proclamation in the last year of his reign ordering the burning
of the works of a number of English reformers, including Tyndale,
Joye, Roye, and Coverdale, Henry included the New Testaments,
not only of Tyndale, but explicitly of Coverdale as well.

It was certainly not all for which the reformers hoped and
struggled, but the English Bible, restricted as it might be,
nonetheless had gained a permanent place in the life of
Church and nation. Coverdale in the preface to his Bible of
1535 had acclaimed Henry "for being our Moses, and for
bringing us out of this old Egypt from the cruel hands of our
spiritual Pharao."[87] When allowance is made for the conventional flattery due royalty in the sixteenth century,
Katherine Parr, Henry's wife in these final years of his reign,
echoed the sentiments of many of her reform-minded cou-
trymen and women when she extended the comparison to
suggest that Henry had not only led his people out of the
"captivetie and bondage" of Rome, but had also brought them
"to the knowledge of the truthe by the light of gods words
whiche was so long hidd and kept under."[88]

Reform, Reaction and the Geneva Bible

A reform-minded Privy Council ruled in the name of the ten-year-old Edward VI, including, from among Henry's chief advisors, Archbishop Cranmer, but not the conservative Bishop Gardiner. Within a year the use of the English Bible was promoted in a wide-ranging series of measures as a cornerstone of a concerted program of reformation in doctrine and liturgy. The council authorized a royal visitation of the kingdom imposing a series of injunctions, in continuity with those of the previous decade, renewing momentum for reform. Within three months, parishes were to provide "the whole Bible of the largest volume ... set up in some convenient place ... whereas their parishioners may commodiously resort ... and read." Repeating the 1538 injunction, the council intended to insure that parishes that had ignored the order and those whose Bibles had been removed would purchase or replace them. The injunction further ordered that parsons

> shall discourage no man (authorized and licensed thereto) from reading any part of the Bible, ... but shall rather comfort and exhort every person to read the same, as the very lively word of God, and the special food of man's soul, that all Christian persons are bound to embrace, believe, and follow, if they look to be saved.[89]

The caveat about "authorized and licensed" persons brought the regulation, issued in the summer of 1547, in line with the parliamentary act of 1543 restricting Bible reading; the act was not repealed until after Parliament convened in November. Parishes were also to secure two other vernacular books: a translation of Erasmus' *Paraphrase of the Gospels*, a free-wheeling rendition which bitingly alluded to contemporary corruption in church life and manners, and the *Book of Homilies*, which Cranmer had had prepared several years earlier for the use of the vast majority of priests who could not deliver their own sermons. Clergy without a theological degree were to obtain New Testaments in both Latin and English and the *Paraphrase*, so that they might compare and study them "diligently."[90]

The scattered episcopal orders of earlier years and that of the 1543 Convocation for liturgical readings at church services were renewed, revised, and imposed throughout the kingdom: epistle and gospel lessons at high mass were to be read in English "and not in Latin," and at Sunday and festival offices, a chapter of the New Testament at Matins and one from the Old at Vespers. On Sundays, when a preacher was not available, a homily was to be read. The injunction declared that the intent of the *Book of Homilies* was to bring people out of the "ignorance and blindness" in which they continued, partly for the lack of competent preachers.[91] The initial homily, by the archbishop himself, was a "fruitful exhortation to the reading and knowledge of holy scripture":

> As drink is pleasant to them that be dry, and meat to them that be hungry; so is the reading, hearing, searching, and studing of holy scripture to them that be desirous to know God, or themselves, and to do his will.... Let us diligently search for the well of life in the books of the New and Old Testament, and not run to the stinking puddles of men's traditions, devised by men's imagination for our justification and salvation.... The words of holy scripture be called words of everlastinglife: for they be God's instrument, ordained for the same purpose.... Those things ... that be plain to understand, and necessary for salvation, every man's duty is to learn them, to print them in memory, and effectually exercise them. And as for the dark mysteries, to be contented to be ignorant of them, until such time as it shall please God to open these things unto him.[92]

In the final homily "against contention" ex-Bishop Latimer, who had resigned in the wake of the conservative swing of policy in 1539 exhorted: "Let us so read the scripture, that by reading thereof we may be made better livers rather than the more contentious disputers."[93] This call for peace reflected the continual concern of English authorities for an orderly progress in the reformation of church life. In his homiliy "on salvation," Cranmer interpreted Scripture to teach a balanced doctrine of justification, thoroughly consonant with the continental reformers: "faith doth not shut out repentance, hope, love, dread, and the fear of God, to be joined with faith in every man that is justified; but it shutteth them out from the office of justifying."[94] The increased use of the English Bible went hand in hand with a doctrinal stance that firmly allied the English Church with Lutheran and Reformed.

The successive Prayer Books of 1549 and 1552 did more than insist on the vernacular epistle and gospel readings at the eucharist and English psalms and course reading of the entire Bible at the daily offices.[95] The language of prayer, already thoroughly laced in its Latin dress with biblical expressions and phrases, was made yet more scriptural as Cranmer and others drew on the Bible for inspiration for their new liturgical compositions. In a new collect in Advent, Cranmer expressed his understanding of the role which the Bible might play in the life of Christians individually and as a community:

> Blessed lord, which hast caused all holy Scriptures to bee written for our learnyng; graunte us that we maye in suche wise heare them, read, marke, learne, and inwardly digeste them; that by pacience, and coumfort of thy holy woorde, we may embrace and ever holde fast the blessed hope of everlasting life, which thou has geven us in our saviour Jesus Christe.[96]

With more consequences for the life of the church, the Ordinal of 1550, included and revised in the 1552 Prayer Book, emphasized the Bible in outlining the responsibilities of deacons, priests, and bishops and in formally examining them for their suitability for ordination. The ordaining bishop was to ask deacons point-blank: "Doe ye unfeynedly beleve all the Canonicall scriptures, of the olde and newe Testament?" Priests and bishops in their ordination were presented with a more carefully crafted doctrinal question:

> Be you perswaded that the holy Scriptures contein sufficiently al doctrine required of necessitie for eternal salvacion, throughe faith in Jesu Christe? And are you determined with the saied scriptures, to enstructe the people committed to your charge, and to teache nothyng, as required of necessitie, to eternal salvacion, but that you

shalbe perswaded may be concluded, and proved by the scripture?

The lengthy exhortation to those to be ordered priest included these words:

> Ye cannot by any other meanes compasse the doyng of so weightie a woorke perteining to the salvacion of man, but with doctryne and exhortacion, taken out of holy scripture and with a life agreable unto the same. Ye perceyve how studyous ye oughte to be in readying and learnyng the holy scriptures, and in framyng the maners, both of yourselves, and of them that specially partein unto you, accordyng to the rule of the same scriptures.... We have a good hope...that you wyll continually praye for the heavenly assistaunce of the holy goste...that by dayly readyng and weighing of the scriptures, ye may waxe riper and stronger in your ministrie.

In the ceremonial delivery of instruments of office, deacons received a full New Testament in place of the medieval Book of the Gospels. To the chalice and paten delivered to priests was added in 1550 the Bible, and in 1552 the Bible alone survived as the liturgical symbol of priestly duties. The Bible, in place of the medieval Book of the Gospels, was in 1550 laid upon the neck of the new bishop before the pastoral staff was delivered to him; in 1552, the staff was omitted and the Bible handed to him. The changes dramatized the new role of scriptural teaching which the reformers placed at the center of pastoral responsibilities.[97]

The reforming ambiance of England under Edward attracted and drew back from the continent some of those who had had a hand in the production of the English Bible including Joye, Rogers, and Coverdale. The Great Bible was reprinted in 1549 and 1553, and during the reign, new editions of the versions of Tyndale and Coverdale and of Matthew's Bible all appeared. The *Book of Common Prayer* itself contained many scriptural passages, including epistles, gospels, and psalms drawn from the Great Bible with only minor variations. A Psalter, substantially that of the Great Bible, "poincted as it shalbe song in Churches" was printed in 1548, and this was frequently bound up with the new Prayer Book after it was published a year later.[98]

In the last year of Edward's reign, the forty-two Articles of Religion staked out the doctrinal stance of the Church of England in the disputed issues of the sixteenth century, as the title described its purpose: "for the avoiding of controversie in opinions, and the establishment of a godlie concorde, in certeine matiers of Religion." The fifth article reflected the declaration required in ordinations:

> Holie Scripture conteineth all thinges necessarie to Salvation: So that whatsoever is neither read therein, nor maie be proved therby ... no manne ought to bee constreigned to beleve it, as an article of faith, or repute it requisite to the necessitie of Salvation.

The following article, directed against tendencies of some anabaptist teachings to regard the Old Testament as fully superseded by the New, insisted that "bothe in the olde and newe Testamentes, everlasting life is offred to mankinde by Christ," so that the Old "is not to bee put awaie as though it were contrarie to the newe."[99]

During Edward's reign, many statues and crucifixes were removed and paintings obscured with whitewash in churches here and there throughout the land. In some places the ornamentation which these had provided was replaced by sentences of Scripture which might both teach the literate and provide them with objects of meditation, much as the statues and paintings had served in earlier years for the illiterate as well as for those who could read. Archbishop Holgate in 1552 ordered in York Cathedral that the monuments and tabernacles which had held images over the high altar be taken down and that the blank spaces "be painted with sentences of Holy Scripture."[100] These could consist of such unexceptional catechetical items as the Ten Commandments, but some zealous reformers seized an opportunity to placard scriptural justifications for their attacks on the old order. Accordingly, a little more than a year

after Mary Tudor had succeeded her brother Edward and had
begun to return the English Church to pre-reformation norms,
Bishop Bonner of London included in a set of visitation articles
of inquiry:

> Whether there be any Scriptures or pictures painted or set
> forth upon the walls of the church, or otherwise within the
> church [as, for example, rood-lofts], and yet remaining,
> which ... tend to the maintenance of carnal liberty,
> especially in eating and drinking upon all days—fasting or
> other—all manner meats and drinks, as for the defence of
> the marriage of priests ... or to express derogation and
> slander of the Blessed Sacrament of the altar?[101]

Carefully excluded from Bonner's inquiry are inoffensive vernacular scriptural quotations; this bishop, who had been
imprisoned and deprived for his resistance to the Edwardian
reforms, had been Cromwell's chief agent in Paris for securing
the release of the materials for the Great Bible from French
authorities. Although concerned to control the reading of
Bible in St. Paul's Cathedral, he had scrupulously set up six
copies to be read, and, as we observed, had ordered the reading
of some part of the English lections before sermons. Bonner's
consistent conservatism left room for what he judged to be the
proper use of the vernacular Bible, but, like Thomas More
before him, as he read the Scriptures, they did not support the
program of the continental reformation. He resisted the program when English reformers attempted to implement it
under Edward and welcomed the opportunity to dislodge it
under Mary—even at the price of accepting the papal obedience he had once repudiated when Henry and Parliament
had broken the ties with Rome.

During the reign of Queen Mary and the restoration of papal
authority, the English Bible was never formally proscribed
although Bibles were destroyed in some places and, throughout
the kingdom, they were removed from the accessible positions
in churches required by earlier injunctions. Presumably the
Great Bible retained its legal standing, and the printing of
1553, largely unsold, was still intact when Mary died. The

Marian bishop of Gloucester required all his "parsons, vicars, and curates, being no preachers . . . earnestly [to] employ themselves to study the Holy Scripture," which, for these non-preachers, would require some use of the English translations.[102] Mary, a product of a renaissance education, had herself translated a portion of Erasmus' *Paraphrase* on the Gospel of St. John. Nonetheless, when the Latin liturgies were restored, liturgical readings in English at services disappeared, and the attitude of many responsible for church policies under Mary is reflected in a pamphlet urging Mary's first Parliament to forbid the vernacular Scriptures:

> Thousands have been brought from the true meaning of God's word through the English Bible: therefore away with it; it hath killed too many souls already. . . . Away with the English damnable translation, and let [the people] learn the mysteries of God by heart.[103]

Enlightened ecclesiastics, such as Bonner and the Cardinal Archbishop Reginald Pole of Canterbury, or the Queen herself might recognize the theoretical value of the vernacular Scriptures, yet these values were outweighed in their minds, as they had been for Thomas More by the necessity of suppressing the rampant heresy that infected the nation. Similarly, they would not allow personal instincts of kindness toward individual men and women to obscure their vision of their responsibilities to society to remove those who carried the infection which had destroyed the religious unity of western christendom and had doomed many English souls to damnation. Along with the more than two hundred simple men and women of little education who died in the flames of the heretic-hunters were a handful of educated leaders, including three who had had key roles in the preparation and promotion of the English Bible: John Rogers, the first of the Marian martyrs, Hugh Latimer, and Thomas Cranmer.

The majority of reforming leaders during Mary's reign either remained in obscure corners of English society or fled to the continent where, with small groups of reform-minded fellow

countrymen and women, they found refuge in cities governed
by protestant magistrates. Of the various cities of refuge,
Geneva attracted a number who found in the theological teaching and ecclesiastical pattern laid down by John Calvin an ideal
that they believed to conform closely to the life of the apostolic
Church of the New Testament. Miles Coverdale, who had been
consecrated bishop of Exeter during Edward's reign, once
again returned to the continent, initially to Denmark, but
eventually settling in Geneva in 1558. The English refugees
arrived in Geneva just at the time that Calvin had achieved a
political victory over those civil leaders who had resisted his
insistence that the presbytery, dominated by the ordained pastors, must determine issues of morality and church discipline
and must be assured of the coercive power of the magistrates to
implement their decisions. During their Genevan residence,
the English patterned their own congregation's life on that of
their hosts, and, when they returned to their homeland on
Elizabeth's accession, many were thoroughly convinced, as one
of them later wrote, that they had resided where "Gods worde is
truly preached, manners best reformed, and in earthe the
chiefest place off true comforte."[104]

Even more important, perhaps, than the memories of godly
Geneva which these former exiles brought back with them to
England was the new vernacular translation which they published and dedicated to Queen Elizabeth in the second year of
her reign. In the years of the exiles' residence in Geneva, biblical
scholarship and translation were major foci of theological
activity. Robert Estienne, who had produced the first critical
edition of the Greek New Testament in Paris in 1550 and had
subsequently moved to Geneva, published in 1553 a French
Bible with each chapter divided into the numbered verses that
thereafter became standard in biblical texts.[105] The Geneva
Bible introduced these into English Scriptures. Theodore
Beza, Calvin's future successor, was revising the Greek New
Testament, to be published in 1565; his fresh Latin translation
appeared in 1557. Refinements of Olivetan's French Bible were
undertaken throughout the decade, and translators were producing Bibles in Italian and Spanish.[106] Biblical commentary,

delivered orally in lectures and printed from time to time, had become a fixed part of the intellectual life of Geneva.

Despite Coverdale's presence from 1558, a younger generation of scholars among the exiles dominated the work of English translation. They published a New Testament in 1557 and a Psalter in 1559 before they completed and produced the whole Bible in 1560. William Whittingham, the principal translator of the 1557 Testament, headed the team that produced the Geneva Bible, and after Elizabeth's accession, he, with others, remained in Geneva to see the edition through the press.[107] The translators used the Great Bible as the ground for the Old Testament; Tyndale served for the 1557 New Testament which went through further revision before 1560. The exiles freely introduced changes, consulting both better Greek and Hebrew texts and new translations into Latin and French. The translators included preface, summary initial descriptions of each book and chapter, maps, a topical index, and variant readings and interpretative annotations in the margins. English words without equivalents in the original tongues, but necessary for the sense, were printed in italics. The Geneva Bible was scholarly, readable, and attractive.

The first three editions of the Bible, two of them in the smaller quarto size, were printed in Geneva, and only in 1576 did editions of this version begin to be printed in England.[108] The annotations reflected the prevalent theology in Geneva; for example, that on Exodus 11:9 declared that "God hardeneth the heartes of the reprobat, that his glorie thereby might be the more set forthe."[109] Yet when the notes appear controversial rather than merely explanatory, they usually attack what the editors perceived to be the errors of Rome rather than the postures of other protestants. The six years of religious reform under Edward had not been undone by the five years of Mary's reign. Convinced reformers, both in England and in exile, kept alive the hope of restoring a religious settlement with the vernacular Scriptures as its cornerstone.

The Bible in the Elizabethan Settlement of Religion

Within six weeks of Elizabeth's accession in 1558, she indicated impending religious change when, in addition to prohibiting controversial preaching for the time being, she authorized clergy to use the English litany and to read "the gospels and epistles" of the day and the decalogue "in the vulgar tongue, without exposition or addition."[110] In the articles of inquiry that she authorized for a royal visitation of the kingdom six months later, visitors were to find out if the Litany and the reading of the lections had been "put in use in your churches."[111] Tutored primarily by humanists who sympathized with the reformers, Elizabeth as a young girl had learned to study the whole Bible and to read the New Testament in its original tongue. Even after she ascended the throne, her former tutor claimed that she read more Greek every day than a clerical prebendary of her chapel at Windsor read Latin in a week.[112] Her education and her developed tastes and convictions were in accord with the religious policy of a renewed separation from Rome and a tempered restoration of the reforming measures of her brother's reign. The Scriptures were a natural centerpiece in the pattern of Elizabeth's religious attitudes and policies. When she had been in custody, suspected of complicity in plots against her sister's reign, she had requested from the Privy Council a small English Bible and a Latin Psalter.[113] In a parliamentary speech in 1585, she acknowledged her reputation for philosophical studies, "and yet," she declared, "amidst my many volumes, I hope God's book hath not been my seldomest lectures."[114] Scraps of evidence suggest that she attended daily Morning Prayer during her reign with its round of course readings from the Bible.[115] As Elizabeth, her newly appointed ecclesiastical officials, her council and Parliament once again changed the direction of English church life, the vernacular Bible resumed its progress, held in check under Mary, from the position it had held in the world of More's *Utopia* toward that which it was to achieve by the time that Bacon wrote *New Atlantis*.

The initial settlement of religion under Elizabeth rested upon two acts of Parliament and the set of royal injunctions which accompanied the visitation in the summer of 1559. Parliament restored England's ecclesiastical independence from Rome and reestablished the vernacular liturgy of the *Book of Common Prayer*. Elizabeth and her advisors drew heavily on the injunctions from the initial 1547 visitation of Edward's reign in framing her own. Among the twenty-six Edwardian injunctions restored were the order to provide both "a whole Bible of the largest volume in English" and Erasmus' *Paraphrases* on the Gospels, the order for clergy with less education to secure and to study the New Testament in English and Latin along with the *Paraphrases*, and the order that the *Homilies* be read on Sundays in the absence of a preacher.[116] Among the twenty-seven new injunctions ordered by Elizabeth were one that no one should "maintain any heresies, errors, or false doctrine, contrary to the faith of Christ and His Holy Scripture" and another that teachers of children "should accustom their scholars reverently to learn such sentences of Scripture as shall be most expedient to induce them to all godliness."[117] These injunctions, which were to be read in churches quarterly, were periodically reprinted, frequently repeated and reinforced in sets of episcopal injunctions, and remained part of the ecclesiastical order throughout the almost half-century of Elizabeth's reign.

From time to time the bishops added their own embellishments to the national standards. Archbishop Grindal in the northern province of York in 1571, in addition to requiring biblical studies of the less well-educated clergy, insisted that *all* clergy daily read a chapter from each of the two testaments "with good advisement." He also required singers in his cathedral church under forty years of age each week to memorize one chapter of Paul's epistles "beginning with the first to the Romans"; those over forty were expected only to be able to recite "the whole sum of the same chapters." Grindal, with his profound concern for a faith grounded in the Bible, attempted to insure that those professionally employed in the worship of the

Church might firmly grasp the purpose of their vocational commitment.[118] As Bishop Latimer had ordered for monks in the first year of the legalized English Bible, so Bishop Bancroft of London inquired of the common table at St. Paul's Cathedral sixty-two years later:

> Whether have you in your Commons a Bible in Latin and English affixed to the public desk, wherein a chapter or some portion of the same is read in dinnertime with an audible voice, those who be at the table giving diligent ear therunto.[119]

As English men and women took part in the worship and life of the national church, the vernacular Bible in innumerable ways became an ever-present part of the fabric of their religious life.

The Prayer Book, revived by the Parliament, maintained the implicit and explicit teachings about the definitive centrality of the Scriptures in the Christian Church. The bishops reflected this teaching when they revised the Edwardian forty-two Articles of Religion in the 1563 Convocation to frame the "Thirty-nine Articles" which, like their predecessors, provided guidelines for parsons and other teachers as they delineated the position of the Church of England amidst the debated theological disagreements of the day. The bishops added three items to their reaffirmation of the two Edwardian articles on the Bible. First, they pointed to the ecclesiastical origin of the canon, or list of authentic biblical books. Old Testament books were listed, those "of whose aucthoritie was never any doubt in the Churche," and all those "of the newe Testament, as they are commonly receaved, we do receave and accompt them for Canonicall." The article recognized the simple fact that the Bible was not a book that had emerged out of a vacuum, but out of the life of the community that had given them birth and had acknowledged their authoritative status. Second, as the Prayer Book lectionary had provided for occasional lessons from the Old Testament Apocrypha, the article listed such books, and, referring to the testimony of Jerome, declared that these "the Church doth reade for example of lyfe and instruction of maners: but yet doth it not applie them to establishe any doctrine." The stance reflected that of the continental Lutheran churches as against those of the Reformed persuasion. Third, while reaffirming the Edwardian article that confirmed the congruity of the Old with the New Testament, the bishops declared that of the three types of laws in the Old Testament, moral, ceremonial, and civil (or judicial), only the moral bind Christian consciences; neither ceremonial nor civil precepts "ought of necessitie to be receaved in any common wealth."[120] Again the English Church took a position akin to that of the Lutherans against some Reformed theologians who looked to Old Testament civil laws for precedents that carried a divine warrant for their enactment into current legislation. Martin Bucer, a Strasbourg reformer who had come to teach at Oxford on Cranmer's invitation in Edward's reign, had urged that the Old Testament guide the king in ordering English society. Although "the ways and the circumstances" of the civil decrees of the Mosaic law may change, their "substance and proper end" remain in force and "whoever does not reckon that such commandments are to be conscientiously observed is certainly not attributing to God either supreme wisdom or righteous care for our salvation." He goes on to urge the death penalty for those "who have dared to injure religion" and for blasphemers and Sabbath-breakers, as well as for murderers, adulterers and kidnappers, all on Old Testament precedent.[121] At the opening of the Convocation, the former Marian exile Alexander Nowell, Dean of St. Paul's, had similarly preached that "by the scriptures, murderers, breakers of the holy day, and maintainers of false religion ought to die by the sword."[122] Yet in the Articles, the bishops ruled out any such rigid application of Old Testament legislation to sixteenth-century England. The three additions were all minor, but according to current interpretation and use of the Bible, they signaled a resistance to the patterns of the continental Reformed which were to be increasingly championed by the more militant reforming clerics of the Church of England.

Bibles remaining in parish churches during Mary's reign, whether set up publicly or stashed away, and copies unsold from Edward's reign began to supply the demand as churches complied with Elizabeth's injunctions. Folio editions of the Great Bible were printed in London in 1562 and in Rouen in 1566, but as early as January 1562 Bishop Cox of Ely suggested a need for "the translation of the bible to be committed to mete men and to be vewed over and amended."[123] In a letter written in March 1566 to William Cecil, Elizabeth's principal secretary, Archbishop Matthew Parker and Bishop Grindal of London referred to a Bible that is "meant by us to be set forthe as convenient tyme and [leisure] hereafter will permytte." They also urged that the Geneva Bible be printed in England: "it shall nothing hindre but rather do moche good to have diversitie of translacions and readinges."[124] By November when the bishops were assembled in London for Parliament and Convocation, Parker reported to Cecil that he had "distributed the bible in partes to dyverse men."[125] Twenty-two months later the Archbishop sent a presentation copy to Elizabeth, urging that she might license the new tanslation and commend it for "public reading in churches, to draw to one uniformity." Parker suggested that the new translation was needed because some parishes still lacked their Bibles and because "in certain places be publicly used some translations which have not been laboured in your realm [that is, the Geneva Bible], having inspersed divers prejudicial notes, which might have been also well spared."[126] The Bishops' Bible, as the translation came to be known, became the version officially authorized to be read in churches. In the following year a quarto edition was published, making the Bishops' Bible more easily available for private use as well as for public reading.

In contrast to earlier English translations, the work was done by individual translators working largely on their own. Parker did state that, after the sections were completed, "some other perusing was had," but this implied minimal supervision and editing which the uneven character of the texts confirms.[127] Twelve or thirteen bishops and four other clerics, all men with extensive administrative pastoral responsibilities, produced the translation. Archbishop Parker himself not only took responsibility for preliminary and introductory material, but also for the books of Genesis and Exodus in the Old Testament and for the Gospels of Matthew and Mark and for the shorter letters of the Pauline corpus in the New.[128] Parker had laid down only a few simple instructions to his fellow translators:

> First, to follow the common English translation used in the churches and not to recede from it but where it varieth manifestly from the Hebrew or Greek original.
> Item, to use sections and divisions in the text as [Santi Pagnini] in his [Latin] translation useth, and for the verity of the Hebrew to follow the said [Pagnini] and Munster specially, and generally others learned in the tongues.
> Item, to make no bitter notes upon any text, or yet to set down any determination in matters of controversy.
> Item, to note such chapters and places as contain matter of genealogies or other such places not edifying...that the reader may eschew them in his public reading.
> Item, that all such words as sound in the old translation to any offence of lightness or obscenity, be expressed with more convenient terms and phrases.[129]

The instructions were variously interpreted as the different translators took time from their other responsibilities to tend to the scholarly task. A modern scholar has described the varying character of the translations:

> Some of the revisers, following the lead of the Archbishop himself, made a careful and conscientious revision of the text of the Great Bible; some, however, simply transplanted the wording of the Great Bible with a few alterations here and there; others were partial to the Geneva Bible and produced a blend of this version with that of the Great Bible; while a few boldly introduced so many novel readings as to make their sections of the work a brand new version in effect.[130]

The character of the Bishops' Bible was as varied as its separate translators. "Bitter notes" were largely absent, although unlike the great Bible, some explanatory notation was included, occasionally identical with the notes in the Geneva Bible. A non-controversial, but clearly protestant tone prevailed in notes and summaries; the heading of Romans 3 declares: "Al are justified by grace through fayth, and not through workes," virtually a slogan of those sixteenth-century Christians who were opposed to what they understood to be the teaching of the Roman Church.[131]

A new folio edition of the Bishops' Bible appeared in 1572, with the text of the Great Bible Psalter printed in a column alongside that of the Bishops' version, with minor corrections in the rest of the Old Testament, and substantial emendations in the New. An Oxford professor of Greek had leveled severe criticisms of parts of the Bishops' work, based on the improved text of the New Testament that Beza had published in 1565. As for the Psalter, Parker had commented in 1568 that, although psalters previously printed for use in churches to accompany the Prayer Book "might remain in quires, as they be much multiplied," he hoped that people, "of their own accord" would switch to the new translation.[132] Parishes, however, resisted changes in the Great Bible psalms. already familiar to many, and even if the 1572 edition suggested in its columnar titles the superiority of the "translation after the Hebrewes" to that "used in common prayer," the older version prevailed and, in fact, completely supplanted the 1568 translations in almost all subsequent editions of the Bishops' Bible.[133] A similar scenario was to follow in 1662 when the Prayer Book was revised: the Psalter and a few other frequently used scriptural passages remained substantially in the words of the Great Bible instead of being conformed to the 1611 Authorized Version.

A dozen more editions of the Bishops' Bible appeared in the next six years, some in folio and others in the smaller quarto size, but after 1578 only five more editions were printed, all of these in the folio size which met the requirements of the injunctions for use in churches.[134] In the year after Archbishop Parker died, the first edition of the Geneva Bible to be printed in England appeared with the notes that Parker had considered "bitter,"[135] Between 1578 and 1611 more than one hundred editions of all sizes of the Geneva Bible were published in England. Although these were not authorized for church use, the appearance of Prayer Book lectionaries bound with many such Bibles suggests that they were often read in church services. For private reading they dominated the field. Richard Hooker, for example, a staunch opponent of militant puritans commonly quoted in his writings from the Genevan version when he did not translate from the original. The Geneva Bible remained more popular in common use even if the words of the Bishops' version were more frequently heard in public worship.

The two biblical versions symbolized the division within the Church of England between supporters of the establishment and more militant reformers who sought to complete what they judged to be the work of reformation. Puritans continued to hammer away at what they insisted were the scholarly inadequacies of the officially authorized Scriptures. Just before the Geneva Bible began to be printed in England, one militant reformer contrasted that version against which "no enemie off god coulde justly finde faulte" with "oure Englishe Bibles" which "are so ill translated (as the lerned report) and so falsely printed (as the simple maie finde)" that only those who know the Scriptures well can "get owte the true meaning and sence." He lamented the "great and intollerable mischeives [that] maie come more and more (by sufferinge suche corrupted Bibles in churches and ells where) to the poore simple flock off Christe."[136]

A revision of the New Testament of the Geneva Bible appeared in 1576. The revisor was Laurence Tomson, a scholarly layman who served on the staff of one of Elizabeth's most militantly reform-minded councillors. Tomson himself had spent many months in Geneva and Heidelberg, and in 1579 he published a translation of a parcel of John Calvin's sermons.[137] The New Testament, like that of the 1572 Bishops' revision, had taken account of Beza's Greek text, but its main innovation is found in the strident tone of the notes which replaced and supplemented those of the original Geneva Bible. The 1560 note on Matthew 18:17, a verse which directed offended brethren to report an unrepentant offender "to the church," mildly suggested the Genevan church order:

He meaneth according to the order that was amongst the Jewes, who had their councel of ancient and expert men to reforme maners, and execute discipline. This assemblie represented the Church, which had appointed them to this charge.

Tomson commented in much greater detail:

> He speaketh not of any kinde of pollicie, but of an ecclesiastical assemblie, for he speaketh afterward of the power of loosing and binding, which belonged to the Church, and hee hath regard to the order used in those dayes, at what time the Elders had the judgement of Church matters in their handes... and used casting out of the Synagogue for a punishment, as wee doe nowe excommunication.

The Genevan translators did not comment on I Timothy 5:17 which speaks of the honor due to "the Elders that rule wel"; Tomson takes full advantage of the opportunity:

> There were two kindes of Elders, the one attended upon the government onely, and looked to the maners of the congregation, the other did beside that, attend upon preaching and prayers, to and for the Congregation.[138]

No presbyterian-minded puritan could wish for a clearer declaration that the Genevan church order, in contrast to England's episcopal ministry, accurately restored the New Testament pattern. Tomson's version appeared in a full Geneva Bible published in 1587; in subsequent printings, more than a third of the Geneva Bible editions and all of the Genevan New Testaments contained Tomson's version with his controversial notes. Just at the end of the sixteenth century, the notes of Francis Junius on the book of Revelation began to be substituted for those of Tomson. Junius, a Frenchman who held professorships in the Reformed theological faculties at Heidelberg and Leyden, in these notes violently attacked the papacy which he identified with the harlot of Revelation 17. By the end of the century, in spite of its general popularity, the Geneva Bible, sometimes bound with Calvin's Catechism and statement on predestination, had become identified with those puritans who, in varying degrees, wished to pattern the English Church more closely on the Genevan model.

The exile community of English Roman Catholics at Rheims in France produced a New Testament in 1582. The chief translator, Gregory Martin, based his work on the Latin Vulgate and heavily annotated it with polemical comments, but he paid careful attention both to the Greek and to the English translations he sought to refute. When William Fulke published the texts of the Bishops' and the Rheims New Testaments in parallel columns with a "confutation of all such annotations as conteine manifest impietie," he helped to bring Martin's text to the notice of those protestants who might appreciate virtuous points of the translation as well as what they might judge to be its infelicities and inadequacies.[139]

"Vernacular" in Britain meant not only English, but also the Celtic tongues that survived in western extremities. Wales represented the major concentration of linguistic nonconformists in the island, and during the first decade of Elizabeth's reign, measures were taken to ensure that the Welsh could hear and read the Scriptures in their own language. Elizabeth's appointment of Welsh-speaking bishops to the sees of Wales made it possible for Parliament to authorize them effectively to oversee the production of a Welsh Bible and Prayer Book. Even if Parliament hoped that the accompanying required English books might help the Welsh "the sooner attayne to the knowldge of the Englyshe tongue," the action essentially reaffirmed the reformation principle of Scriptures and worship in languages understood by the people. New Testament and Prayer Book with Psalter were published by 1567, and the Old Testament finally appeared in 1588. An English historian has recently commented that without these books the language of Wales "would have declined to the status of Breton—a peasant patois."[140] Owen Tudor could have been proud of the way in which his royal great-granddaughter solicitously cared for the culture and religion of his people.

Elizabeth had no Irish forebears, but she, her government, and a few of her episcopal appointees to the Church of Ireland made earnest, but less successful attempts to provide the Bible in the Gaelic of Ireland. Communications between the Council of Ireland and the English Privy Council reveal that by 1567 the queen had given money to the Irish bishops "for the making of [type] for the testement in irishe."[141] Although in 1571 a primer with catechism, the first Irish book to be printed, was produced on the queen's type and, by 1585, an Irish bishop had prepared a manuscript of the New Testament, no Scriptures had yet appeared. The Privy Council in 1587 urged Irish officials to take measures so that "the woorke of the Testament might be taken in hand and fynyshed as soone as might be."[142] The Irish New Testament was finally being printed while Queen Elizabeth was dying in 1603; the Prayer Book was printed later in the decade, and the Old Testament did not appear until 1685.[143] Through most of Elizabeth's reign, the crown's control of Ireland seldom extended beyond the "English Pale" about Dublin, and by the time the royal authorities imposed their rule, the "Church of Ireland" had become identified with English domination and Irish national resistance with the Roman Catholic faith. The Irish New Testament with its tardy arrival a half century after the reformation settlement could not duplicate the role that its Welsh cousin had performed across the Irish Sea.

Anglicans and Puritans in Disagreement and Collaboration

Both those English who pressed for further reforms in the Church and those who were substantially content with the religious settlement agreed, in large measure, on the importance and use of the vernacular Scriptures, but they nonetheless differed on significant points over and above their preference in translations. Puritans continued to press for the elimination of Old Testament Apocrypha readings from the Prayer Book lectionary, although the Apocrypha usually continued to be printed in Geneva Bibles. The militant reformers emphasized the importance of preaching to the point of deprecating what they termed "bare reading" of the Bible when a licensed preacher was not present:

By the word of God, [the ministry] is an office of preaching. They make it an office of reading.... They make the chiefest part, which is preaching, but an accessory.... For bare reading of the word, and single service saying, is bare feeding.[144]

Richard Hooker's response to those who wished to make over the Church of England in the pattern of Geneva has remained a classic of Anglican theology; he valued the place of preaching in the church, but he insisted:

When we reade or recite the scripture, we then deliver to the people *properlie* the worde of God. As for our sermons, be they never so sound and perfect, his worde they are not as the sermons of the prophetes [in the Bible] were, no they are but ambiguouslie termed his worde.[145]

Hooker's own writings were saturated with biblical phrases. When he quoted from the New Testament, he usually translated freely from the Greek. Although he commonly quoted Old Testament passages from the Geneva Bible, he himself had been a lecturer in Hebrew at Oxford.

The larger area of disagreement between puritans and theologians such as Hooker was more subtle. It reflected, to some degree, different perspectives on the Bible between continental Reformed and Lutherans. Hooker's use of the Bible presumed both the Lutheran understanding that, in church life, those things not expressly prohibited were permitted, and also the humanist tradition, still strong in England that left room for a historical perspective in interpreting Scripture. Militant English reformers, like their continental Reformed brethren, tended to look to the Bible alone for direction to guide them in the ordering of church life and worship, and, somewhat less consistently, for direction in all areas of human life. The learned conforming puritan theologian at Cambridge, Wiliam Perkins, describing how Christians are to determine their vocation in life, rested his case squarely on Scripture:

God ordaineth a calling when he prescribeth and commandeth the same in and by his word: and those callings

and states of life which have no warrent from God's word
are unlawful.... The word of God must be our rule and
square whereby we are to frame and fashion all our actions
and according to the direction received thence, we must do
the things we do, or leave them undone.[146]

The puritan propensity to urge, as Bucer had proposed, that
Old Testament judicial laws guide English legislation led a
cleric writing an exposition of the Articles of Religion to insist
against this notion that such laws are "not necessarily to be
received or established in any commonwealth."[147] Hooker
treated seriously the historical circumstances within the biblical
narratives, developing a characteristic implied in earlier
humanists such as Erasmus. Writing of Old Testament ordi-
nances, given by God to the Jews to be continually observed,
Hooker declared:

> Almightie God in framing their Lawes had an eye unto the
> nature of that people, and to the countrey where they were
> to dwell; if these peculiar and proper considerations were
> respected in the making of theyr Lawes, and must bee also
> regarded in the Positive Lawes of all other Nations besides;
> then seeing that Nations are not all alike, surely the geving
> of one kinde of positive Lawes unto one onely people,
> without anye libertie to alter them, is but a slender proofe,
> that therefore one kinde should in like sort be given to
> serve everlastingly for all.[148]

Hooker placed the disagreements in a wider framework. We
learn of God and of our responsibilities as his creatures from
nature, he contended, as well as from Scripture. The capacity of
our senses to observe and of our minds to reason enables us to
apprehend a major portion of the law from God that is necessary for the ordering of our personal lives and for establishing
the rules and structures of human society. "Albeit scripture do
professe to conteyne in it all things which are necessary unto
salvation; yet the meaning cannot be simplye of all things that
are necessarye."[149] Rather, Hooker explains:

> The absolute perfection of scripture is seene by relation

unto that end wherto it tendeth, . . . a full instruction in all things unto salvation necessary, the knowledge wherof man by nature could not otherwise in this life attaine unto.[150]

Even in the life of the Church, Hooker insisted, changing circumstances require a reordering of structures and law. In the particular issue of the exercise of spiritual discipline, for which, according to puritans, the Bible provided a definitive pattern, Hooker argued that although Christ's laws as recorded in the Gospels

bee the only ground and foundation, whereupon the prac-tise of the Church must susteyne itself, yet, as all multi-tudes, once growen to the forme of societies, are . . . warranted to enforce . . . those things which publick wisdome shall judge expedient: soe it were absurd to imag-ine the Church itselfe, the most glorious amongst them, abridged of this libertie, or to thinck that noe law, constitu-tion, or canon can be further made . . . through varietie of tymes . . . during the state of this inconstant world, which bringing forth dayly such new evills, as must of necessitie, by new remedies bee redrest, . . . in summe [the Church needs] often to varie, alter, and chaunge customes, incident [to] the manner of exercising that power, which doth itselfe continue allwayes one and the same.[151]

Hooker argues that "it is no more disgrace for scripture to have left a number of . . . things free to be ordered at the discretion of the Church, then for nature to have left it unto the wit of man to devise his own attyre."[152] Hooker consciously positioned his understanding of "the sufficiencie of holy scripture" between two extremes, each

opposite unto the other, and both repugnant unto truth. The schooles of Rome teach scripture to be so unsufficient, as if, except traditions were added, it did not conteine all revealed and supernaturall truth, which is absolutely nec-essarie for the children of men in this life to know that they may in the next be saved. Others justly condemning this opinion growe likewise unto a daungerous extremitie, as if scripture did not onely containe all thinges in that kinde necessary, but al thinges simply, and in such sorte that to doe any thing according to any other lawe were not onely unnecessary, but even opposite unto salvation, unlawfull and sinfull.... We must ... take great heede, lest in attributing unto scripture more than it can have, the incredibillitie of that do cause even those thinges which indeed it hath most aboundantly to be lesse reverendly esteemed.[153]

The puritan position regarding Scripture remained a legitimate and accepted strain within the Church of England, even after the seventeenth-century events of the civil war, commonwealth, restoration, and the advent of toleration had resulted in the separation of many descendents of the puritans into the nonconformist free churches. Hooker, nonetheless, expressed the theological stance that proved to be most influential in the development of Anglicanism as a distinct way of understanding and practicing the Christian faith.

As James VI of Scotland traveled south in 1603 to add the royal responsibilities of England to those he already possessed, he was met by puritan representatives who hoped that the new king would bring in the "due and godly reformation" that had been frustrated by Elizabeth's consistent adherence to the settlement of the initial months of her reign. James had been brought up on the pure milk of the presbyterianism that the firm hand of John Knox had established in Scotland after returning from his Genevan duties as pastor of the English exiles during Mary Tudor's reign. The petition presented by the puritans to James requested that he remove abuses "yet remaining and practised in the Church of England." Among these requests, they asked that "only the canonical Scrptures"— not the Apocrypha—be read in Church.[154] None of the other points of the petition directly touched the use of the Bible, but nonetheless, the major consequence of the Hampton Court Conference of bishops and puritan divines that James held in response to the petition was a decision to prepare a new English translation of the Scriptures.

The preface to the 1611 Authorized Version of the Bible described the volume's origins:

Upon the importunate petitions of the Puritanes at his Majesties comming to this Crowne, the conference at Hampton Court having been appointed for hearing their complaints: when by force of reason they were put from all other grounds, they had recourse at the last, to this shift, that they could not with good conscience subscribe to the Communion booke, since it maintained the Bible as it was there translated, which was, as they said, a most corrupted translation. And although this was judged to be but a very poore and emptie shift; yet even hereupon did his Mejestie beginne to bethinke himself of the good that might ensue by a new translation, and presently after gave order for this Translation which is now presented unto thee.[155]

The anti-puritan tone of the account does not obscure the fact, substantiated from other evidence, that the suggestion for the new Bible came from the militant reformers at the conference although it was not part of the collective agenda which they brought with them. More than conventional flattery of royalty is involved in the attribution of the subsequent initiative to James, for the initial reaction of the soon-to-be Archbishop of Canterbury and eventual manager of the translation project, Richard Bancroft, was negative. The king, expressing his dislike of existing English Bibles and his opinion that the Geneva was "worst of all," proposed that the translation be undertaken "by the best learned in both the Universities, after them to be reviewed by the Bishops, and the chiefe learned of the Church" and finally to be given to the Privy Council and ratified by the King. Pointing out marginal notes in the Geneva Bible encouraging resistance to royal authority, James, encouraged by Bancroft, directed that "no marginall notes should be added" to the new edition.[156] Within six months Bancroft sent his fellow bishops a circular letter including a communication from James asking that appointments to church posts which offered adequate income be given to the fifty-four "learned men" to whom he entrusted responsibility for the translation.[157]

The work of translation was carefully orchestrated. The three centers where English scholars congregated, London and the two universities, were each assigned a section of the Hebrew and a section of the Greek Scriptures, and teams made up of seven to ten members were given responsibility for each section. Bancroft laid down a set of fifteen rules to be observed. The Bishops' Bible was to serve as the basic text, "as little altered as the Truth of the original will permit," but the Tyndale, Matthews, Coverdale, Great, and Geneva Bibles were commended to the translators. Notes were to be limited to cross-references and explanations of words which could not be expressed in the text itself "without some circumlocution." The teams were jointly to review the initial translations of individual members, teams were to exchange their drafts, and "the chief Persons of each Company" were to make final judgments in disputed matters. Specialists were to be consulted when necessary and were invited to offer their "particular Observations" to the various teams. Reflecting disputes in the times of Tyndale and Coverdale, Bancroft opted for the traditional practice when he ordered that "the old Ecclesiastical Words to be kept, *viz.*, the Word *Church* not to be translated *Congregation* &c."[158] Two later accounts of the procedures suggest that a committee of twelve, composed of two from each company, performed the major task of editing the drafts of the various sections.[159] Staunch supporters of the religious establishment worked hand in hand with fellow churchmen who longed for further reformation. Never perhaps in the history of human literary achievements has organized committee work, rather than individual genius, produced a work of the literary quality of the King James Bible.

The members of the teams must have encouraged one another's scholarly interests, and that peculiar combination of collaborative and competitive instincts that characterize many academic groups redounded to the benefit of the work. A few fresh translations from the original languages had provided additions to the resources available to them. A new edition of the Polyglot Bible published in Antwerp in 1572 included a new interlinear Latin translation of the Hebrew text. Tremellius, the converted Jew who had taught at Cambridge in Edward's reign, in 1579 published another Latin translation of the Old Testament. Attached to it was the Apocrypha rendered into Latin by his son-in-law Francis Junius, the author of the commentary on Revelation that was sometimes included in the Geneva Bible.

Three years earlier Tremellius' Latin translation of the Syriac New Testament, in parallel with the Syriac itself, the Vulgate, and the Greek, had been published in Geneva. In the years since the Bishops' Bible, revisions of French, Italian, and Spanish Bibles had appeared.[160] Accordingly the preface of the King James' Bible reports that the translators did not hesitate "to consult the Translators or Commentators, Chaldee, Hebrewe, Syrian, Greeke, or Latine, no nor the Spanish, French, Italian, or Dutch."[161] The corps of competent scholars who shared initial drafts with one another and submitted their work to review helped to ensure that the new Bible would reflect the best scholarship of the day.

In the use of the English texts which had preceded their work, the translators of the Authorized Version drew on wording of all their predecessors of the previous century, including that in the New Testament of the Roman Catholic exiles in Rheims. Although unmentioned in Bancroft's instructions, the work significantly contributed words not used in earlier translations. In an analysis of "literary units," that is, phrases and clauses, in representative sections from the Old and New Testaments, a modern scholar has estimated that 39 percent were contributed by the King James translators, 4 percent of these units reflect phrases used in the pre-Reformation Lollard Bibles or in sermons by John Wyclif himself, 18 percent originate with Tyndale, 13 percent with Coverdale, 19 percent with the Geneva translators, 4 percent with the Bishops' Bibles, and the remaining 3 percent from other vernacular sources.[162] The contributions of the various translations vary considerably, as might be expected, in different parts of the Bible. For example Tyndale is the chief formative influence in the Pentateuch, but "the Geneva Bible is supreme" in the prophetic books.[163] The low contribution of the Bishops' Bible does not mean that the translators ignored their instructions to use it as the foundation from which they were to work, for the contributions of a large portion of the earlier editions was mediated through the text of the Bishops' Bible which had maintained the readings of existing translations.

The Authorized Version was published in 1611, some seven

years after the king had set in motion the machinery for its production. Never actually submitted to Privy Council or ratified by the king, this work, whose scholarly craftsmen represented the spectrum of religious convictions within the early seventeenth-century Church of England, gradually took the place of earlier versions among English protestants, and even later editions of Roman Catholic Rheims-Douay Bibles were not free from the influence of its wording and cadence. It fulfilled the canonical requirement for church Bibles "of the largest volume" and won on its merits the affection of both scholars and literate church people of all degrees of educaiton for private reading and study. By the time that Francis Bacon wrote his *New Atlantis*, the King James Bible was well on its way to the position it was to occupy for more than three hundred years— and still occupies in the hearts and minds of many:

> Its victory was so complete that its text acquired a sanctity properly ascribable only to the unmediated voice of God; to multitudes of English-speaking Christians it has seemed little less than blasphemy to tamper with the words of the King James Version.[164]

The achievement of the King James Bible gave evidence that puritans and those later to be known as Anglicans could find common ground in the writings they both took to contain the word of God. Disagreements over the interpretation and proper use of Scripture were to continue, and increasingly members of the established Church were to develop the understandings suggested in the ways that Richard Hooker approached the sacred writings. Overshadowing these disagreements, the vernacular Bible had become so firmly fixed in English life and thought that we may imagine that scarcely an eyebrow was raised by those who read Bacon's story of the Bible's role in the conversion of the inhabitants of New Atlantis.

2

The Bible in Worship

by Marion J. Hatchett

The renewed emphasis on the holy Scriptures during the renaissance and reformation fostered a renewed emphasis on preaching[1] and affected greatly the revision of the liturgical books. Cranmer was concerned that the Book of Common Prayer set forth the Scriptures in its lectionaries and that liturgical forms be true to the Scriptures, and subsequent revisers have been concerned that the songs of the choir and of the people be instruments for winging scriptural texts or scriptural teaching into their hearts.

Scripture Read

The Daily Offices

One of the first effects of the English reformation on worship was inclusion in the rites of Scripture readings in the vernacular. In 1543 Convocation ordered:

> that every Sunday and holy day throughout the year, the curate of every parish church after the *Te Deum*, and *Magnificat*, should openly read unto the people one chapter of the New Testament in English, without exposition; and when the New Testament was read over, then to begin the Old.[2]

Medieval Matins included lessons, but Vespers did not; from 1543 a lesson in English was included in both rites. Soon after this, if not before, Cranmer began work toward a revision of the breviary.[3] One of his schemes was based on the reformed breviary of Cardinal Quiñones[4]; another is more closely related to German Church Orders.[5] One scheme was arranged according to the church year with three lessons at Matins, one at Lauds, and one at Vespers.[6] The wisdom literature is to be read at Lauds; Romans, 1 Corinthians, and most of the Old Testament as the first and second lessons at Matins and the lesson at Vespers; Luke, Matthew, John 1–10, the remaining Epistles, and portions of Jeremiah as the third lesson at Matins. Another scheme, arranged according to the civil rather than the church year, called for three lessons at Matins and one at Vespers.[7] Old Testament historical books and most of the New Testament were to be read at Matins, and selections from the Prophets and the wisdom literature at Vespers. Both of these schemes called for Isaiah to be read out of course in Advent. A third scheme, arranged according to the civil calendar, calls for the Old Testament historical and wisdom literature to be read as the first lessons at Matins and Vespers, the Prophets and the Apocalypse as a second lesson at Matins, the Gospels and Acts to be repeated every four months as a third lesson at Matins, and the Epistles to be repeated every four months as a second lesson at Vespers.[8] The preface to Cranmer's schemes is dependent on the prefaces to the first and second recensions of Quiñones' breviary.[9]

The preface of the first Book of Common Prayer of 1549 is an apologia for the lectionary of its Daily Offices, drawn largely from the preface of Cranmer's Liturgical Projects.[10] What Cranmer saw as the order of the ancient fathers in which the people heard each year in their own language "all the whole Bible (or the greatest parts thereof)" read for their edification was to be restored along with a periodic recitation of the whole Psalter. The rites were to be purified and simplified by the elimination of "uncertain stories," legends, anthems, reponsories, invitatories, etc. Nothing is to be read "but the very pure word of God, the holy scriptures, or that which is evidently grounded upon the same." In the late medieval period the office was a private obligation for the clergy; the Book of Common Prayer bound clergy with cures to say the office publicly.

For the sake of simplicity and to avoid substantial omissions in some years the 1549 Daily Office lectionary is arranged according to the civil calendar rather than the church year. The Psalter is to be read through each month[11] and the Old Testament each year, "except certain books and chapters, which be least edifying, and might best be spared."[12] The New Testament, except for the Apocalypse (which was omitted in two of Cranmer's schemes), is to be read through every four months, the Gospels and Acts at Morning Prayer and the Epistles at Evening Prayer (as in one of Cranmer's schemes). Except for Isaiah, begun on November 28 and ended on December 31, the books are read in their biblical order. Course readings were interrupted for certain fixed holy days.[13] The only times, however, when proper lessons would displace course readings were from Evening Prayer on Wednesday before Easter through Evening Prayer on Tuesday after Easter, and on Ascension Day, Pentecost, and Trinity Sunday.[14] The system assured reading of almost the whole of the Scriptures, but it resulted in some incongruous relations to the church year. Depending on the date of Easter, post-resurrection material from John and Acts might be read in Holy Week or the account of the Passion in Easter Week.

One of the weak points of this lectionary was that those who attended the Daily Offices only on Sundays and Holy Days would often get Old Testament lessons which made little sense out of context. The Elizabethan Prayer Book of 1559 provided a year's course of proper Old Testament lessons for Sundays.[15] Selected passages from Isaiah were to be read in course on the Sundays of Advent, Christmas, and Epiphany,[16] and chapters from the historical books from Septuagesima through the Thirteenth Sunday after Trinity.[17] These were arranged so that Exodus 12 and 14 would be read on Easter and Deuteronomy 17 and 18 on Pentecost.[18] The series is broken only for Morning Prayer on Trinity Sunday (Genesis 18). Selected chapters from the Prophets were to be read in course from the Fourteenth Sunday after Trinity through Morning Prayer on the Twenty-first Sunday after Trinity.[19] Lessons from Proverbs were to be read for the remainder of the year, except for the Twenty-seventh Sunday after Trinity, for which no proper lections were appointed.[20] The only Sundays for which proper New Testament lessons were appointed were Easter, Pentecost, and Trinity Sunday (Morning Prayer only).[21] This calendar also provided what is apparently an alternative series of Old Testament readings in course from the wisdom literature for the fixed Holy Days which did not have proper lessons assigned in the calendar.[22] These lessons were worked into the calendar itself in the 1561 revision.[23]

Except for the provision of these proper lessons only minor changes were made in the lectionary revisions of 1552, 1559, 1561, and 1604.[24] The Scottish revision of 1637[25] shifted Isaiah to its biblical order and omitted course readings from the Apocrypha (though readings from Wisdom and Ecclesiasticus were appointed for six Holy Days[26]). To fill out the lectionary, readings from 1 and 2 Chronicles were appointed from November 23 to December 16,[27] and Isaiah 47–66 was repeated December 17–31. The 1662 lectionary was a conservative revision of that of 1604.[28] From 1662 the King James Version of 1611 was used for the Epistles and Gospels as well as for the lessons of the Daily Offices.

Objections to readings from the Apocrypha arose in Elizabethan times and affected the revisions of 1604, 1637, and 1662.[29] Late seventeenth- and eighteenth-century proposals for Prayer Book revision from various schools of thought urged the omission of lessons from the Apocrypha,[30] and the first American Book of Common Prayer of 1789 eliminated Apocryphal lessons from the Daily Office lectionary though not from the lessons for Holy Days.[31] The Gospels and Acts were to be read twice rather than three times each year. The Table of Proper Lessons for Sundays was revised, increasing substantially the number of lessons from the Prophets. Isaiah would continue to be read in Advent, Christmas, and Epiphany, but readings from the Prophets would be used from Septuagesima to Pentecost and course readings from the historical books would extend from Trinity Sunday through the Twentieth Sunday after Trinity; Daniel 6 and 7 would be read on the Twenty-first Sunday, and readings from Proverbs on the remaining Sundays of the year.[32] This was the first Book of Common Prayer to appoint proper lessons for Ash Wednesday.[33] It was also the first Prayer Book to appoint New Testament lessons for all Sundays. At Morning Prayer events from the life of our Lord filled the Sundays from Advent through the Sixth Sunday of Lent, the Acts of the Apostles was read from the First Sunday after Easter through the Tenth Sunday after Trinity, and selected chapters from the Gospels filled out the remaining Sundays.[34] Selections from the Epistles, largely in biblical order, were appointed for Evening Prayer.[35] Proper lessons were also provided for each of the days of Holy Week.[36]

The other issues in eighteenth-century lectionary revision, in addition to the use of the Apocrypha, were the Psalter translation to be used and the "promiscuous" use of the Psalms. Various revisions or proposals for revision removed from the Psalter, or from use in the services, the imprecatory Psalms and others which were felt not to be suitable for use in Christian worship.[37] The 1786 Proposed Book of Common Prayer[38] defends in its preface the abridgment of the Psalter (for the use of the whole Psalter is not suitable for "christian societies") and its use in places of the King James Version rather than the Prayer Book translation. Typical of the editing is Psalm 5: verses 9-11, a castigation of enemies and a petition to God to destroy them, were omitted, and verses 1 and 13 are in the King James Version. Rather than appointing proper Psalms for Christmas, Ash Wednesday, Good Friday, Easter, Ascension, and Pentecost, the Proposed Book provided anthems to take the place of the Venite made up almost altogether of verses from the Psalms appointed in the English Book. These provisions regarding the Psalter were highly controversial. The 1789 Prayer Book restored the whole Psalter, but also provided ten "Selections of Psalms, to be used instead of the Psalms for the Day, at the discretion of the Minister."[39] The book restored the table of Proper Psalms, but also retained the anthems from the

Proposed Book, for use when one of the Selections would be used rather than the Proper Psalms for the Day.

In 1871 the Church of England adopted a new lectionary for the Daily Office, which was taken into the Irish Prayer Book of 1877 in a revised form which included the whole of Revelation and omitted the lessons from the Apocrypha. The English version was approved for trial use by the American General Convention of 1877 and was included in the Scottish book of 1912. Many lessons were shortened, and many were divided; the number of lessons from the Apocrypha was drastically reduced, and the number of lessons from Ezekiel substantially increased. Lessons from 1 and 2 Chronicles (not represented in previous English or American books) were inserted at appropriate places among the readings from 1 and 2 Kings. The Gospels, Acts, and the Epistles were read twice a year, once in the morning and once in the evening, in the biblical order in the morning, beginning with Acts and the Epistles followed by the Gospels in the evening. Previous Daily Office lectionaries did not include readings from Revelation,[40] but this lectionary appointed selected chapters, morning and evening, beginning December 17.[41] The table of proper lessons for Sundays was revised, with two lessons being listed for evening, either of which might be used at Evening Prayer or at a "Third Service." A slightly different selection of chapters was given from some books, and a few lessons were shortened. The series from Isaiah was brought to an end on the Third Sunday after the Epiphany, and lessons from Job and Proverbs appointed for the remainder of the season. Isaiah 6:1-10 was appointed for Morning Prayer on Trinity Sunday. Lessons from the Prophets were substituted for the lessons from Proverbs on the last Sundays after Trinity. Changes were made among the few proper New Testament lections.[42] Suitable lessons were substituted for the course readings from the wisdom literature on the fixed Saints' Days, and some additions and substitutions were made among the New Testament lessons. Following the precedent of the American book, proper lessons were provided for Ash Wednesday and all the days of Holy Week.

The Daily Office lectionary of the 1892 American Prayer

Book is an adaptation of the English 1871 lectionary, with fewer readings from Ezekiel and the Apocrypha, but with the whole of Revelation. For the Sunday lessons the 1892 book retained the 1789 lectionary in a slightly revised form.[43] The 1892 book also provided a table of proper lessons for optional use for the forty days of Lent and for the Rogation and Ember Days.[44] The table of Proper Psalms was expanded to include fourteen days,[45] and twenty rather than ten Selections of Psalms were listed.[46] The 1910 General Convention set an example, later followed by other provinces, in allowing use of other translations as well as the King James Version.

Out of the 1908 Lambeth Conference came recommendations that proper Psalms be appointed for each Sunday and that lectionaries follow the church year.[47] With the lectionary arranged according to the civil calendar proper lessons for Sundays and Holy Days displaced course readings on all Sundays and on at least twelve weekdays dependent on the date of Easter.

In 1922 the Church of England adopted a new alternative lectionary which, with revisions, was accepted in the 1922 Canadian Prayer Book, the 1927 Irish, the 1928 English, the 1929 Scottish, the 1954 South African, and the 1960 Indian. Proper New Testament lessons (generally with alternatives) were provided for Sundays, so that a large proportion of the New Testament could be read on Sundays. The Scottish version provided a three-year cycle of Sunday lessons. Lessons were provided for eves of Holy Days. In the period from Advent to Trinity Sunday the Daily Office lessons related more appropriately to the seasons. In keeping with ancient tradition Isaiah is begun in Advent, Genesis on Septuagesima, and Acts at Easter. After Trinity Sunday lessons were generally consecutive. The proportion of readings from the Apocrypha increased, but the Irish version omits Aprocryphal readings and the Canadian, South African, and Indian provide alternatives. In a few cases lessons from the prophets take their place in the historical narrative. At Evening Prayer the first eleven weeks after Trinity Sunday selections from the Synoptic Gospels were arranged to form a composite life of Christ. Pauline Epistles were to be read in the order in which they were supposed to have been written.

The Irish, English, Scottish, South African, and Indian books provided similar but different tables of proper Psalms for all Sundays, so that a large part of the Psalter would be read on Sundays each year, and selections of Psalms for certain occasions. The Canadian book expanded the table of proper Psalms for certain days, and provided sixteen Selections of Psalms for use in place of the Psalms of the Day. The English, Scottish, South African, and Indian books allowed the omission of certain unedifying Psalms or portions of Psalms.[48]

The 1928 American lectionary is quite different from the 1922 English, but did incorporate some of the same principles. Proper Psalms were provided for certain seasons and days, a revised version of the twenty Selections of Psalms was retained from the 1892 book, optional proper Psalms were provided for each Sunday in a table similar to others of the period, and a listing of Psalms for special occasions was provided. The Daily Office lectionary was arranged according to the church year rather than the civil year. Selections from Genesis through 1 Kings 10, followed by Proverbs and Ecclesiasticus, were read at Morning Prayer, and 1 Kings 11 through the remainder of the Old Testament and Apocrypha at Evening Prayer, largely in their biblical order except for certain special days and seasons. Mark, the Epistles, Matthew, Luke, John, and Revelation 1–3 were read at Morning Prayer, and Revelation 4–22, John, Matthew (selections), Luke, Acts, and the Epistles at Evening Prayer. In the Sunday lectionary the principle of selections in course was abandoned for a new series of lessons related to the Sunday Eucharistic lections. The table for fixed Holy Days and their eves retained many lessons from 1892 but brought in a number from the 1922 English lectionary. Proper lessons were also provided for a number of special occasions.

The 1928 lectionary was not well received. The weekday lectionary was not sufficiently related to the church year, and the Sunday lectionary was given over too much to narrative material at the expense of prophetic and wisdom literature and Epistles. After eight years of trial use, a new lectionary was approved in 1943 by General Convention.[49] The table of Selections of Psalms was revised and enlarged, and for the first time in any Anglican lectionary proper Psalms were appointed for each day of the church year. The Psalms recur, more or less in course, in cycles of from four to seven weeks. Attention was given to the suitability of particular Psalms for morning or for evening, and Psalms of a penitential flavor were assigned to Fridays, whereas in the traditional Anglican daily system all of the traditional Compline Psalms were used in the morning and Psalms traditionally associated with morning (such as 51 and 147–150) came up in the evening; the most exuberant Psalms of praise could come up on fast days or penitential Psalms on festal occasions. Seven Psalms were omitted altogether from the lectionary.[50] The Daily Office lectionary recovered certain historic associations. A substantial portion of Isaiah is to be read in Advent and the Christmas Season; Genesis is begun at Septuagesima; Jeremiah is read during Lent, and Lamentations in Holy Week. Other books were assigned with more sensitivity to the days and seasons of the church year: Revelation to Advent; 1 John, Hebrews, and Ephesians to the Christmas and Epiphany seasons; 1 Corinthians to Lent; Hebrews, 1 Peter, and Ephesians to the Easter Season; and 1 and 2 Peter, 1 and 2 Thessalonians, and Jude to the weeks immediately preceding Advent. A continuous narrative of salvation history from the creation through the fall of Jerusalem (Genesis through 2 Kings) is to be read at Morning Prayer from Septuagesima to the Twenty-fourth Sunday after Trinity. At Evening Prayer readings concerning the return from the Exile and literature from the period begin immediately after Trinity Sunday. Acts is begun at Ascension. Mark and John are interwoven, beginning with Advent; Luke is begun immediately after Trinity Sunday at Morning Prayer, and Matthew takes up in Evening Prayer when Luke ends at the Thirteenth Sunday after Trinity. Alternative sets of lessons, for both morning and evening, related to the Eucharistic lectionary are provided for the Sundays of the church year. In the season after Trinity Sunday, two additional sets of Sunday lessons are provided. Course readings covering creation through the Conquest are linked with related New Testament passages at Morning Prayer, and readings covering the period from the birth of Samuel through the fall of

Jerusalem are read as Old Testament lessons with readings from Acts as New Testament lessons at Evening Prayer. The tables of lessons for fixed Holy Days and for special occasions were revised, and the latter substantially enlarged.

The Church of England produced a two-year table of Sunday lessons in 1947 and a conservative revision of the 1922 lectionary in 1955 with a two-year cycle of Sunday lessons. This revision was picked up in the Prayer Book of the Anglican Church of Ghana. The 1959 Canadian version also provided a table for reading the Psalter over a two-month period; several Psalms and portions of Psalms were omitted from the book altogether.[51]

In 1963 a Joint Liturgical Group was founded by representatives of the major communions in the British Isles. In 1968 it published a Daily Office[52] which would influence later revisions. The Psalms were spread over a thirteen-week period.[53] An Old Testament lesson, an "Epistle," and a Gospel are provided for each weekday in a two-year cycle, which begins with the Monday after the Ninth Sunday before Christmas. Most of the Old Testament was to be read once and most of the New Testament twice every two years. No Anglican revision has adopted this lectionary per se, but various features have been picked up.

The 1979 American Book of Common Prayer contains a new translation of the Psalter. Except for the period from the Fourth Sunday in Advent to the First Sunday after the Epiphany and for Holy Week and Easter Week, the Psalms are spread over a seven-week period. Seventeen Psalms or portions of Psalms are bracketed for possible omission.[54] Psalms with a penitential flavor are normally used on Fridays; Wednesdays are marked by the use of portions of Psalm 119, and Psalms dealing with creation and paschal deliverance are used on Saturday evenings and Sundays.[55] There are slight variations for the seasons of Lent and Easter.[56] The two-year lectionary appoints three lessons (Old Testament; Acts, Epistles, or Revelation; and Gospel), although if an Old Testament lesson is desired at both Daily Offices, that from the other year may be used at Evening Prayer. Many of the associations of particular books with particular seasons were retained from the 1943 lectionary. Seasons are enriched by the use of two cycles. In Year One, for example, Advent has Isaiah and substantial John the Baptist material; in Year Two, Amos, Haggai, and Zechariah, Revelation, and Matthaean apocalyptic material. In Year One, in Lent the principal readings are from Jeremiah, Romans, and John, and in Year Two from Genesis and Exodus, 1 and 2 Corinthians, and Mark. Since many of the lessons for fixed holy days were little more than commons of saints, with no reference to the particular saint, permission is given to maintain sequences by lengthening, combining, or omitting lessons. This translation of the Psalter and this lectionary have also been included in the 1983 Canadian revision.

The 1978 Australian Prayer Book and the English Alternative Services 1980 share another new translation of the Psalter. In the Australian book, except for days near Christmas and Easter, the Psalter is read more or less in course every eight weeks, except for Psalms used as Invitatories and Psalms 53, 70, and 108; Psalm 4 is bracketed for possible omission and a number of verses are listed which may be omitted.[57] In the English book the Psalter is read in course six times each year, except for some services from Christmas Eve through Epiphany and for Holy Week; Psalms 58 and 109 are bracketed for possible omission. The closely related weekday lectionaries provide for most of the Scriptures to be read every year, with two lessons both morning and evening. Lessons read in the morning one year are read in the evening the next, and vice versa. Lessons from the Apocrypha are alternatives to lessons from canonical Scripture. Sundays have proper Psalms and a two-year cycle of lessons related to the new English Eucharistic lectionary.

Through all the revisions over the centuries the Anglican Daily Offices are still based on Cranmer's rationale of regular reading of the Psalter and of most of the Scriptures.

The Eucharist

The Edwardian Injunctions of 1547 ordered that the Eucharistic Epistle and Gospel be read "in English and not in

Latin," and that a homily be read.[58] In addition to the Epistle and Gospel the Sarum Mass included snippets of Scripture, generally from the Psalms, at four points in the rite: as an introit, after the Epistle (both "Gradual" and "Alleluia" or "Tract"), at the offertory, and after the Communion. Cranmer substituted short Psalms or sections of Psalm 119 (beginning the First Sunday after Trinity) for the Sarum introits. These were appointed mostly in course, though a few were chosen for the relationship to the day.[59] He completely eliminated the selections between the Epistle and Gospel, possibly because these were associated with preparation of the elements. For the proper offertories of the Sarum missal Cranmer substituted a series of sentences designed to encourage the giving of alms, printed mostly in the biblical order, one or more of which were to be sung as the people placed their offerings in the "poor men's box." Another series of sentences in biblical order, exhorting people to be good and do good and to prepare for the Second Coming, took the place of the proper postcommunion selections of the Sarum rite. For Sundays and major Holy Days Cranmer retained the Epistles and Gospels of the Sarum missal, though he made some substitutions, lengthened some lessons, and abbreviated a few.[60] Minor changes were made in the revisions of 1552, 1662, 1892, and 1928.[61]

The Eucharistic lectionary itself did not expose people to a large amount of Scripture and hardly any Old Testament. Until the English "Shortened Services" Act of 1872[62] and the American 1892 Prayer Book, however, the morning service on Sundays and Holy Days was always to include Morning Prayer as well as Ante-Communion. People were therefore exposed to a substantial amount of Scripture in the principal services, and the whole Psalter would be read almost twice each year. Many of the old Anglican Sunday and Holy Day rites were quite rich. On Epiphany, for example, in early Prayer Books Isaiah 60 ("Your light has come"), Luke 3:1-22 (the baptism of Jesus), Ephesians 3:1-12 ("that the Gentiles should be fellow-heirs"), and Matthew 2:1-12 (the story of the Wise Men) would be read in the morning, and Isaiah 49 ("All flesh shall know that I am the Lord your Saviour ") and John 2:1-11 (the wedding at Cana) in the evening. The Easter rites were rich in paschal and baptismal imagery, with Psalms 2, 62, and 111, Exodus 12 (the Passover), Romans 6 (baptism into the death of Christ), Colossians 3:1-7 ("If ye be risen again with Christ") preceding the Gospel of the resurrection in the morning, and Psalms 113, 114, and 118 and Acts 2 (the Pentecost event) in the evening.

The 1958 Lambeth Conference called for subsequent Prayer Book revisions of Eucharistic rites to include Psalmody and Old Testament lessons.[63] The 1960 Indian book included Old Testament lessons, generally related to the Epistles and Gospels, but with some short periods of course readings. The newly united Church of South India authorized in 1962 The Book of Common Worship, with a new Eucharistic lectionary based on principles which would be adopted by some later revisions. An Old Testament lesson, a Gradual Psalm, an Epistle, and a Gospel were appointed for each Sunday and Holy Day, and the lessons develop a theme. The Sundays after Pentecost are devoted to the Christian life: God's Call (2–5), Bible, Church, and Sacraments (6–11), the life of devotion (12–17), life in the world (18–23), and the End (24–27).

The 1978 Australian, 1979 American, and 1983 Canadian Prayer Books have all adopted revised versions of the lectionary adopted by the Roman Catholic Church after the Second Vatican Council.[64] Most of the New Testament and a large portion of the Old are read in a three-year cycle.[65] The foundation of the lectionary is the reading from the Gospels. The Gospel according to John is read in the seasons of Lent and Easter and on certain other occasions; each year one of the synoptic Gospels is read in course throughout the remainder of the church year, except for certain special days or seasons. The first of the three readings is from the Old Testament, except in the Easter season when, in accordance with an old tradition, the first choice is a reading from Acts. In Lent the Old Testament readings each year provide a conspectus of salvation history, but through most of the year the Old Testament readings were chosen for their relationship to the Gospel of the day. The Psalm appointed for the gradual is often linked to the lesson preceding it. In Lent the Epistles tend to correspond to the Old

Testament readings. In the Easter season the second reading, following ancient traditions, is from 1 Peter or 1 John because of their baptismal significance, or from Revelation because of its portrayals of the life of the world to come. In the periods between the First and the Last Sundays after the Epiphany and between Trinity Sunday and the Last Sunday after Pentecost the Pauline Epistles are read in course.

This new three-year ecumenical lectionary gives more shape to the church year and heightens or recovers certain traditional emphases. The First Sunday of Advent has an eschatological emphasis, the Second and Third center on John the Baptist, and the Fourth (in accordance with Gallican tradition) is devoted to the Annunciation. The First Sunday after the Epiphany is always a feast of the Baptism of Christ, and the Last (in accordance with Lutheran tradition) a celebration of the Transfiguration.[66] The baptismal nature of the seasons of Lent and Easter is heightened. A Palm Sunday rite that deals with both the entry into Jerusalem and the passion, and Easter and Pentecost baptismal vigils, are recovered. The last three Sundays after Pentecost have eschatological themes, with the last devoted to the kingship of Christ.

The 1980 English book provides a three-lesson, thematic, two-year Eucharistic lectionary developed by the Joint Liturgical Group. The lectionary begins with the Ninth Sunday before Christmas. The five Sundays preceding Advent are devoted to Old Testament preparation. The Sundays after Pentecost are devoted to the Christian life, with the theme of the last being "Citizens of Heaven."

Until recent years no Anglican Prayer Book provided Eucharistic propers for weekdays that were not Holy Days; normally those of the preceding Sunday were repeated. Recent Anglican books, however, have made provision for Black Letter Days and other occasions.[67] The 1979 American book provides common propers for Black Letter Days and propers for twenty-five "Various Occasions." The current Lesser Feasts and Fasts, authorized by the 1979 General Convention (a revision of earlier editions published in 1963 and 1973), provides a two-lesson and Psalm lectionary for the weekdays of Lent and Easter (Old

Testament lesson and Gospel in Lent, a lesson from Acts and a Johannine Gospel for Easter) and two lessons and Psalm for each of the Black Letter Days listed in the Calendar of the 1979 Prayer Book. The 1980 English and 1983 Canadian books also provide propers for several categories of saints and for various occasions and a daily two-lesson and Psalm Eucharistic lectionary, with a two-year cycle of first lessons for the periods after Epiphany and after Pentecost. The American, English, and Canadian provisions are all indebted to the Roman lectionary.

Other Rites

The early Prayer Books were based on the principle that baptism and most of the pastoral offices would normally be celebrated within the principal Sunday liturgy; they therefore contained few Psalms or lessons.

The baptismal rite contained one lesson, Mark 10:13-16, "Suffer little children to come unto me," used as an apologia for infant baptism. When a rite for adults was added in 1662, John 3:1-8 (the story of Nicodemus) was the lesson. The 1928 American book combined the rites and added a third lesson, Matthew 28:18-20 (the great commission) for occasions when both infants and adults would be baptized at the same service.

The 1892 book was the first to include a lesson in the confirmation rite. Acts 8:14-17 was inserted as an optional reading, apparently as a scriptural warrant for the rite, a use few New Testament scholars would defend. Yet it was picked up by the 1922 Canadian, 1928 English, 1929 Scottish, and 1954 South African revisions.

The marriage rite of the early Prayer Books contained two alternative Psalms, 128 and 67, and an exhortation consisting of scriptural quotations for use when the sermon did not expound the duties of husbands and wives. The 1789 revision, however, dropped the concluding portion of the rite, including the Psalms and exhortation. The 1912 Scottish book appointed an Epistle (Ephesians 5:25-33) and a Gospel (Matthew 19:4-6) for a Eucharist at a marriage, and most later revisions have followed suit. The early rites for churching of women contained Psalm 121. The 1662 revision substituted Psalm 116:1-13a and 16b or Psalm 127.

The 1549 Visitation of the Sick contained Psalms 143 and 71 and Psalm 13 for use at the anointing. The anointing, with its Psalm, and Psalm 143 were dropped at the 1552 revision. Psalm 71 was abbreviated to verses 1-17 in the 1662 revision, and Psalm 130 was substituted in 1789. Beginning with the 1922 Canadian book most revisions have provided alternative Psalms and suggested suitable lessons. From 1549 the Prayer Book provided a brief Epistle (Hebrews 12:5b-6) and Gospel (John 5:24) for Communion of the Sick. Beginning with the 1927 Irish book most revisions have provided alternatives.

The 1549 Prayer Book contained for a burial provisions for a procession accompanied by scriptural sentences,[68] an office including Psalms 116, 139, and 146 and 1 Corinthians 15:20-58, a Eucharist with introit (Psalm 42), Epistle (1 Thessalonians 4:13-18), and Gospel (John 6:37-40), and a committal including scriptural texts among its anthems.[69] The 1552 book retained special provision only for the procession and the committal, at which 1 Corinthians 15:20-58 was to be read. The 1662 book appointed Psalms 39 and 90 and the Corinthian lesson for use in the church. The 1877 Irish book provided an alternative lesson (1 Thessalonians 4:13-18). Beginning with the 1912 Scottish book most revisions have provided alternative Psalms and lessons for the burial office and an Epistle and Gospel for use at a Eucharist.

The Sarum pontifical did not appoint proper lessons for ordination rites. The 1550 Ordinal provided alternatives for the Epistle at the ordination of deacons (1 Timothy 3:8-16 or Acts 6:2-7), introits for the ordination of priests or bishops (Psalms 40, 132, or 135), Epistle (Acts 20:17-35 or 1 Timothy 3) and Gospel (Matthew 28:18-20, John 10:1-16, or John 20:19-23) for the ordination of priests, and Epistle (1 Timothy 3:1-7) and Gospel (John 21:15-17 or John 10:1-16) for the ordination of bishops. All of these Psalms and lessons except Acts 6:2-7 had been suggested by Martin Bucer's *De ordinatione legitima*.[70] In 1552 the introits were dropped. The

1662 book appointed a proper Gospel for the ordination of deacons (Luke 12:35-38) and shifted both of the Epistles and the Matthew 28 and John 20 Gospels from the rite for priests to that for bishops to prevent presbyterian interpretations. Ephesians 4:7-13 was appointed as the Epistle at the ordination of priests and Matthew 9:36-38 was provided as the first choice for Gospel.

The latest Prayer Book revisions, the 1978 Australian, 1979 American, 1980 English, and 1983 Canadian, recognizing that the pastoral offices are seldom associated with a regular service, and that baptisms, confirmations, and ordinations are not always associated with the principal services of a congregation, have provided much richer lectionaries for these rites. Each provides for a full liturgy of the word with Old Testament lesson, Psalm, New Testament lesson, and Gospel for baptisms, confirmations, marriages, rites for the sick, burials, and ordinations. The American book, unlike the others, includes rites for the celebration of a new ministry and for the consecration of a church, and these rites, also, have provisions for a full liturgy of the word. The Book of Occasional Services, authorized by the 1979 General Convention, provides additional rites with substantial readings from the Scriptures.

Scripture Prayed

The order of December 25, 1549, calling in the old service books says of the 1549 Book of Common Prayer that it is "grounded upon the holy Scripture,"[71] and the Act of Uniformity establishing the revision of 1552 speaks of the 1549 book as "a very godly order . . . agreeable to the word of God."[72] The preface of the 1549 book speaks of it as an "order for prayer" in which "is ordained nothing to be read but the very pure word of God, the holy Scriptures, or that which is evidently grounded upon the same."

Unscriptural Forms Deleted

Cranmer revised or deleted texts that he felt were contrary to scriptural teaching, but he did not take the stance of many continental reformers that anything must be rejected which did not have clear scriptural warrant. The basic structure of the church year was retained, but dozens of saints' days and other days, some of which were considered among the most important in the late medieval period, such as Corpus Christi, the feasts of the Conception and of the Assumption of Mary, and All Souls' Day, were swept away. The only Holy Days retained were feasts of our Lord, and the days of apostles and evangelists, St. Stephen the protomartyr, the Holy Innocents, St. Mary Magdalene, St. Michael and All Angels,[73] and All Saints. The only saints given propers or even listed in the calendar were New Testament saints.[74]

Many forms were retained from the Sarum rite in translation, and many others in revised versions, but many were not brought over into the 1549 book, evidently because they were considered unscriptural. Primary concerns were ideas of merit, the intercession of saints, and false eucharistic doctrine. Except for the Lord's Prayer and the Collect for Purity (which was revised) all of the priest's prayers and blessings which had preceded the Mass were swept away. Troped forms of the Kyrie were deleted, and the phrases inserted in the Gloria in excelsis on occasion ("Spirit, and kind comforter of orphans," "First born of Mary virgin mother," "to the glory of Mary," "sanctifying Mary," "governing Mary," "crowning Mary") were omitted. A prayer for the king took the place of the memorial collects which often involved intercession of saints or reference to Mary. The Sarum missal provided a sequence for almost every day that rated an Alleluia, but many contained nonbiblical legendary material or intercession of saints, and they were all deleted. All the offertory prayers were omitted. Only five proper prefaces were retained.[75] The occasional variation in the Sanctus, "Blessed be the Son of Mary that comes in the Name of the Lord," was deleted. Substantial portions of the Eucharistic Prayer dealing with offering or with the commemoration of the living or the departed have no parallel in the prayer of the 1549 book. The embolism following the Lord's Prayer was deleted, as well as the priest's prayers of preparation and thanksgiving. The baptismal rite, the Daily Offices, and the pastoral offices were stripped in the same manner of forms deemed unscriptural.[76] The Sarum baptismal rite set the Ave Maria alongside the Lord's Prayer and the Apostles' Creed as a third text to be learned by every child; the 1549 book substituted the Decalogue and eliminated the Ave Maria altogether from the book.

Another issue in the first Book of Common Prayer and subsequent revisions was prayer for the departed. The 1549 version of the Prayer for the Whole State of Christ's Church ended with a commemoration of saints, a petition that we might follow their examples, and a commendation of those "departed hence from us with the sign of faith." The highly elaborate Sarum burial rite was simplified and abbreviated; the absolutions of the body and most of the petitions for the departed were omitted. The 1552 revision omitted the concluding section of the Prayer for the Whole State of Christ's Church and drastically abbreviated the burial rite, revising many of the forms that were retained. One prayer was formed by joining portions of two 1549 prayers and adding a conclusion "beseeching... that we with this our brother, and all other departed in the true faith of thy holy name, may have our perfect consummation and bliss, both in body, and soul, in thy eternal and everlasting glory." This was the closest the 1552 book came to a petition for the departed, but even this was too much for the Puritans, who also objected to the phrase "as our hope is this our brother doth" in another prayer. The 1637 Scottish book restored a commemoration of saints based on that of 1549, but not prayer for the departed. In the 1662 revision a thanksgiving for the departed and a petition that we might follow their good examples were added to the Prayer for the Whole State of Christ's Church, but no petition for the departed. In the first prayer of the burial office "with all those that are departed" replaced "with this our brother, and all other departed." Yet phrases in the burial office continued to be a problem through the late seventeenth and the eighteenth centuries.[77] The 1789 book revised the committal and the prayers to eliminate the last vestiges of prayer for the departed. The custom was reintroduced in the nineteenth century, and by the time of the 1928 American revision, amid great controversy, a petition for the departed was inserted in the Prayer for the Whole State of Christ's Church and optional prayers for the departed were brought into the burial rite, for sufficient people had been convinced that prayer for the departed was not contrary to Holy Scripture. Petitions for the departed also made their way into the 1928 English, 1929 Scottish, 1954 South African, and 1959 Canadian books.

Forms Revised

Many of the Sarum forms which were retained were very much revised by Cranmer. Of special significance is the reworking of the Eucharistic Prayer. The Benedictus qui venit was followed in the Sarum rite by a petition to accept "these holy unspotted sacrifices," then by a petition for those who offer and their intentions, commemorating the saints and praying that through their merits and prayers we may be defended. Another petition for the acceptance of this oblation led into a petition to bless it "that it may become for us the body and blood of thy most dearly beloved Son our Lord Jesus Christ." The Institution Narrative was followed by the offering of "a pure, holy, spotless, victim." God is asked to accept this offering that it may be borne to his altar on high. Prayers for the departed and for fellowship with the saints lead into a concluding doxology. In the 1549 book the Benedictus qui venit leads into a prayer "for the whole state of Christ's church," modeled after prayers of the people of German Church Orders. The initial quotation from 1 Timothy 2:1 sets the stage for broader intercessions than those of the Roman prayer, and the prayer emphasizes the preaching and receiving of the word. The intercessions are followed by a recalling of the one sacrifice of the cross, and a petition, "with thy Holy Spirit and word, vouchsafe to bless and sanctify these thy gifts, and creatures of bread and wine, that they may be unto us the body and blood of thy most dearly beloved son Jesus Christ."

The Institution Narrative is a conflation of the four biblical accounts, but the nonscriptural phrases in the Roman form are all excised. The anamnesis leads into a petition to accept "our sacrifice of praise and thanksgiving" and our offering of "our self, our souls, and bodies." The prayer ends with a petition not that "our offerings" but that "our prayers and supplications" might be borne to God's altar on high. Though using some material from the Roman prayer Cranmer systematically excised all references to an oblation of the elements and to the merits and prayers of the saints. The 1552 revisers dealt harshly with this prayer, placing the intercessions immediately after the giving of alms, substituting a petition for worthy reception for the epiclesis, and retaining a truncated version of the portion which came after the Institution Narrative as one of two alternative forms for use after the administration of Communion. With minor revisions this is the form retained in the 1662 book. The Scottish book of 1637, however, restored a revised form of the 1549 prayer. It came into use in Scotland through a series of "Wee Bookies," the first of which was published in 1722. The edition of 1735 inserted the phrase "which we now offer thee" in the anamnesis, the revisers being aware that such a phrase was found in ancient and Eastern prayers and convinced that it was not unbiblical. A revised version of the Scottish form, minus the phrase "that they may be unto us the body and blood of thy most dearly beloved Son," came into the first American book. Most twentieth-century Anglican revisions other than the Scottish and the American have shied away from an oblation, but many have substituted an epiclesis for the petition for worthy reception of the 1552 and subsequent English books.[78] Most recent Anglican revisions have, in the preface and/or post-Sanctus, incorporated thanksgiving for creation and redemption with specific mention of the incarnation and have incorporated anticipation of the second coming in the anamnesis. Cranmer was concerned that there be nothing unbiblical in the Eucharistic Prayer and that it set forth a Eucharistic doctrine founded on the Scriptures. Cranmer's prayer has been revised and a number of other Eucharistic Prayers included in more recent Prayer Books, but the revisers have worked under the constraint of these same concerns.

Cranmer's concern in regard to the invocation of saints and of angels can be seen in his 1544 litany, the first rite officially set forth in English. The numerous invocations addressed to Mary, the angels, and the saints were compressed into three petitions, one asking the prayers of Mary, one the prayers of the angels, and a third the prayers of all the saints. These three petitions were deleted in the 1549 revision.

Cranmer eliminated the insertions in the Sarum rite's farced or troped versions of the Kyrie and Gloria in excelsis. That rite also had farced or troped scriptural passages as the Institution Narrative, as songs of the people,[79] and as lessons.[80] No troped version was brought over into the 1549 book. The full biblical text of the Benedicite omnia opera was substituted for the condensed version of the Sarum rite.

Many of the collects retained from the Sarum rite were revised to conform to Cranmer's view of scriptural teaching.[81] Though the old Latin collects were basically Augustinian, Cranmer took no chances. In three collects the verb form *mereamur* ("we may merit") is omitted from the translation.[82] Forms of the word *propitius* are always translated by some form of the word "mercy"—"mercy,"[83] "mercifully,"[84] "by thy great mercy,"[85] or "by thy grace and mercy."[86] In one collect "guiding" becomes "merciful guiding,"[87] and in another "may be relieved" becomes "may mercifully be relieved."[88] A petition for the protection of the Doctor of the Gentiles is changed to a plea that we may be defended "by thy power."[89] The petition "that we may by his example advance toward thee" becomes a petition that we "may follow and fulfill the holy doctrine that he taught."[90] In two cases the word *spero* is translated not "hope" but "trust."[91] Other collects are changed or amplified to stress the weakness of humanity and humanity's dependence upon God's grace. The phrase "through the satisfaction of thy Son our Lord" is inserted in one collect.[92] *Convalescent* is expanded to "have grace and power."[93] "By thy goodness" is added to a petition for forgiveness.[94] The word "all" is inserted in the petition "nourish us with all goodness."[95] In the address, "God, of whose only gift it cometh, that thy faithful people do unto thee true and laudable service," the word "only" is not in the Latin.[96] The inability of humanity to do good is stressed by the addition of the word "good" in "the weakness of our mortal nature can do no good thing without thee."[97] On the other hand, Cranmer changes some collects to lay stress on the idea that faith brings forth the fruit of good works. A petition that might be translated "bring the same to good effect" becomes "so by thy continual help we may bring the same to good effect."[98] "May by thee be able to live" becomes "may by thee be able to live according to thy will."[99] Other changes have to do with Cranmer's view of the Church and ministry. "Thy bishops" becomes "our bishops and curates [those in charge of a cure]."[100] One prayer in the Good Friday rite which in the original was for those in holy orders becomes a prayer for every member of the Church. Another contains a reference, not in the original, to the Church as the true Israel. The word *ecclesia* is sometimes translated "Church"[101] but sometimes "congregation."[102] Many of the Latin collects came from times when the Church was threatened by exernal forces. At a time when the Church in England was divided between those of the "old learning" and those of the "new learning," and threatened by Papists on the one hand and Anabaptists on the other, Cranmer tends to turn these prayers into a petition to defend the Church from enemies within or enemies both without and within.[103] Certain other changes either introduce or intensify the thought of heaven and its attainment.[104] At least one translation shows a more pessimistic view of this world: "we may so pass through temporal good things" becomes "we may so pass through things temporal."[105] Cranmer was fearful of any word which might allow for an interpretation of the Mass which denigrated the all-sufficient sacrifice of Christ; he also seems to have been wary of the use of words which might be used to interpret the feasts of the church year as in any sense a renewal of our redemption. In the collect for the First Communion on Christmas Day the word *expectatione* is changed to "remembrance," as is *colimus* in the Collect for the Conversion of St. Paul. Eight of the Latin collects retained say that on this day, *hodie*, a certain event took place; in five *hodie* is left untranslated.[106]

New Forms

The 1549 Prayer Book contained many forms not in the Sarum rite. Some of these came from other sources, but many were apparently newly composed.

The only saints' day collects retained even in a revised form were those for the feast days of St. Stephen, St. John, the Holy Innocents, the Conversion of St. Paul, St. Bartholomew, and St. Michael and All Angels. The others were all rejected because they asked for the prayers or the protection of or a share in the merits of the saint. With one exception, Cranmer turned to the Scriptures to provide the content for the new collects. If the saint was one about whom anything was known, the new collect is based on biblical references to the saint, recalling some lesson, commending the example of the saint, or leading into an appropriate petition. The one exception is the collect for St. Andrew's Day which alludes to a nonscriptural story of his death by crucifixion, but this was replaced in the 1552 revision by a new collect which refers to his call.

Freed from the restraint of translating or revising a Latin original Cranmer looked to the Scriptures for content and manner of expression in the new collects for saints' days and in other new collects and prayers as well. The new collect for the First Sunday of Advent is based on the Epistle (Romans 13:8-14). The new collect for the Second Sunday, based on the opening verse of the Epistle (Romans 15:4), reflects the new emphasis on the Scriptures:

> Blessed Lord, which hast caused all holy Scriptures to be written for our learning; grant us that we may in such wise hear them, read, mark, learn, and inwardly digest them, that by patience, and comfort of thy holy word, we may

embrace, and ever hold fast the blessed hope of everlasting life, which thou hast given us in our Saviour Jesus Christ.

New collects were also provided for Christmas Day (the Second Communion), Circumcision, Quinquagesima, Ash Wednesday, the First Sunday in Lent, Easter Day (the Second Communion), the Second Sunday after Easter, and the Sunday after Ascension Day. The new collect for Ash Wednesday, inspired by Psalm 51, used that day in the commination rite, places the emphasis on penitence rather than fasting. That for the First Sunday in Lent avoids the Pelagian overtones of the Sarum collect, and bases the practice of fasting on our Lord's example, related in the day's Gospel. The new collects for Circumcision, Quinquagesima, Easter Day, and the Second Sunday after Easter were all clearly inspired by the Epistle, and that for the Sunday after Ascension Day by the Gospel. Very much the same principles and style have marked new collects that have come into the Prayer Book with successive revisions.[107]

The Sarum missal provided a proper postcommunion prayer for each Mass. Though many would be unexceptionable, several spoke of attaining worthiness, a few spoke of the Mass as a sacrifice or in some other manner which would have been objectionable to Cranmer, and those for saints' days frequently invoked their prayers. He therefore provided in the 1549 book one fixed postcommunion prayer remarkable for its biblical descriptions of the Eucharist and the Church and Christian vocation.[108]

The homily printed after the marriage rite and that which introduced the commination rite were constructed almost altogether by linking biblical quotations. This tendency to turn to the Scriptures themselves for new forms can be seen in subsequent revisions. The general confession appended to Morning Prayer in the 1552 revision, for example, is based on Romans 7:8-25 and includes allusions to Isaiah 53:6, Psalm 119:176, 1 Peter 2:25, Psalm 51:13, Romans 15:8, 1 John 2:12, Titus 2:11-12, and John 14:13.

Forms which came from other sources were also biblical in content and wording. For the prayers over the baptismal water

Cranmer turned to an ancient Gallican form richer in biblical baptismal imagery.[109] Many forms which met this test were brought in from German Lutheran sources: for example, the "Flood Prayer" (which dates back to Martin Luther himself), the prayer following the exhortation to the godparents, and substantial portions of the exhortations and other forms in the rite for public baptism, most of the text of the rite for private baptism, and the prayer following the laying on of hands in the confirmation rite. The two exhortations and the invitation, general confession, absolution, and "Comfortable Words" in the Eucharistic rite are all heavily dependent on the *Consultation* of Hermann von Wied, the reforming archbishop of Cologne. Portions of the marriage rite, the rites for the sick, and the burial rite also stem from Lutheran sources. Many forms in the 1550 ordination rites were based on Bucer's *De ordinatione legitima*.

Scripture Sung

Invitatory Psalms and Anthems and Canticles

For the sake of simplicity, and possibly to encourage congregational participation, Cranmer retained in Matins only one Invitatory Psalm, Venite (Psalm 95), and three canticles: Te Deum laudamus for use after the first lesson; Benedicite omnia opera for use in its place in Lent; and Benedictus Dominus Deus for use after the second lesson. He retained the Magnificat from Vespers and the Nunc dimittis from Compline for use after the two lessons at Evensong. He also provided a special anthem for Easter, composed of Romans 6:9-11 and 1 Corinthians 15:20-22. Possibly because of objections to the Apocrypha, the restrictions on the use of the Te Deum were removed at the 1552 revision, and because of objections to general use of the songs of Zechariah, Mary, and Simeon, Psalms were provided as alternatives to the Gospel canticles: Psalm 100, Jubilate, for the Benedictus; Psalm 98, Cantate Domino, for the Magnificat; and Psalm 67, Deus misereatur, for the Nunc dimittis. Objections to the Benedicite continued, and Psalm 23 was substituted in the 1637 Scottish book, but the Benedicite was retained in the 1662 revision. That revision prefixed 1 Corinthians 5:7-8 to the Easter Anthems. Objections to the last verses of the Venite, to the Benedicite, and to the Gospel canticles continued through the late seventeenth and the eighteenth centuries,[110] and the 1789 American revision in the Venite substituted Psalm 96:9 and 13 for Psalm 95:8-11, abbreviated the Benedictus to four verses, and substituted Psalm 92:1-4, Bonum est confiteri, for the Magnificat and Psalm 103:1-4, 20-22, Benedic, anima mea, for the Nunc dimittis. The 1892 revision restored the Magnificat and Nunc dimittis and the concluding verses of the Benedictus. Twentieth-century Prayer Book revisions have enlarged the selection of biblical canticles, and some have shifted the place of the Jubilate to that of an alternative to the Venite. The 1922 Canadian book added two canticles, Cantate Domino (Isaiah 42:10-12) and Surge, illuminare (Isaiah 60:1-3, 11a, 14, 18-19). The 1927 Irish book added Urbs fortitudinis (Isaiah 26:1b-4, 7-8) and Dignus es (Revelation 5:12, 9-10, 13). The 1928 American book added Benedictus es (Song of the Three Young Men 29-34), and the 1928 English Misere mei, Deus (Psalm 51:1-18). The most recent Australian and English revisions appoint different Invitatory Psalms or anthems and different canticles for the various days of the week, and the American and Canadian revisions provide tables suggesting appropriate days for the use of the various canticles. The 1979 American book added to those included in the 1928 book seven biblical canticles: The Song of Moses (Exodus 15:1-6, 11-13, 17-18), three Songs of Isaiah (12:2-6; 55:6-11; 60:1-3, 11a, 14c, 18-19), A Song of Penitence (Prayer of Manasseh 1-2, 4, 6-7, 11-15), A Song to the Lamb (Revelation 4:11, 5:9-10, 13), and The Song of the Redeemed (Revelation 15:3-4). The 1980 English book picked up the two canticles from Revelation and added another new to Anglican Prayer Books, Philippians 2:6-11. The 1983 Canadian book has picked up all of these except the canticle from the Prayer of Manasseh, appoints Psalm 134 as an Invitatory Psalm at Evening Prayer (following the Australian book), and has added other canticles: three from Isaiah (2:2-5; 40:9-11, 53:3-6), Jeremiah 31:10-14a, Ezekiel 36:24-28, three from Wisdom (3:1-8; 10:15-19, 20b-21; 16:20-21, 26), Matthew 5:3-12, Ephesians 1:3-7 (from the Australian book), and Colossians 1:15-20. The 1978 Australian book also treats as an Invitatory Psalm or anthem or as a canticle several passages not found in other books: Psalms 23, 93, 96:1-6, 96:7-13, and 150; Tobit 13:1-4; Judith 16:13-15; John 1:1-5, 10-14, 16; Ephesians 2:4-7; and Hebrews 10:19-22. These more recent Prayer Books bring into use as Invitatory Psalms or anthems or as canticles a much larger portion of the Scriptures.

Metrical Psalms and Hymns

The 1549 Prayer Book did not contain a single metrical hymn or rubrical permission for the use of any hymn. Cranmer had attempted to translate some Latin hymns, but had not been pleased with the results.[111] Possibly as early as 1539 Miles Coverdale had published a collection of *Ghoostly Psalmes and Spirituall Songes Drawen Out of the Holy Scripture* based on the Wittenberg hymnals,[112] but it was prohibited in 1546. The 1550 Ordinal did include a translation, apparently by Cranmer, of one metrical hymn, Veni Creator Spiritus. Aside from this hymn there is no permission to use any hymnody in either the 1552 or 1559 books.

In 1547 Thomas Sternhold published a small collection of metrical versions of Psalms in ballad metre. An enlarged edition was published in 1549, and another in 1551 with additional Psalms by John Hopkins. Exiles in Geneva and Strassburg continued work on the Psalter and brought out an edition in 1556. After the return of the exiles work continued, and in 1562 the edition which became the staple musical diet of Anglicans for two centuries or more was published, *The Whole Book of Psalms, Collected into English Metre by Thomas Sternhold, John Hopkins, and Others. Set Forth and Allowed To Be Sung in All Churches, of All the People Together, Before and After Morning and Evening Prayer; and Also Before and After Sermons; and Moreover in Private Houses, for Their Godly Solace and Comfort, Laying Apart All Ungodly Songs and Ballads, Which Tend Only to the Nourishing of Vice, and Corrupting of Youth.*[113] (The Elizabethan Injunctions of 1559 allowed a "hymn, or suchlike song" before and after Morning and Evening Prayer.)[114] In addition to the metrical versions of the Psalms, this book contained metrical versions of the Veni Creator, the canticles, the Lord's Prayer, the Decalogue, the Athanasian and Apostles' Creeds, two hymns which are translations from German,[115] and six English hymns.[116] One of these is a prayer for use before a sermon, one a thanksgiving after Communion, and four are general confessions. There were slight additions and subtractions in successive editions. In the larger foundations anthems, mostly in the words of Scripture, and plainchant or polyphonic settings of canticles, Psalms and service music continued to be sung.[117]

The first Anglican hymnal was George Wither's *Hymns and Songs of the Church*, published in 1623.[118] It contains thirty-six metrical versions of scriptural passages, paraphrases of the Decalogue, the Lord's Prayer, the Apostles' and Athanasian Creeds, the Benedicite, the Te Deum, the Veni Creator, and the scriptural anthems of the burial rite. These are followed by hymns for the principal days of the church year and for all the saints' days (thirty-five in all), and eleven "Spiritual Songs fitted for other Solemnities." These are hymns rather than biblical paraphrases, but the content is truly biblical. Wither obtained a patent from King James ordering that his work be bound with each copy of the metrical Psalter, but the Company of Stationers succeeded in securing its revocation.

Certainly part of the opposition in Scotland to the imposition of the 1637 Prayer Book was due to the fact that bound with it was *The Psalmes of King David Translated by King James*,[119] designed to take the place of the beloved Scottish Psalter.

During the Interregnum there were attempts to displace the Sternhold and Hopkins version with a "purer" version, either that of Francis Rous[120] or that of William Barton,[121] both of which contributed to the Scottish Psalter of 1650. At the Restoration what was probably a common practice in the larger foundations was legitimized by the addition of a rubric after the fixed collects in both Morning and Evening Prayer, "In Quires and places where they sing here followeth the Anthem." Soon after the Restoration Anglican chant developed as a medium for Psalms and canticles, and the Verse Anthem as a vehicle for other scriptural texts, though use of Anglican chant and of anthems was mostly confined to the larger foundations with choirs.

In 1696 *A New Version of the Psalms of David, Fitted to the Tunes Used in Churches*, by Nicholas Brady and Nahum Tate, was first published. This "New Version," with or without *A Supplement to the New Version of the Psalms*, a small supplement of hymns, which first appeared in 1700 or earlier, began more and more to displace the "Old Version" by Sternhold and Hopkins. In addition to paraphrases of the usual items it contained a paraphrase of the Gloria in excelsis, and five scriptural paraphrases, one designated for Christmas (the familiar "While shepherds watched their flocks by night"), two for Easter Day, and two for Holy Communion. The number of hymns was increased slgihtly in later editions of the supplement.

Though the Church of England limited itself almost altogether to metrical paraphrases of scriptural and Prayer Book texts, Presbyterians and Independents in the last decades of the seventeenth century accepted freer paraphrases of the Scripture and hymns inspired by Scripture. Isaac Watts, often called "Father of English Hymnody," published two volumes with descriptive titles which found great favor among his fellow Nonconformists, *Hymns and Spiritual Songs. In Three Books. I. Collected from the Scriptures. II. Composed on Divine Subjects. III. Prepared for the Lord's Supper*[122] and *The Psalms of David Imitated in the Language of the New Testament, and Applied to the Christian State and Worship.*[123] Among the Nonconformists there was a great proliferation of hymn-writing. One of the best and most prolific of these writers was Philip Doddridge who wrote many hymns based on the texts for his sermons, three hundred seventy-four of which were collected after his death and published in 1755.[124] Among Anglicans this tendency to deal more loosely with the Scriptures and the singing of songs "of human composition" was resisted. Many eighteenth-century printings of either the Old or the New Version of the metrical Psalter lacked the usual supplement of metrical versions of other biblical or Prayer Book texts and hymns. Possibly as an effort to offset use of the growing body of hymnody, Edmund Gibson, soon after he became bishop of London, published *Directions Given to the Clergy of the Diocese of London, in the Year 1724*, in which he sets forth a six-months' course for singing selections from the Psalms. Proper Psalms are designated for only four days (Christmas, Easter, Pentecost, and "King's Inauguration-Day"), and for four special occasions, burials, "Rain after much Dry Weather," "Fair Weather after much Rain," and "on the Days of [Charity] Collection." Others published similar courses. Prayer Books printed in the eighteenth century for use in Ireland lack the supplement and contain a listing of "Proper Psalms suited to the Feasts and Fasts of the Church."

Even before his Aldersgate experience, during his ministry in Savannah, Georgia, John Wesley published a hymnal, *A Collection of Psalms and Hymns*,[125] which includes some of his own translations of German hymns and hymns and metrical Psalms from the works of Joseph Addison, John Austin, George Herbert, Thomas Ken, Isaac Watts, his own father and his elder brother, Samuel, Jr. Soon after returning to England and entering upon their evangelical mission, John and Charles Wesley found that hymns were their most effective instrument and between them composed more than six thousand. Some of the Wesley hymns are inspired by particular passages of Scripture, but many, though imbued with scriptural content, are much freer, with particular emphasis on the individual's appropriation of religious experience. The evangelical party in the Church of England was influenced by the Wesleyan hymnody and began to produce substantial hymnals, the most notable of which was that produced by John Newton and William Cowper, *Olney Hymns in Three Books. Book I. On Select Texts of Scripture. Book II. On Occasional Subjects. Book III. On the Progress and Changes of the Spiritual Life*.[126]

From the mid-eighteenth century some of the parishes not caught up in the evangelical revival began to use small parochial collections of additional hymns. Those of Watts, Doddridge, and Addison were particularly favored. One, typical of these parochial collections, which had special influence on the first American "Prayer Book Collection," was *The Hymns, Anthems and Tunes with the Ode Used at the Magdalen Chapel: Set for the Organ, Harpsichord, Voice, German-Flute or Guitar*.[127] It includes twenty-seven hymns, mostly by Addison, Doddridge, Dryden, Ken, Samuel Wesley, Jr., and Watts.

The American 1786 Proposed Book contained a collection of "Singing Psalms" abridged from the Tate and Brady Psalter, arranged in four sections: "Praise," "Prayer," "Thanksgiving," and "Instructive Psalms." It also contained fifty-one "Hymns," fourteen of which, in whole or in part, are selected verses from the Tate and Brady Psalter, and six from its supplement. Sixteen are, in whole or in part, from the Psalms and hymns of Isaac Watts. Six are by Doddridge, five by Addison, one each by Samuel Wesley, Jr., John Dryden, John Patrick, James Maxwell, and Francis Hopkinson, and one probably by Arthur Bedford. The book also contained an appendix, edited by Francis Hopkinson, of eighteen metrical tunes and four Anglican chant tunes. Though in England chanting was still confined to choirs, congregations in America were beginning to chant the canticles and Psalms.[128]

The 1789 book contained the whole Tate and Brady Psalter and twenty-seven of the hymns from the Proposed Book, preceded by a preface which authorizes their use "before and after Morning and Evening Prayer; and also before and after Sermons, at the discretion of the Minister." At the end of the hymns is the note "End of the Prayer-Book." The 1789 Prayer Book withdrew permission for an anthem after the fixed collects, but required a hymn immediately before the Communions. This collection was too meager for some parishes; supplements appeared as early as 1792. In 1808 General Convention authorized thirty additional hymns. Charles Wesley was represented for the first time in this collection.[129] A new hymn by Anne Steele, "Father of mercies! in thy word," was published under the heading "The Excellency and Sufficiency of the Scriptures."

In the first decades of the nineteenth century British writers continued to produce hymns and new metrical versions of the Psalms. Among the more outstanding of these authors were Thomas Kelly, Richard Mant, James Montgomery, and Reginald Heber. Heber began to assemble a collection which was not published until 1827, the year after his death, *Hymns Written and Adapted to the Weekly Church Service of the Year*.[130] Included were three translations by William Drummond of Latin hymns. The metrical Psalms which were included were not given pride of place but printed in appropriate places among the hymns. An increasing number of Anglican parishes were beginning to make more use of hymns, and controversy concerning their use died down after the famous Cotterill incident in 1819.[131]

The General Convention of 1826 authorized a collection of two hundred twelve hymns, with more adequate provisions for the various days and seasons and for the different rites. The first two hymns were devoted to the Holy Scriptures—"Great God, with wonder and with praise" by Isaac Watts and "Father of mercies! in thy word." The number of Wesleyan hymns was increased, and hymns by Montgomery, Newton, Cowper, and Heber were included. The 1832 convention authorized an abbreviated and revised metrical Psalter. The one hundred twenty-four selections came mostly from Tate and Brady, but Watts, Montgomery, Mant, and other authors were represented.

The Oxford Movement sparked the publication of translations from Greek, Latin (from both the Roman breviary and the Paris Breviary of 1736), and German, and the writing of many new hymns.[132] Because of the concern to be true to the Scriptures Anglican translators often dealt selectively and freely with the originals, and editors were selective and did not hesitate to abbreviate or revise. A number of new hymnals were published in England, culminating in the 1861 *Hymns Ancient and Modern*, the sales of which in the first three years reached 350,000. The editor, Henry Williams Baker, contributed one of several hymns on the Scriptures, "Lord, thy word abideth." Collections drawing largely from the new English hymnals were printed and put to use in this country, and the 1865 General Convention authorized the addition of sixty-five hymns to the "Prayer Book Collection." The 1871 convention authorized a new book containing five hundred twenty Psalms and hymns, arranged as one collection rather than two, and bound separately from the Prayer Book. This book contained several hymns on the Scriptures, including William Walsham How's "O Word of God incarnate," with its note of the Church as the bearer of Scripture. This hymnal was revised slighly in 1874 and more thoroughly in 1892, 1916, and 1940. Each edition tended to reduce the number of metrical paraphrases and to broaden the scope of other texts.

The 1892 and the 1928 American Prayer Book included a rubric permitting "Hymns set forth and allowed by the authority of this Church, and Anthems in the words of Holy Scripture or the Book of Common Prayer" before and after any rite or sermon. The 1892 revision made permissive the rubric concerning a hymn before the Communions and allowed a hymn or anthem at the presentation of the alms and oblations, and also an anthem after the fixed collects at Evening Prayer. The 1928 book allowed a hymn or anthem between the Epistle and the Gospel.

The 1979 American book deleted the general rubric on hymns and anthems and designates in the rubrics of the various rites points at which Psalms, authorized hymns, or anthems in the words of the Bible or Book of Common Prayer or "texts congruent with them" may be used. The rubrics encourage a recovery of Psalms at the entrance of the ministers, the offertory, and the Communion of the people in addition to those appointed in the lectionary. Antiphons are provided for the Venite, and scriptural antiphons may be used with the Psalms and biblical canticles.

Recent revisions of Anglican hymnals, in particular the American Hymnal 1982, reflect a growing concern that the hymns used within rites be related to the Scripture readings, and a growing recognition that hymns are the people's "take home package," probably exerting more influence on their theology and piety than readings, sermons, or prayers. Concern for biblical content and biblical orthodoxy was, therefore, a major influence in the selection of new texts for the Hymnal 1982 and the primary reason for the elimination of some popular texts which had come into the Hymnal in recent revisions (for example, "Once to every man and nation" and "Turn back, O man, forswear they foolish ways").

No communion has been more concerned than the Anglican that in its worship the Scriptures be proclaimed in their wholeness and that nothing be read, prayed, or sung except the Scriptures or texts "evidently grounded upon the same."

3

Reformers and Missionaries: The Bible in Eighteenth and Early Nineteenth Century England

by John Booty

The Bible and the Eighteenth-century Church of England

Christianity in eighteenth-century England was influenced intellectually by religious rationalism and practically, in day-to-day church life, by latitudinarianism. Both rationalism and latitudinarianism tended toward the diminishment of the authority of the Bible as understood during the Middle Ages and beyond, into that period familiarly known as the Reformation.

The rationalism to which I refer asserts the supremacy of reason over revelation. Reason is then neither the "right reason" of Christian humanism nor Richard Hooker's "moral law of reason," but amoral, quasi-mathematical deduction which in time issues in the qualitative inductive reasoning of the physical sciences. Reason as such logically culminated in the teaching of such a deist as Thomas Woolston, who in his *Discourses on the Miracles of our Saviour* (1727–1729) argued that the miracles recorded in the New Testament were so fantastic that at best they could only be accepted as conveying some spiritual truth, but could not be regarded as historical events by any rational, reasoning person. He proceeded thence to ridicule miracle after miracle. Matthew Tindal, author of *Christianity as Old as Creation* (1730) deserves to be taken more seriously as he struggled to reconcile the supreme being of deistic belief with the God of the Christian Scriptures who chose to reveal himself to an inferior people in an obscure part of the world, "and in a series of trivial and sometimes outrageous laws and anecdotes."[1]

Those who did battle with the deists were also rationalists, in their own fashion. John Locke's *The Reasonableness of Christianity as delivered in the Scriptures* (1695) was an attempt to demonstrate convincingly that reason and revelation were not in opposition, one to the other. As Norman Sykes said:

> Locke's *The Reasonableness of Christianity* popularized a new version of Christianity by reducing its doctrine to the lowest common denominator of belief in Jesus as the Messiah, whose advent had been foretold in the prophecies of the Old Testament and whose mission had been authenticated by the miracles of the New Testament. Even this reduced creed was to be measured against the background of Natural Religion and the religion of Natural Science, so that Revelation in addition to being required to justify itself by Locke's standard, had to present itself as a republication of Natural Religion. For a time indeed the Word of God assumed a secondary position to his works as set forth in the created universe.[2]

And Joseph Butler (1692–1752), the most able defender of the orthodoxy of the English Church, contributed without intention to the growth of rational scepticism as, seeking to protect the authority of biblical revelation, he argued that both the natural order and revelation exceeded the bounds of rational inquiry, ending in mystery. In the process Butler raised doubts concerning the certitude of revealed knowledge and suggested that neither reason nor revelation could satisfactorily arrive at the verity of Christian theism or even the existence and reality of a Supreme Being. As William Neil has written:

> The net result of the Deist controversy, as it affected Holy Scripture, was to leave the traditional view of the Bible in a

much weakened position. It is of little moment that on paper the victory went to orthodoxy. Its champions were abler and it was supported by the powerful assistance of law, traditions and convention. But to bandy about the sacred texts in public dispute, and to make the Scriptures the small change of pamphleteers, was at once to unseat the Bible from the pedestal on which it had been placed in the seventeenth century.[3]

Norman Sykes had done much to challenge and correct the familiar and harshly critical view of the eighteenth-century Church of England as being worldly and corrupt. The administrative abuses of pluralism and non-residence and the poverty of the parish clergy were all abuses inherited from the medieval Church and left unreformed through the sixteenth and seventeenth centuries. Latitudinarianism had its reason for being. With its capacity for compromise and its concern for peace and tranquility, latitudinarianism was defensible as a corrective to the bitter conflicts of religious devotees disturbing the public order in the seventeenth century. And the doctrines of the men of latitude were not altogether unworthy, nor were they without roots in the Scriptures of the Old and New Testaments. Writing of the latitudinarian movement as it effected belief and practice in the Georgian Church, Sykes reported:

Its doctrines were marked by plainness and directness; and the essential content of the Christian evangel was epitomized in the proclamation of the Fatherhood of God and the duty of benevolence in Man. Persuaded of the centrality of this cardinal tenet of the beneficence of the Creator towards his creatures, the men of Latitude deduced the obligation on the part of mankind to imitate the divine charity by the performance of good works towards each other. Public worship was designed ... for the adoration of the Supreme Being and the inculcation of the duties of men living in society. Thus conceived religion was in no wise divorced from the affairs of the world. Its profession did not involve abstention from the innocent relationships of social life, but rather supplied the best motive for the conduct of citizens whose membership of an earthly kingdom was the preparation for that of an heavenly city.[4]

However, this view of religion, as preached by divines ranging from Archbishop Tillotson to Anthony Hastwell, priest of Kildale and Great Ayton in the north riding of Yorkshire,[5] also contributed to the gradual diminution of respect for the authority of Scripture. Most importantly, latitudinarian teachings de-emphasized certain central biblical doctrines. As Sykes remarks, the latitudinarian view of Christianity "tended to decline in popular estimate into the idea of religion as supplying an additional bonus to a course of moderation and virtue rather than as sounding a call to renunciation and asceticism."[6] Henry Venn (1725–1797), an evangelical of the Clapham Sect, attacked the preachers of the eighteenth-century Church of England as largely moralistic in their preaching, clergymen who, neglecting such key biblical doctrines as sin and salvation, "press the necessity of moral practice without first giving plain and full directions how to master the great impediment to welldoing, which is no better than reading our sentence of condemnation. What we all want is power to surmount... difficulties and ... assurance of its vouchsafement."[7]

In addition, the latitudinarianism of the Georgian Church was faulted for its lack of seriousness in religious matters. John Wesley characterized its worship—to a degree unfairly caricaturing that worship—in terms of an assembly of "gay, giddy" people, participating in divine service "in a careless, hurrying, slovenly manner," with prayers interrupted "by the formal drawl of a parish clerk, the screaming of boys who bawl out what they neither feel nor understand."[8] Sykes notes the unfairness of Wesley's criticism while admitting that there was some basis for it in fact and in particular "the indecorous behavior of many worshippers, nestled securely within their pews designed more for slumber than devotion," the fact that the poor were seated in places such as encouraged non-attendance, the uncleanness of many churches, and the inadequacy of many parish clerks.[9]

Anglican Evangelical Reform

The emergence of the evangelical reform movement in Wales during the first decades of the eighteenth century, spreading from thence through all the United Kingdom and beyond, into the New World, constituted a revolution, such a revolution as worked a radical change in the religious life and thought of the English-speaking peoples. Deriving inspiration and energy from seventeenth-century Puritanism, from the High Church piety of William Law and others, and from Moravian pietism, the evangelical movement brought the rationalistic controversies effectually to an end. A new seriousness in religion and in life generally spread through the society, with an emphasis on heart over mind and of feelings over concepts. The fearful sinner prayed for conversion knowing that the unconverted, those who were not washed in the blood of the Lamb, whose lives did not radiate with the fruits of sanctification, would surely be damned for eternity. Those who experienced the assurance which Wesley felt were intensely concerned for the souls of those around them. William Wilberforce (1759–1833), the parliamentarian, wrote to his son Samuel on his ninth birthday saying how much he hoped that soon he would see "decisive marks of your having begun to undergo the great change." Anabella Mirbanke allowed herself to be married to Lord Byron in 1812 in hope that, although she did not love him, she might be the agent for his conversion. The fear of being found wanting on judgment day drove the serious-minded evangelical to intense self-examination and soul-searching. In his diary, Henry Thornton (1760–1815), the banker, whose house was a center for the Clapham Sect, recorded the results of his self-examination.

First, I lie idly in bed often and even generally longer than I need. 2. I am not steady and punctual enough in reading the Scriptures. 3. In my prayers I am idle. 4. In my secret thoughts and imaginations I am far from having learnt self-denial. 5. I am not self-denying in my business.[10]

The reform centered upon a revival in the Church of England and the English nation of the quest for perfection and holiness in life according to biblical precepts. This is the quest for "real Christianity" as Wilberforce was wont to say. It is the quest for holiness in personal and corporate life, not unlike the quest at the heart of earlier Puritan and High Church piety. The evangelicals were not all of one mind in all things. There were Calvinists and there were Arminians. Some stayed within the Church of England and others left it to form the Methodist Church. But the same character of seriousness was to be found among them all.

The evangelicals who stayed in the Church of England tended to be Calvinistic in doctrine. They emphasized the fallen condition of mankind and the desperate need for redemption. Such a doctrine necessitated belief in a divine Redeemer, and rejected the concept of an impersonal, distant deity. Their faith centered in a fully divine Person. Whereas earlier generations had been concerned primarily with Trinitarian doctrine, with cosmology, or with natural theology, the eighteenth-century evangelicals emphasized soteriology—the salvation of sinful, fallen, miserable human beings. As a result, Sykes concludes, the Bible

> was restored to its position of authority and popularity as the foundation of doctrine and the inspiration and source of piety, until the nineteenth century witnesses a further assault upon its authenticity at the hands of the new movement of literary and historical criticism. Meantime, however, it resumed its traditional prestige as the fount of study on the part of learned divines and as the vademecum of Christian in his pilgrimmage from the City of Destruction to the City of God.[11]

For the evangelicals the power and assurance needed by all Christians in the face of the Fall and the realities of personal and corporate sin—power and assurance that Henry Venn claimed the preaching of the Georgian Church did not provide—was to be found in the Scriptures understood and preached as God's Word. Such power provoked the person to self-examination, contrition, repentance, and a lively faith. William Wilberforce who was a lay leader of the movement, wrote:

We must be deeply conscious of our guilt and misery,

heartily repenting of our sins and firmly resolving to forsake them: and thus penitently 'fleeing for refuge to the hope set before us,' we must found altogether on the merit of the crucified Redeemer our hopes of escape from deserved punishment, and of deliverance from their enslaving power. This must be our first, our last, our only plea. We are to surrender ourselves up to him to 'be washed in his blood,' to be sanctified by his Spirit, resolving to receive him for our Lord and Master, to learn in his School, to obey all his commandments.[12]

It would be difficult to find a more accurate, succinct, and biblical statement of the evangelical point of view than this.

The Anglican-Evangelical Understanding of the Bible

William Romaine (1714–1795), the evangelical scholar and preacher who labored in the vineyard called London, reflected a widely held evangelical point of view when he wrote of the Holy Scripture as God's Word whereby to govern all of life. It is, he believed, the Word of God as revealed and illuminated by the Holy Spirit. Romaine spoke of the sweetness of the Word for Christians in times of trouble. "All people in distress look out for some comfort and the Holy Spirit directs believers to the Scriptures," and he quoted: "whatsoever things were written aforetime, were written for our learning, that we, through patience and comfort of the Scriptures, might have hope."[13] Charles Simeon (1759–1836), the Vicar of Holy Trinity in Cambridge and a leading evangelical in the University, commenting on Jeremiah 15:16, asked who can possibly live without the Bible? The answer is that no one can truly live or possess just knowledge of God and God's mercy toward sinful persons without God's Word in Scripture.

The greatest philosophers of Greece and Rome were entirely in the dark on all subjects connected with the soul; nor could unenlightened reason ever have explored those mysteries which the inspired volume alone has revealed to man. Even at this present day, notwithstanding the light of revelation, the great and learned amongst ourselves are still ignorant of divine truth, if they have not been taught of God by the effectual application of his word to their souls. It is by the word that the knowledge of salvation is communicated to every one of us: and we must all study it for ourselves, receiving its testimony with a believing heart, and submitting both our reason and our passions to its enlightening and sanctifying influence.[14]

Here Simeon indicates something of the context in which evangelicals understood the Scripture and its authority. John Wesley helpfully spoke (in a sermon on 1 Cor. 14:20) of his times in which men seemed to run to extremes, either undervaluing reason or over-valuing it, people of "weak understanding" for whom "pride...supplies the void of sense," or people of "strong understanding" who "suppose they can know all things." Both do damage to Scripture, but those "that are prejudiced against Christian revelation, who do not receive the Scriptures as the oracles of God," are usually rationalists. Wesley argued for a middle course between the two extremes, defining reason as understanding, including simple apprehension, judgment, and discourse.[15] Asking what function reason serves in religion, Wesley answered that reason, assisted by the Holy Spirit, "enables us to understand what the Holy Scriptures declare" regarding God, his being and attributes. "It is by reason that God enables us, in some measure, to comprehend his method of dealing with children of men; the nature of his various dispensations, of the old and new covenant, of the law and the gospel."[16] But, on the other hand, reason is limited; it cannot produce faith.[17]

Thomas Scott (1747–1821), John Newton's successor as curate of Olney, Buckinghamshire, was one of the most influential Anglican evangelicals in his day. His influence came in large part from the widespread use of his commentary on the Bible, first published in weekly installments from 1788 to 1792, and then subsequently published as an entirety and used all through the English-speaking parts of the world by evangelicals and others. He was convinced that there was no religion without revelation and no revelation without the Bible. He had little patience with natural religion based on reason alone. None of the truths and precepts proposed as "the oracles of reason" were ever "proposed by reason without revelation, with such certainty, clearness, and authority, as to become a constant principle and rule of action, in secret and in public, towards God, and towards man."[18] Indeed, Scott argued, the internal and external evidence concerning the absolute necessity of revelation as found in the Bible, is such that were people open to the truth in this matter, "as they are in mathematical investigations, they could no more reject" the Bible as the vehicle of divine revelation, "than they could contradict an evident demonstration."[19]

The Christian hope, Scott taught, is "grounded upon this principle, *The Bible is the Word of God.*'" It is divinely inspired. His definition here expressed a prime belief on the part of evangelicals. By divine inspiration Scott meant:

Such a complete and immediate communication, by the Holy Spirit, to the minds of the sacred writers, of those things which could not have been otherwise known; and such an effectual superintendency, as to those particulars, concerning which they might otherwise obtain information, as sufficed absolutely to preserve them from every degree of error, in all things, which could in the least affect any of the doctrines, or precepts, contained in their writings, or mislead any person who considered them as a divine and infallible standard of truth and duty.[20]

The conclusions are clear. Every sentence of Scripture must be regarded as "the sure testimony of God." Any idea of difference or disparity among the biblical writers must be denied. Such writers, from Moses to John, are the voices and the Holy Spirit is the speaker. Where errors can be proven they are attributed to the transcribers of the written works, not to the authors, the voices of the divine speaker.

Scott then set forth his reasons for believing that the Scriptures are the infallible word of God, such as the fact that so many "wise and good men" through the ages have so regarded the Scriptures, the existence of miracles, the agreement of the

writers among themselves, the fulfillment of biblical proph-
ecies, the depiction of God, his character and works as presented in the Bible, and the positive effects of Scripture in
molding the characters of men. Finally, "He that believeth hath
the witness in himself. The discourses which he hath made by
the light of the Scripture; the experience which he hath had,
that the Lord fulfils its promises to those who trust in them ... "
tend to corroborate the assertion that the Scriptures are the
infallible word of God.[21] Thus reason and experience confirm
what authority and faith attest.

But, after all of these considerations, Scott argued that it is
only through faith that believers know the Scriptures to be "the
testimony of God to truths and facts ... to become principles of
our habitual conduct," and this is the chief end of the Bible: to
nurture us in holiness. The relation of faith to reason is clear.
Acknowledging that faith is the exercise of our rational faculties, Scott wrote:

> Faith, receiving and appropriating the testimony of God, is
> to reason not unlike what the telescope is to the eye of the
> astronomer; who by it discerns objects invisible to all oth-
> ers; and sees clearly and distinctly those things, which to
> others appear obscure and confused. Reason, thus appro-
> priating by faith, the information communicated by revela-
> tion, adds immensely to her former scanty stock of
> knowledge; possessing, at the same time, *certainty* instead
> of *conjecture*; and thus, in the posture of a humble disciple,
> she receives that instruction, which must forever be with-
> held from her, while she proudly affects to be the
> teacher.[22]

Reason is, thus, not without importance. Properly subordi-
nated to revelation, it is the faculty required to make judgments
concerning the evidence supporting biblical authority, it is
useful in the process of understanding and explaining the
language through which revelation is communicated, and
much else, besides. Nor does Scott deny that when interpretations of biblical texts are contrary to the demonstrable evidence
present to the senses they must be rejected as false. But if an
interpretation is not demonstrably untrue and is rather simply

mysterious, beyond our comprehension or contrary to ordinary human perceptions, notions or reasoning, "to reject, on such grounds the testimony of God, must be *irrational* in the highest degree; unless man be indeed wiser than his Creator."[23]

In a further qualification, Scott stated that he and those like him, do not maintain "that all truths of revelation are of equal importance, because they are not stated in scripture to be so."[24] Without fully developing the point, Scott here sounded not unlike Wesley, who, in keeping with Anglican tradition, sought to locate and emphasize within the great mass of biblical teaching that which is deemed essential. Wesley identified this work of discrimination with the proper function of reason. He wrote that true religion is founded upon "the oracles of God"—on the prophets and apostles with Jesus Christ being the chief cornerstone. Reason functions to help us understand and explain the living oracles. "And how is it possible without it, to understand [we might add, and ascertain] the essential truths contained therein? A beautiful summary for which we have in that which is called the apostles' creed."[25] Reason is thus, in its own way, essential. That at times Scott and others make reason seem to be *adiaphora* has more to do with the circumstances which pitted evangelicals against rationalists, who endowed reason with authority far in excess of that justly due to reason as the evangelicals understood it and as it was understood in Christian and Anglican tradition.

Simeon and the Christological Interpretation of the Bible

Not all evangelicals viewed scriptural authority and inspiration in exactly the same way as did Scott. Charles Simeon, to whom reference was made earlier, was on the whole a man of broader spirits. He admitted that the Scriptures were written by men but added that the writers "only wrote what was dictated to them." It was as if the books of the Bible were written by the finger of God. Therefore we dare not ignore or suppress one word of the Bible. This attitude of respect for Scripture lay behind his refusal to participate in the bitter theological battles of his day. He was no friend to systematizers. As Hugh Evan Hopkins says, Simeon "hardly ever quotes any authority other than the actual text of the Scriptures. He was really never happier than when shut in his room with a chance of uninterrupted Bible study."[26] He gladly accepted the Church of England's assertion of the supremacy of Scripture in all that concerns salvation. At the same time he recognized that while "no error in doctrine or other important matter is allowed; yet there are inexactnesses in reference to philosophical and scientific matters because of its popular style." He realized that not everything in Scripture should be taken literally, but insisted that every page be treated with reverence. As Hopkins says:

> When he was pressed to be more specific, he would distinguish between what he called 'plenary' and 'supervisory' inspiration. The former involved revealing 'those things which man could not know, and which the writer did know, to prevent him from going wrong.'[27]

Simeon also insisted that the Bible be taken and understood as whole and not as a vast collection of precepts. To regard it this way is to be steeped in it. It was one of the benefits of the Church's liturgy, to his mind, that it presented a public opportunity for such steeping and an inspiration in its lessons and preaching for the individual to study the Scriptures as a whole and not select portions.

C. M. Chavasse makes a further important observation on Simeon's understanding of the Bible: "Simeon's *Biblicism* did not in fact rest upon the doctrine of verbal inspiration. It was founded upon the inseparable connection between Holy Scripture and Christ Himself: an intimate and vital relationship that is independent of any particular theory of Inspiration, which, indeed the Bible itself has never defined."[28] Simeon complained, as has been noted, that the Scriptures were not always viewed as a whole. They are a whole, he argued, the same from the beginning to end. To human observation the Bible is a body of many parts, but it is penetrated in every segment by a soul, invisible but real, "and that soul is Christ." This is true of the

Old Testament as well as of the new Testament. Christ is the substance of the law and the law is a revelation of Him. It is the schoolmaster that leads us to Christ.

Simeon also taught that in addition to being the lively soul of the Bible, Christ speaks to contemporary humanity from the Scripture's word. In notes for a sermon on Col. 3:16, Simeon wrote:

> Let us suppose that the Lord Jesus Christ were now to come among us, and to teach in our Churches... Were we to hear him speaking... the word would not more certainly be his than this word which we now possess: and therefore whatever sentiments of fear or love or gratitude we should feel... we ought to feel in reference to that sacred volume which we have in our hands: whenever we look upon it, we should say, This is the word of Him who came down from heaven to instruct me; of Him who died upon the cross to save me; of Him who now sits enthroned in glory, and will hereafter fix my doom according to it.[29]

Simeon's Christological interpretation of Scripture provides a major and serious qualification to his at times dogmatic and rigid affirmation of verbal inspiration, and it is in part his Christological premise that makes him assert verbal inspiration on occasion so flatly. If Christ is the animating Spirit of the whole Bible then the faithful must be prepared to hear him speak to them from any part of it, any sentence, any word. And yet it is Christ who is expected to speak, the Christ of the synoptics, of John and of Paul, amongst others of the New Testament writers. This is the Christ as perceived and interpreted in the late eighteenth century, we might add, prior to the emergence in full force of literary and historical criticism, of Darwin and Huxley, but after the defeat of deism and the full blossoming of pietism and of the evangelical revival.

The Anglican Evangelical Use of the Scripture

The evangelical understanding of the Bible is further elucidated by consideration of the use of the Bible in preaching,

Bible study, and prayer. The preaching of the evangelicals tended to be biblical and Christ-centered. John Wesley, writing to a friend in 1751 said that preaching the Gospel meant "preaching the life, death, and resurrection of Christ," and preaching the law meant "explaining and enforcing the commands of Christ, briefly comprised in the Sermon on the Mount."[30] Simeon would have agreed. It was his intent "to know nothing but Jesus Christ and Him Crucified." In order to know Christ he turned to the Bible, studied it intensely, and made it the basis of all of his preaching. Preaching was the instrument to bring people to Christ through the faithful and evangelical exposition and application of the Word of God in and through the words of Scripture. In preparing sermons he (1) asked, "What is the principal scope and meaning of the text," for he always began with a text from the Bible. Next, (2) he asked, "Of what parts does the text consist, or into what parts may it be most easily and naturally resolved?" He then (3) proceeded to examine in greater detail the parts that emerged. Then (4) came the application. "The nature of the application must depend in some measure on the subject that has been discussed, and on the state of the congregation to whom it is addressed." Finally, (5) there was the exordium, the introduction which was to be composed last.[31] In all of this Simeon aimed at simplicity and directness. He could not abide preaching that went over the heads of the congregation. His intent was the same whether he was preaching to a country congregation or to dons and undergraduates at Cambridge. He wrote: "Most of my sermons before the university have given satisfaction from their plainness, clearness, and simplicity; for it is a mistake to suppose that men of science will not be pleased unless the sermon be abstruse or profound."[32]

As a preacher, Simeon was a Bible expositor and it was in part this, as well as his personality, that made him such a highly respected preacher. As Chavasse says:

The secret of his power in the pulpit...was that Simeon allowed the Holy Spirit to speak directly to individual consciences through the inspired Word. As an undergraduate testified, 'Never before or since have I heard a preacher who seemed to take me by the hand and lead me aside into close communion with himself.'[33]

Such could be, and was, often said of other evangelical preachers. Since the Scriptures were so vital to them, the preaching of the Word, the careful, lively, and enlivening exposition of the biblical text was of vital importance in the promotion of the gospel.

The evangelicals also emphasized Bible reading and study. John Newton, the ex-slaver who became the curate of Olney before Scott, extolled the reading of the Bible and recommended that the faithful begin by reading the Bible through, from Genesis to Revelation, and proceed by reading it through again and again.

> We shall meet with many passages which we can make little improvement of, but not so many in the second reading as in the first, and fewer in the third than in the second: provided we pray to him who has the keys to open our understanding, and to anoint our eyes with his spiritual ointment. The course of reading to-day will prepare some lights for what we shall read to-morrow and throw a further light upon what we read yesterday.[34]

This procedure depended, of course, on persistence and it was also reliant upon the reading being done in the context of prayer with a certain attitude.

Simeon wrote of three essentials for fruitful Bible reading. The first was humility and openness to learning from God's word. Secondly, there must be a praying heart, for the Scriptures are a sealed book to those not enlightened by prayer. Simeon wrote: "Without such a special illumination of the mind, the most learned philosophers cannot comprehend them; and by such an illumination the most untutored savage shall be made wise unto salvation." He therefore cautioned that "it is not sufficient to study the Scriptures merely as we read other books: we must search into them for his treasure...digging into them...and praying earnestly to God that

he would open our understanding to understand them."[35]
Thirdly, there is needed an obedient will, a willingness to
accept the direction of Scripture for personal and social
behavior without debate, but with childlike simplicity, wearing
the oracles of God as frontlets before our eyes, "binding them,
as it were, upon our fingers, 'so as to be ever ready to carry them
into execution.'"[36]

It is clear, then, that the Bible constituted the chief book of
devotions for the evangelical. Other books, such as Doddridge's
Family Expositor, were revered for their reproduction of and
fidelity to the Bible. As William Meade, third Bishop of Virginia, said, the true churchman "loves the liturgy because he
believes it to be according to the doctrines of the bible and
prayer." And the prayer book Meade conjoins to the Bible as
being biblical through and through. Thus he wrote, as to the
Church's worship, the true churchman of the Anglican communion

> seeks to enter into its deep spirit of devotion, without
> which all his admiration and praise of it will be of no avail.
> If he be a minister he will read it as one who feels its truth,
> and will seek to induce his congregation to unite audibly
> and heartily with him. If a parent, he will not only open his
> mouth and utter it as one not ashamed of it, but seek to
> lead his children and others to do the same.[37]

With such conviction and with a strong belief that the public
worship of the Church was biblical as well as providing a proper
framework for the public reading of the Bible, the evangelical
clergy encouraged Bible reading and exposition in their
churches not only on Sundays but at mid-week services as well,
and in family devotions.

Family devotions became commonplace in evangelical households. It is reported that in the Hey family the head of the
house began morning devotions by reading a section of Doddridge's *Family Expositor*. Following the reading the family sang a
psalm or hymn, and Mr. Hey prayed, sometimes using the
prayer book. The family gathered again between nine and ten
in the evening for the reading of a psalm or a portion of the Old

Testament, ending with prayer and singing. It is reported that Mr. Hey conducted these devotions in a manner serious and impressive: "he read the Scripture slowly and reverently, now and then offering a very short and pious remark on any particular text that occurred. His prayer was offered up with a devout solemnity and reverence, which indicated his due recollection of the greatness and majesty of Him whom he was addressing."[38]

The individual Christian, reading the Bible daily, would examine his or her life according to the precepts of the Gospel, pray for forgiveness and direction, as well as for the needs and wants of others. William Romaine's three books, *The Life of Faith* (1763), *The Walk of Faith* (1771), and *The Triumph of Faith* (1795) were widely used as books of personal devotions. Each chapter is a meditation both edifying and designed to stir the affections to action. The traditional emphasis on intellect and affections with the affections receiving most attention is all through each book, as it is in the works of meditation written in the late middle ages.[39] In one place, for instance Romaine addressed God, saying:

> Thou art the Giver of every grace. I acknowledge Thee to be the Author of my spiritual life; I was dead in trespasses and sins, and Thou hast quickened me. It is of Thy mere gift that I have any faith, and that upon the trial it was found to be true faith; I bless Thee for this grace, and humbly pray for the continuance and increase of it. Meet me in the use of all means, and enable me to grow in faith, rooted and grounded in Christ Jesus, that I may also grow in love to His Father and to my Father.[40]

Evangelical piety was simple and clear and rooted, as they firmly believed, in the Bible. It was the outcome of intense, close study of the whole Bible, interpreted Christologically and soteriologically, using biblical words and phrases, sometimes without any acknowledgement for the words and phrases were so ingrained in the evangelical's mind that they were the believer's own words and phrases. This was a piety that fashioned and refashioned lives and had its effect not only on those involved but on the whole Church and peoples in general.

World Missions and the Bible

A major result of the evangelical revivals in Great Britain and America was the beginning and development of missionary movements among non-Roman Catholic churches, There were, of course, earlier movements. The Society for Promoting Christian Knowledge (S.P.C.K.) had been founded in 1698 "to promote and encourage the erection of charity schools in all parts of England and Wales; to disperse, both at home and abroad, Bibles and tracts of religion, and in general to advance the honor of God and the good of mankind, by promoting Christian knowledge both at home and in other parts of the world by the best methods that should offer." The Society for the Propagation of the Gospel (S.P.G.) was founded in 1701 to support the missionary work begun by the S.P.C.K., to provide clerical support to British citizens living overseas, and to propagate the gospel among non-Christians in British possessions abroad. The two societies exemplified the concerns of English Christians of the established church of the time, were limited to the missionary work of the Church of England, especially abroad, and were dedicated to providing Bibles and other literature and missionaries. They were effective within their limits but lacked that which was necessary to spark a vigorous, ecumenical movement.

The evangelical revivals provided that which was needed: a serious and zealous concern to evangelize the world, based upon the recovery of biblical authority and piety in the churches, relatively free from the constraints of national and denominational ties and directions. Something of the evangelical attitude is to be found in Henry Venn's statement:

> Every Christian must be a Missionary, if his Christianity is vital and effective. Your calling in life may be a humble one, and it may be your duty to "abide therein"; nev-

ertheless, in that calling, who may not speak of Christ, and extol His love and grace? Yet beyond this, there is special work, full of honour and responsibility, to which God gives, as He sees right, a special call. Distant lands must be visited: the Gospel must be preached there: The Scriptures must be translated: Churches must be founded! The work is divinely appointed, and He who has appointed the work will not fail to confer the gifts and graces needful for its accomplishment.[41]

When William Carey pled for the founding of the Baptist Missionary Society, he met the familiar objection when he was told, "Sit down, young man; when God wishes to convert the heathen, He will do it without your help." Now, at the end of the eighteenth century, evangelical leaders were speaking of responding to God's Word in Scripture, obediently to preach the Gospel to the Gentiles. The aim was no less than that of the evangelization of the world. The effort was to involve all people, of whatever denomination, lay and clerical, male and female, young and old, some called to go out to the far ends of the world, others to stay at home, praying, recruiting, raising money, sending out more people and more supplies. Some of the inspiration came from the Moravians of Herrnhut, the focal point of the pietist movement in Germany during the eighteenth century. The Moravians, who influenced John Wesley and the evangelical revival in England, regarded themselves as a missionary brotherhood, and reached out to non-Christians, to Jews and to Muslims. But basically the inspiration came from that biblical understanding that led revivalists to evangelize others, near and far, after the example of the early Church, and to engage in field preaching if necessary in order to reach lukewarm Christians and unchurched men and women, in rural England but now also in the burgeoning industrial urban centers where the established parish churches were simply unable to meet the challenge. Furthermore, the evangelical faith tended to emphasize "Bible-Christians" rather than denominational affiliations. The universal faith, grounded in Scripture, above all party strife and theological disputes, was the faith that motivated evangelicals to be missionaries. Their spirit was expressed by Simeon when he wrote that the author

> bitterly regrets that men will range themselves under
> human banners and leaders, and employ themselves in
> converting the Inspired Writers [of the Bible] into friends
> and partisans of their own peculiar principles. Into this
> fault he trusts that he had never fallen. One thing he
> knows, namely, that pious men, both of the Calvinistic and
> Arminian persuasions, approximate very nearly when
> they are upon their knees before God in prayer.[42]

It was this universal, fundamentally biblical and evangelical
faith that was to be promoted abroad. In 1795 the London
Missionary Society was founded, destined to be the inter-
denominational spearhead for world missions in the nineteenth century. In 1799 the Church Missionary Society (C.M.S.)
was founded by Anglican evangelicals. The C.M.S. was the
conduit through which evangelical zeal in the established
Church flowed to support and enliven Anglican missionary
efforts, especially in Africa.

Supportive of these endeavors were the Bible societies. The
British and Foreign Bible Society began in 1804. The founding
is described in an official report of 1875:

> In the year 1802 the Rev. Thomas Charles, of Bala, met a
> Welsh girl who told him that she journeyed seven miles
> over the hills every week to get sight of a Bible. This
> incident directed his attention to the dearth of Scripture in
> the Principality, and led him, when next he visited
> London, to urge the Committee of the Religious Tract
> Society to consider how the need might be met. While he
> was speaking, it occurred to the Rev. Joseph Hughes, who
> was present, 'Surely a Society might be formed for the
> purpose; and if for Wales, why not for the Empire, and the
> World?'[43]

The result was the founding of the society with the support of
wealthy and influential evangelical laymen of the Clapham
Sect, such as Lord Teignmouth, the first President, William
Wilberforce, Zachary Macaulay and Charles Grant. The object
of the society was "to promote the circulation of the Holy

Scriptures, without note or comment, at home and abroad." The affairs of the society were conducted by a committee, all laymen, six "foreigners" resident in or near London, fifteen members of the Church of England, and fifteen representatives of other denominations. Following the pattern of the benevolent societies, this society was supported by local auxiliary and branch societies and its business was conducted by paid agents. Other Bible societies followed, the first in this country being founded at Philadelphia in 1808, the national American Bible Society dating its formal beginning from 1817, the latter being supported initially by a grant from the British and Foreign Bible Society.

The accomplishments of the Bible societies were phenomenal. William Carey, who helped found the Baptist Missionary Society and went to India in 1793, was responsible, with the aid of colleagues, for the translation of parts of the Bible into thirty-four Asian languages and dialects by 1834. This he did with financial support from the British and Foreign Bible Society. Henry Martyn, an Anglican inspired by what he heard of Carey from Charles Simeon, was ordained in 1803 and went out to India in 1805 as a chaplain of the East India Company. During his short ministry there he translated the New Testament into Hindustani and then into Persian. While planning an edition of the New Testament in Arabic he died in 1812.

Bible translation was perforce a major concern for the evangelical, missionary-minded Christian. By 1854 the British and Foreign Bible Society had translations of some portion of the Bible in 152 languages and distributed in that year alone more than 570,000 Bibles, 744,000 New Testaments, and 52,000 portions of the Bible. By the same date the American Bible Society had translations of some portion of the Bible in 9 languages and distributed in the year 1854 more than 250,000 Bibles, 490,000 New Testaments, and 454 portions. The work was to continue so that by the end of the next hundred years some part of the Bible was available from the British and Foreign Bible Society in 852 languages and in 101 from the American Bible Society. In 1954 the societies distributed over a million Bibles each and over four million portions (British,

4,500,000; American, 12,600,000).[44] Early in the nineteenth
century, Henry Venn was able to write:

> The difficulties of languages have been overcome, in great
> degree, in every Mission-field. Bibles in the vernacular are
> provided in great abundance, through the liberality of the
> British and Foreign Bible Society. Philological skill has
> been so brought to bear upon the reduction of unwritten
> languages, that portions of the Scripture are prepared as
> soon as Missionaries have entered a new country.[45]

The distribution of the Bible or some portion of it, was a
major first step in the missionary work of the evangelicals in the
nineteenth century. Bibles, New Testaments, and portions were
distributed either by missionaries themselves or by agents,
called colporteurs. Whether an agent of a bible society or a
native Christian volunteer, the colporteur has been "the hero of
Bible Society literature." In time the colporteur was customarily
a native Christian of great conviction who went "out alone day
after day, with his bag of books, often uncertain of his reception."[46] There was wastage in this distribution, but there was
also measurable gain. The 1875 report of the British and Foreign Bible Society naturally considered that the work of the
society had made a tremendous impact on the world and was
the basis for the evangelization of a world where "the great
need, alike of heathen lands and Christendom itself, is the
enlightening, emancipating Word of God."[47]

Critics of the Evangelicals

There were those critical of the evangelical emphasis on the
use of the Bible. Within Anglicanism some of that criticism
concerned the seeming neglect of the Church and its authority.
The criticism could be as simple and direct as that of the woman
who believed that the C.M.S. was neglecting the *Book of Common
Prayer*—that which distinguished Anglicanism from other
denominations. Henry Venn answered the objection, saying
that the society "uniformly sends out the prayer book with the

Bible, wherever a Christian Church exists and has done more to extend the use of the prayer book in different languages than has been done by any other society or agency since the prayer book existed." He went on to say, however, that the "prayer book is intended for an established Christian congregation, and it is necessary to train up new converts by shorter and more elementary forms of worship."[48]

More serious was the criticism that the evangelicals so emphasized the Bible as interpreted by the pious individual that the reality and authority of the Church, so clearly necessary to preserve the faith in modern times, and to maintain the unity of the people of God in the one Body, was either neglected or ignored. Such evangelicals prided themselves on being "Biblemen" not Churchmen, so it was derisively claimed by some. Tractarians such as J. H. Newman believed that the evangelicals were standing by, doing nothing, while the Church of England was being destroyed by the very rationalist liberalism in theology and politics that the evangelicals themselves should be fighting and protested that they were opposing. What was needed, so members of the Oxford movement believed, was a new reformation (Newman spoke of a "second reformation"), the restoration of ancient beliefs and practices, such as were so obviously inspired by the working of the Holy Spirit in the early Church. The need seemed now to be not so much for an emphasis on Scriptures as on the One, Holy, Catholic, and Apostolic Church, a divine, organic body that no secular powers could rightly meddle with or change. Liberals interpreted the Church to be, somewhat vaguely, the sum of all Christians. Newman scoffed and wrote:

> Doubtless the only true and satisfactory meaning [of "Church"] is that which our Divines have ever taken, that there is on earth an exciting Society. Apostolic as founded by the Apostles, Catholic because it spread its branches in every place; i.e. the Church Visible with its Bishops, Priests, and Deacons. And this surely *is* a most important doctrine; for what can be better news to the bulk of mankind than to be told that Christ, when He ascended, did

not leave us orphans, but appointed representatives of Himself to the end of time.[49]

Thus among Tractarians there was a shifting of focus. The Bible held a central and indispensable place, but that place was within the ongoing life of the Church and its tradition.

It has been said that the basic teachings of the nineteenth century Tractarians were anticipated in virtually every detail by the teachings of the Old High Churchmen and in particular with those identified as the Hackney phalanx, men such as Van Mildert of Durham, Hugh James Rose, Alexander Knox, Christopher Wordsworth, the brother of the poet, Thomas Sikes, and others. In pre-Tractarian days this "orthodox" party was not large. It lacked the zeal, or "interiority" that characterized the Anglican evangelicals and was to characterize Newman and his followers. Its members had a high view of Scripture, so high a view that in one place Charles Daubeny (1744–1827) could write:

> To the Scripture ... we must go for information in spiritual things: and the more that Scripture is made the Interpreter of itself, the better reason shall we have to be satisfied, that the information derived from it is correct.[50]

But Archdeacon Daubeny is known, not for his promotion of the Bible, but rather for his teachings concerning church polity and the sacraments. He emphasized the doctrine of apostolic succession. The Church is composed of men who, with respect to the Church's constitution, are "duly commissioned to their office by those who can trace back their descent to the Apostles."[51] In the context of his understanding of the Church he could not approve the operation of private judgment. Where the Church's polity was concerned, Daubeny believed that the Bible was not designed to furnish all that we need to know. He wrote this:

> we have no information but what is derived from the mere recital of the fact, that our Saviour did, after his resurrection, deliver a commission to his eleven disciples, relative to

the government of his Church. The manner in which this commission was to be carried into effect, is to be ascertained by the subsequent practice of the Apostles; which doubltess conformed to the direction they had received from their Divine Master.[52]

The apostolic tradition as preserved in and by the Church stands alongside Scripture, if not on an equal level, then a step or two below.

John Keble (1792–1866), one of the early Tractarian leaders, echoed Richard Hooker when he argued that Christians do not first gain faith by applying their reasons to the study of the Bible. They rather learn from others in the body of the faithful and thus being led obtain evidence themselves for the truths of Scripture. The faithful must then be involved in the life of the Church and exposed to the tradition that existed most purely in the primitive Church. As Owen Chadwick summarizes Keble's thought on this matter, the Church puts the Bible in our minds and "prepares our minds to penetrate into its truth. It arranges the doctrines of the Bible into a system as it delivers them, distinguishes the essentials from the inessentials, gives us help by its treasures of interpretation, and a mode of government and worship which forms the context in which the Scriptures are declared."[53]

In tune with this Keble emphasized tradition, the tradition of the apostles. With reference to his knowledge of the development of the New Testament canon, Keble argued that the "Apostolic Tradition was divinely appointed in the Church as the touchstone of canonical Scripture itself." He went on with conviction to say:

Here is a tradition so highly honoured by the Almighty Founder and Guide of the Church, as to be made the standard and rule of His own divine Scriptures. The very writings of the Apostles were to be first tried by it, before they could be incorporated into the canon. Thus the Scriptures themselves, as it were, do homage to the tradition of the Apostles; the despisers, therefore, of that tradition take part, inadvertently or profanely, with the despisers of Scripture itself.[54]

That tradition found particular focus in creed, but it also involved a developing consensus and the discipline and worship of the Church.

By the time Keble was writing, the dogmatisms of evangelicals and Tractarians alike were being challenged anew by rising voices from Germany, from those who proposed to study the Bible critically from the point of view of historic investigation and from those who were examining the apostolic period of the church without reverence and without benefit of participation in the Church's life. Bernard Reardon remarks, "The issue between religion and science was first clearly posed by geology. Between 1800 and 1834 four different series of the Bampton lectures had dealt with the subject, and three of them...were strongly critical of the claims being made for geological study...always the clinching argument was that to question the accuracy of Scripture in any matter is to impugn divine revelation itself."[55] Clearly, a new day was emerging in which the presuppositions of devout Christians such as the evangelical reformers and missionaries were to be challenged as never before.

4

Historical Criticism and the Bible

by Reginald H. Fuller

It is often asserted that Christianity is a historical religion. This can mean many things. In a sense all religions are historical. They are historical phenomena, the products of humanity in history, and we are by nature historical beings. Most religions, including say Mohammedanism and Buddhism, have historical founders, and Christianity is no exception, whether we think its founder was Jesus of Nazareth, or as the older liberals sometimes asserted, the apostle Paul.[1] But properly speaking much more is meant when we make this claim for Christianity. We mean thereby that Christianity claims that God has acted in history, and above all that he has acted in the historical person of Jesus of Nazareth. Two Anglican biblical scholars, Sir Edwyn Hoskyns (1883–1937) and his pupil, Francis Noel Davey (1904–73) made a typically Anglican statement in the opening of *The Riddle of the New Testament:*

> When the Catholic Christian kneels at the words *incarnatus est* or at the words *and was incarnate*, he marks with proper solemnity his recognition that the Christian Religion has its origin neither in general religious experience, nor in some esoteric mysticism, nor in a dogma, and he declares that his faith rests upon a particular event in history. Nor is the Catholic Christian peculiar in this concentration of faith. This is Christian Orthodoxy, both Catholic and Protestant. In consequence, the Christian religion is not merely open to historical investigation, but

demands it, and its piety depends on it... The critical and historical study of the New Testament is therefore the prime activity of the Church.[2]

Allowing for the rhetorical exaggeration (other activities such as evangelism, prayer or worship could legitimately compete) we could agree that the historical study of the New Testament is a necessary part of the Church's activity, something that is integral to the gospel. The Bible itself, both the Old and New Testaments, frequently refers to the centrality of remembering (*zikaron* and *anamnesis*), a recalling of the past that it might become presently effective. Today, if we are to recall the past, we must use every aid that we have, and that includes historical criticism.

The Rise of Historical Criticism

The historical-critical method is a modern phenomenon. In the early Church and indeed right through the middle ages there was little sense of a critical approach to the past. People lacked the feeling of the pastness of the past. A typical expression of the medieval attitude to the past is the way artists portrayed biblical scenes. There is a triptych by one of the Dutch masters showing Abraham's meeting with Melchizedek as he returned from the battle of the kings. Abraham appears as a medieval knight in black armor! True, Augustine of Hippo had some sense of the historical problematic, as is shown by his wrestling over the agreements and differences between the synoptic Gospels. He settled for the priority of Matthew, thought that Mark followed after him "as a lackey" and that Luke used both his predecessors. But that problem was practically shelved until the 1770s, and instead the Bible was treated as a source of timeless truths of religion and ethics.

It has been said that theology is created in Germany, corrected in England and corrupted in America. One might debate the third of these clauses, but the first two are by and large true as far as historical criticism is concerned.

The methods in question may be summed up under the three headings: criticism, analogy and correlation.[3] A historian approaches his documents with a certain methodological skepticism. The statements of a document must be confirmed whether by analogy (the things asserted to have happened must be the kind of thing we know within our own experience to be the kind of things that are likely to have happened) or by correlation (the things alleged by the text must be correlated with evidence in other texts of inscriptions or later on archaeological remains). Where analogy does not hold or correlation breaks down the historian is skeptical about the statements in his text. The historian thus seeks to establish "what really happened."

The application of such methods to the Bible began (as we have already noted) in the 1770s. The pioneers were Johann Salamo Semler (1725–91) and Johann David Michaelis (1717–91).[4] A little later, J. J. Griesbach (1745–1812) reopened the synoptic problem and opted for the order Matthew-Luke-Mark, Matthew being the first Gospel, Luke using Matthew, and Mark combining and abbreviating Matthew and Luke.[5] Herbert Marsh (1757–1839) fellow of St. John's College, Cambridge and later Bishop of Peterborough studied in Germany and became acquainted with the new critical methods. After returning to England he published a translation of Michaelis' *Introduction to the New Testament* mentioned above (4 volumes 1793–1801). He also wrote a "Dissertation on the Origin of Our Three First Canonical Gospels" which he included in volume 3 of Michaelis. This was an extensive discussion of the synoptic problem, concluding with his own advocacy of an "Ur-Gospel" hypothesis (viz., that the three Gospels were all derived from a primitive Gospel now lost). As Lady Margaret's Professor at Cambridge Marsh lectured on biblical criticism between 1809 and 1816. One would have thought from this that German critical methods would soon be firmly established in England. But this was not to be the case. The two universities were only slowly coming out of their eighteenth-century doldrums. And for the next half-century theologians had other preoccupations, largely arising from the Oxford

Movement. After Marsh, English sholarship returned to its habitual isolation from the Continent. A fog descended over the Channel and it was lifted only briefly with the publication by the novelist George Eliot of Strauss' *Life of Jesus* (1840) in English translation.[6] This work engaged the attention of the Cambridge "Apostles," a group of intellectuals of which F. D. Maurice and R. C. Trench were members.

Although the publication of Charles Darwin's *The Origin of Species* in 1859 threw doubt on the literal truth of Genesis, the full effect of German "higher criticism" was not felt until the appearance of *Essays and Reviews* in 1860.[7] This was the first instance of what was to become a characteristic Anglican literary genre. Later on we shall have occasion to note the successors of this volume. It might almost be said that we could write the history of Anglican theology—including biblical scholarship since 1860—from a study of these successive volumes of essays.

Seven Oxford dons combined together to write the series of essays on biblical and theological subjects in *Essays and Reviews* and the work was edited by Benjamin Jowett of Balliol College, best known as the translator of Plato. One of the contributors tells how the project came into being:

> The book owes its origin to some conversation between Mr. Jowett and myself, as far back as eight or nine years ago, on the great amount of reticence in every class of society in regard to religious views—the melancholy unwillingness of people to state honestly their opinions on points of doctrine. We thought it might encourage free and honest discussion of Biblical topics, if we were to combine with others and publish a volume of essays ... one stipulation being made, that nothing should be written which was inconsistent with the position of ministers of our Church.[8]

Particularly interesting for our purposes is the essay by Rowland Williams who was Professor of Theology and Hebrrew at St. David's College, Lampeter, a chair which the present writer also held from 1950–55. Through the Harfords, who lived at Falcondale House just outside of Lampeter, Williams came into contact with Baron Bunsen, a German Lutheran layman, who was a diplomat and amateur theologian.[9] Bunsen put Williams in touch with the vast amount of biblical criticism that was going on in Germany. Rowland Williams set himself in his essay to introduce British readers to some of the conclusions which the German critics had reached. In particular he sought to familiarize them with the new views about the growth of the Pentateuch and the mysteries of J, E, D, and P, about Deutero-Isaiah, and the second-century date of Daniel. Then, in New Testament criticism, he introduced his readers to the fact that Hebrews was the work, not of Paul as the title in the King James Version claimed, but (probably) of Apollos, and finally that 2 Peter was not authentic.

Although a few scholars had known what was going on in Germany, to most of the bishops and other clergy (to say nothing of the laity) all this was new and shocking, as also was the contention of the editor, Benjamin Jowett, that the Bible should be studied with the same methods as any other ancient literature: "Interpret the Scripture like any other book." People forgot that Jowett went on to add the caveat: "There are many respects in which Scripture is not like any other book." *Essays and Reviews* provoked a major crisis in the Church of England and Ireland (as it was then). True, the tone of some of the essays, especially that of Williams, a fiery Welshman, did not help matters. Tractarians, old-fashioned High Churchmen like Samuel Wilberforce, and even Broad Churchmen like Stanley, reacted negatively to the work. The redoubtable John William Burgon, Newman's successor at St. Mary's, later Dean of Chichester and throughout his life a High Churchman of the old school, thundered from the University pulpit:

> The Bible is none other than the voice of Him that sitteth upon the throne. Every book of it, every chapter of it, every verse of it, every word of it, every syllable of it (where are we to stop?) every letter of it, is the direct utterance of the Most High. The Bible is none other than the Word of God, not some part of it more, some part of it less, but all alike the utterance of Him who sitteth upon the throne, faultless, unerring, supreme.[10]

No less than 8,500 of the clergy sent a petition to the Archbishop of Canterbury (Longley) requesting the bishops to bring the essayists to judgment. In the end Rowland Williams and one other essayist (Wilson) had suits brought against them and were sentenced to one year's suspension by the Dean of the Arches, the supreme judicatory of the Church. On appeal to the Judicial Committee of the Privy Council the sentences were squashed on the ground that the positions held by Williams and Wilson were within the limits of comprehensiveness allowable under the Anglican formularies. Panic ensued in the Church at large. This time there was a petition from 11,000 clergy and another from 137,000 of the laity thanking the Archbishop (who had dissented from the decision of the Judicial Committee). In the end, *Essays and Reviews* was condemned by Convocation. Poor Rowland Williams was hounded from his chair at Lampeter and banished to his living in Wiltshire. I often wondered what would have happened to myself 90 years later. I taught everything Williams had asserted, plus much more besides, like form criticism and demythologizing, but continued in the Lampeter chair undisturbed. The saddest part of the whole business is that Williams' own bishop, Connup Thirlwall of St. David's (1797–1875) never lifted so much as his little finger to defend his protegé—although Thirlwall, as a Cambridge don, had done much to introduce German historical-critical method into Britain through his *History of Greece* (8 vols., 1835–44).

We must let Bishop Tait (at that time of London, later of Canterbury) have the last word on the subject: "The great evil is that the liberals are deficient in religion and the religious are deficient in liberality." Things, fortunately, were to change later.

Meanwhile another crisis arose over the historical criticism of the Bible. John William Colenso, a Cornishman and a Cambridge scholar, had been appointed Bishop of Natal in 1853. In 1861 he published *A Commentary on the Epistle to the Romans* in which he attacked the doctrine of everlasting punishment and questioned much of the traditional doctrine of the sacraments. But the real offense came the year after, when he turned to historical criticism proper, in Part I of a work entitled

The Pentateuch and the Book of Joshua Critically Examined. Colenso, who was a mathematician, made evident the great statistical and logistical difficulties in the Book of Exodus. It was impossible, he said, for the number of the people given at the Exodus to have traveled to the Red Sea in the time stated. Such things pointed to the unhistorical character of books hitherto accepted as verbally inspired. We need not pursue the Colenso case any further except to say that the Bishop of Cape Town, Robert Gray (1809–72), deposed and excommunicated him. Thirlwall, it is worth noting, was more courageous this time and invited Colenso to preach in his diocese.

One more interesting point: it was largely in order to secure a wider Anglican condemnation of Colenso that the first Lambeth Conference was summoned in 1867. As it turned out, the bishops took no action in the matter, despite the recommendation of one of their committees that they support Bishop Grey's action in deposing Colenso and declaring his seat vacant. *Essays and Reviews* and the Colenso affair were part of the growing pains which many other parts of Christendom had to endure before the historical-critical method was fully accepted. In 1881 W. Robertson Smith, Professor of Oriental Languages and Old Testament exegesis at the Free Church College in Aberdeen, Scotland, was dismissed from his chair for his espousal of German critical views on the origin of the Pentateuch. And following him there was Charles Augustus Briggs, Professor of Hebrew at Union Theological Seminary in New York. As editor of the *Presbyterian Review* Briggs propagated the German views in this country during the 1870s. This led to his suspension as a Presbyterian minister in 1893, and incidentally he became a priest in the Episcopal Church in 1899 (see below). Evidently, by that time he felt there was more freedom for critical scholarship with Episcopalians than with the Presbyterians!

The Cambridge School

Cutting right across all the controversies of the orthodox conservative versus the critics was the work of the famous

Cambridge School during the second half of the nineteenth century. The "school" consisted of three Anglican scholars, Brooke Foss Westcott (1825–1901), John Barber Lightfoot (1828–89), and Fenton John Anthony Hort (1828–92).[1] Their work was Anglicanism's response to the *Tendenzkritik* of the "Tübingen school." The founder of the Tübingen school was Ferdinand Christain Baur (1792–1860). In a study published in 1831 Baur noted that in 1 Corinthians 1:12 Paul speaks of four parties at Corinth associated with the names of Paul, Apollos, Kephas, and Christ.[12] Of these the important ones were the Paul and Cephas parties. Paul as we know from the "four principal letters" (Galatians, 1 and 2 Corinthians, and Romans), contended for a Christianity free from the Jewish law. His opponents were the Judaizers, who contended that the observance of the Jewish law was necessary for salvation even for Gentiles. The leaders of the Judaizing Party, according to Baur, were the original Jerusalem apostles, including Peter and James the brother of the Lord.

Starting with this notion of a struggle between the two parties, Baur developed an interpretation of the history of early Christianity along Hegelian lines (the so-called dialectical process of thesis, antithesis, and synthesis). The thesis was Jewish Christianity, the antithesis Paulinism, and the synthesis what Baur called "old catholicism." On this threefold grid Baur proceeded to place all the writings of early Christianity including the New Testament writings. In the Jewish Christian thesis he placed Matthew and Revelation.[13] The only Pauline letters he recognized as genuine were the four principal letters (see above). All the other New Testament writings were assigned to the synthesis stage. Since "old catholicism" was according to Baur a second-century phenomenon, it meant that all these other writings were pseudonymous and written after 130. John's Gospel for instance he placed between 150 and 175 (!).[14]

Lightfoot began his refutation of Baur not with the New Testament documents, but with the Apostolic Fathers, Clement and Ignatius. By careful historical criticism of the documents in question, Lightfoot demonstrated (1) that they emanated from the late first and early second century, i.e., just at the time to which Baur assigned the main part of the New Testament literature; and (2) that there was no trace in them of an attempt to synthesize Judaizing Christianity and Paulinism. The documents in question therefore fail to support Baur's reconstruction of first- and second-century Christian history.

In 1860 the three Cambridge scholars planned to write a series of commentaries on all the books of the New Testament. Lightfoot was to take the Epistles of Paul, Hort the three synoptic Gospels and James, Peter, Jude and Revelation, and Westcott the Fourth Gospel, the Johannine Epistles and Hebrews. The plan proved to be far too ambitious. Lightfoot did indeed complete Galatians (1865), Philippians (1868), Colossians and Philemon (1875). At his death he left behind him some notes of the other Pauline Epistles and these were published posthumously in 1895. Hort, who was preoccupied with his work on textual criticism (see below) and who was a meticulous writer, did not complete a single commentary but left behind him three unfinished commentaries, 1 Peter, the Apocalypse and James, all of which were published posthumously. Westcott came somewhat closer to completing his assignments. The Epistles of John appeared in 1883 and Hebrews in 1889. As for the Gospel of John, Westcott did complete a commentary on the King James Version in 1880, which was published in another series, and after his death it was posthumously adapted to the Greek text in 1908.

A recent assessment of the work of these three scholars is worth quoting:

> The members of the Cambridge trio were sufficiently different in outlook and temperament to impose limitations on any attempt to make a complete appraisal of their work: yet it can readily be said that all of them were characterized by a wide, deep and exact scholarship which refused to take short cuts or to cut corners. Their linguistic equipment was complete and detailed; for the rest, Lightfoot's strength lay in the historical interpretation of the documents which he handled, while Westcott was gifted with a rare theological insight, which served him particularly well in his exposition of the thought of the Fourth Gospel.[15]

To this assessment we might add that Hort was primarily a textual critic, but in what survives of his exegetical work he displays a meticulous accuracy, coupled with reticence and modesty.

Their commentaries were published by Macmillans of London and the series was continued by other scholars of the same school after their deaths:

1892	J. B. Mayor on *James*
1898	H. B. Swete on *Mark*
1904	J. Armitage Robinson on *Ephesians*
1906	H. B. Swete on *Revelation*
1907	J. B. Mayor on *Jude and 2 Peter*
1908	G. Milligan in *1 and 2 Thessalonians*

All of these scholars except Milligan were Anglicans and their work is typical of Anglican scholarship: a primary emphasis on the linguistic and historical problems of the text at the expense of the theological aspects, and always (especially as compared with much German work) cautious and conservative in their conclusions.

Hort's major contribution, as we have noted, was in the field of textual criticism. There was a long-standing Anglican interest in this field of biblical study, going back to the arrival of the Codex Alexandrinus (A), a text which represented an earlier text type than the Textus Receptus on which King James Version was based. Among earlier Anglican text critics were Brian Walton (c. 1600–36), who published his famous *Polygot* and John Fell (1625–86), Dean of Christ Church and later Bishop of Oxford, who published a Greek New Testament, the first to be published at Oxford with a critical apparatus (i.e., a list of variant readings). Another Oxford scholar, John Mill (1645–1707) spent many years working on textual problems and just before his death published the results of his studies in an edition of the Textus Receptus with a far richer critical apparatus drawn from 78 manuscripts plus the evidence of versions (Latin and Syriac) and patristic quotations. In his prologomena Mill also laid down the principles of New Testament text criticism for the first time. Richard Bentley

(1662–1742) the Master of Trinity College, Cambridge, and a great classical scholar, planned a critical edition of the Greek New Testament but, owing to his other preoccupations, the work never got off the ground. But Edward Wells (1667–1727), Rector of Bletchley, did produce a revised text of the New Testament. This, however, failed to break the dominance of the Textus Receptus in England. Oxford and Cambridge sank into their eighteenth-century lethargy and the leadership in this field passed to Germany, where it remained for another 100 years.

In the nineteenth century Westcott and Hort, whose general work in the New Testament area we have already considered, took up the task of producing a critical text. Having worked on the project for some 30 years, they published their text without apparatus but with extensive Prolegomena in 1881. Its publication coincided with the appearance of the English Revised Version (of which the American Standard Version of 1901 was an adaptation). The Prolegomena set out the principles of text criticism and a classification of the manuscripts into four main families labeled "Neutral," Alexandrian, Western and Syrian. Syrian indicated the later post-Constantinian standardized text on which the Textus Receptus was based, while the term "Neutral" called attention to a particular theory of Westcott and Hort. In the nineteenth century two ancient manuscripts became available to scholars. These were Vaticanus (B) which had become known after Napoleon transported it temporarily to Paris from the Vatican, and Sinaiticus, which was discovered by the German scholar Constantin Tischendorf (1815–74) in 1844 at St. Catherine's Monastery at Mt. Sinai. The Wescott-Hort theory was that these two manuscripts represented a text type relatively uncontaminated by the common later corruptions and standardized revisions, and therefore closest to the autographs. In one respect, however, Westcott and Hort departed from the "Neutral text." This was in the case of the so-called "Western non-interpolations." Normally the Western text type is longer compared with the other text types, especially in the Acts of the Apostles. Thus, for instance, at Acts 19:9 Paul preached in the lecture hall of Tyrannus "from the fifth hour to the tenth"—i.e., from 11 a.m. to 4 p.m., during the midday recess when the hall would be otherwise unoccupied. However, there are occasions, especially in Luke-Acts, when the Western text preserves a shorter reading. So contrary was this to the normal tendency that Westcott and Hort had a high regard for these readings and dubbed them "Western non-interpolations." This view had a great influence especially in Britain and America and lasted long after it was generally abandoned in Germany. Thus, for instance, in the earlier editions of the Revised Standard Version many of the "Western non-interpolations" were relegated to the margin and only recently (1971) have some of them been restored. A case in point is Luke 22:19b-20, the words of institution at the Last Supper.

Westcott and Hort's work met with a negative reception in some quarters. Many people were still devoted to the King James Version and the new text was condemned as too radical. The chief opponent was again J. W. Burgon (see above). He vigorously defended the Textus Receptus even in such places as the longer ending of Mark (16:9-20). But Burgon was for the most part fighting a losing cause. Perhaps it was he more than anyone who was responsible for the quip that Oxford was the home of lost causes! But even allowing for new discoveries, especially of papyri, and refined views on the history of the text in which Anglicans, e.g., B. H. Streeter (see below) have played a major role, most of Westcott and Hort's work still stands today. For example, the United Bible Society's *Greek New Testament* is basically the Westcott and Hort text. In a lecture delivered at Cambridge in 1981, the centennial of the Westcott-Hort text and of the Revised Version, the Princeton New Testament scholar and text critic Bruce Metzger delivered this final verdict: "It is not extravagant to say that, in textual studies of the New Testament, Westcott and preeminently Hort were veritable giants."[16]

Lux Mundi

In the 1880s the scene once more shifts from Cambridge to Oxford. That University had been the site of the Tractarian movement, and Oxford High Churchmen were by and large preoccupied with the issues raised by the Catholic revival. They had been in the forefront of the opposition to *Essays and Reviews*. But in the 1880s a group of younger dons of Anglo-Catholic persuasion met together in the vacations for reading parties. Their aim was to reconcile Anglican Catholicism with modern thought, including biblical criticism. We might say that their intention was to synthesize the theology of the Oxford Movement with the historical criticism of the Cambridge school.[17]

The final fruit of these reading parties (the group used to call themselves "the Holy Party") was the publication of a volume entitled *Lux Mundi: A Series of Studies in the Religion of the Incarnation*. It was edited by Charles Gore (1853–1932). Most of the essays were devoted to questions of systematic theology and philosophy (the essayists were very much under the influence of the then reigning Oxford Hegelianism of the Cairds and T. H. Green). But inevitably some of the essays had implications for biblical criticism. Aubrey Moore, for instance, welcomed Darwinism and that implied a critical attitude to Genesis 1–3. But it was Gore's essay on "The Holy Spirit and Inspiration" that raised the question of the historical criticism of the Bible head-on.

Gore abandoned the venerable doctrine of verbal inspiration and frankly recognized the human element in the Bible. "The human activity is none the less free, conscious, rational, because the Spirit inspires it. The poet is a poet, the philosopher a philosopher, the historian an historian, each with his own idiosyncracies, ways and methods, to be interpreted each by the laws of his own literature." It was to take the Roman Catholic Church another 50 or 60 years to admit that, which it finally did in *Divino Afflante Spiritu* (1943).

Gore then proceeded to draw out the implications of this for the understanding of the biblical text. In Genesis "the first traditions of the race are all given there from *a special point of view*."[18] By this Gore seemed to mean that it is not a historical or scientific but a theological account; its truth lies in the realm not of science or history but of theology. In the historical books we find the recorders "acting like the recorders of other nations,

collecting, sorting, adapting, combining their materials."[19]
The prophets at times "foreshorten the distance" of the coming
day of the Lord, as St. Paul did with regard to the parousia.
Gore can here speak of "erroneous anticipations."[20] Overall
Gore recognized that the Old Testament is "imperfect."[21] True,
there is "a profound air of truthfulness pervading the Old
Testament from Abraham downward,"[22] but the Church cannot insist on the historical truth of the Old Testament in detail
"as she can on the historical character of the Gospels or the Acts
of the Apostles."[23] Here we come upon the limitations of Gore's
admission of the historical-critical standpoint. He admits it
fully for the Old Testament but only to a limited degree for the
New Testament. All through his life Gore upheld this limitation
of the historical-critical method. This is because for him the
catholic creeds were inviolate. Thus, as he made clear in his later
writings, it is necessary to defend the traditional authorship of
the Fourth Gospel as well as the historicity of the synoptic
miracle stories in order to maintain the truth of the doctrine of
the incarnation. The virgin birth requires the defense of the
historicity of the infancy narratives. The resurrection and
ascension require *inter alia* the reliability of St. Luke as a historian and his identification with the companion of Paul. The
necessity of episcopacy likewise required maintaining the
Pauline authorhship for the Pastoral Epistles.

In his *Lux Mundi* essay Gore was compelled to broach another
problem which had to do both with biblical criticism and with
systematic theology. He was ready to recognize that the Book of
Jonah was a dramatic composition rather than a historical
account. But Jesus had taken it to be historical. Gore was
prepared to accept the non-Davidic authorship of the Psalms;
yet Jesus had ascribed Psalm 110 to David. Jesus assumed the
historicity of the flood, and Gore met this problem by a doctrine
of "kenosis." The incarnation involved a process of self-empty-
ing (the idea was based on Phil 2:7, though that was not exactly
what the passage meant) on the part of the pre-existent Son of
God at the moment of his incarnation. He emptied himself of
his omniscience as well as of his omnipresence. He "*used* human
nature, its relation to God, its conditions of experience, its
growth of knowledge, its limitations of knowledge."

Gore's essay, more than all the others, caused consternation in strict Tractarian circles, and it is said to have hastened the death of H. P. Liddon in the following year (1890). Liddon had been preoccupied since 1882 with writing the life of Pusey, and had not realized the change of mental climate among the younger Anglo-Catholics.

A. M. Ramsey has noted three points in which criticism of the *Lux Mundi* position was justified: its kenotic theory; its blurring of the distinction between divine revelation and acquired human knowledge; its overemphasis on the incarnation at the expense of the cross.[24] But the reader will notice that none of these criticims affect the use of the historical-critical method. Gore and his colleagues had made possible a new kind of liberal Anglican Catholicism: one which, while firmly grounded on the ecclesiology and spirituality and sacramental theology of the Tractarians, was nevertheless unlike them open to the historical criticism of the Bible. In this they were faithful to the basic Anglican method, which allowed a place for reason and experience alongside scripture and tradition. Of course, there were limits to their work. It was only a beginning. And while Gore was willing, as his later works show, to accept the modern solution to the snyoptic problem, he drew the line against the more radical results of historical criticism as applied to the New Testament. But the door had been opened, and as we shall show, younger scholars of the *Lux Mundi* tradition were not reluctant to pass through it.

From Lux Mundi to Essays Catholic and Critical

One of the most prominent figures in Anglican biblical criticism was William Sanday (1843–1920), Lady Margaret Professor at Oxford from 1895–1919. He probably did more than anyone to win the Anglican clergy over to acceptance of the historical-critical method in biblical study. For many years he held a seminar on the synoptic problem, and this study and research more than anything else established the two-document hypothesis as the accepted solution to the relationship between the Gospels.[25] The same view prevailed at Cambridge through the work of Vincent Henry Stanton and Francis Crawford Burkitt.[26] No longer was it possible to maintain, as Westcott had done, that agreements between the first three gospels were the result of common dependence upon oral tradition. With few exceptions, only Roman Catholics and fundamentalists still clung to the Augustinian hypothesis (priority of Matthew). Acceptance of the two document theory became the touchstone of one's acceptance of biblical criticism in the early part of this century. A member of Sanday's seminar, Burnett Hillman Streeter (1874–1937), Fellow of Queen's College Oxford and Canon of Hereford, later refined the theory into a four-document hypothesis (Mark, Q, M, and L, the latter being the special material of Matthew and Luke respectively). To this Streeter added his proto-Luke theory, according to which Luke composed his Gospel in two stages, the first consisting of Q + L, the second of (Q + L) + Mark. These Streeterian refinements have never won widespread acceptance, even in Oxford, and one of my teachers, John Martin Creed (1887–1940) dismissed them in a footnote to his Commentary on Luke (!).

Gore and the *Lux Mundi* school generally had no difficulty in going along with these developments in biblical criticism. But where articles of the creeds were affected, Gore continued to draw the line as we have seen.

In 1911, by which time Gore was Bishop of Oxford, an Oxford don named J. M. Thompson wrote a book entitled *The Miracles of the New Testament* which denied completely the miraculous element in the New Testament including the virgin birth.[27] The *Lux Mundi* stalwarts took part in an interesting meeting (reported by G. L. Prestige in his biography of Gore)[28] at which Streeter and Sanday spoke on the other side. Gore, later expressing himself in typical fashion, said he was "solidly convinced of the peremptory necessity" of some action being taken by the bishops to maintain the creeds. All that happened was that E. S. Talbot, a *Lux Mundi* bishop, withdrew Thompson's license to officiate. Next year there was another storm, this time over a further volume of Oxford Essays, *Foundations*.[29] This is usually described as the work of Anglican liberals, but several of the contributors were actually epigoni of the *Lux Mundi* school: Neville Talbot (son of E. S. Talbot), A. E. J. Rawlinson (who later became Bishop of Derby and ordained the present writer) and E. H. Moberley and W. H. (later Sir Walter) Moberley (son of R. C. Moberley, another contributor to *Lux Mundi*). However, it was the liberal B. H. Streeter's essay that, ironically, distressed Gore almost as much as Gore himself had distressed Liddon back in 1889. For Streeter seemed to deny the resurrection by downgrading the appearances to subjective visions conveying the truth that Jesus was indeed alive. Fortunately, Scott Holland persuaded Gore that Streeter did not really deny the resurrection itself as a real event, and Gore refrained from any disciplinary action. But he later pressed for an episcopal declaration that the belief in the historical miracles of the creeds was obligatory upon the clergy. Archbishop Davidson, assisted by two scholars of the Cambridge school who were thoroughly at home in historical criticism but also thoroughly orthodox, namely J. Armitage Robinson (1858–1933) and F. H. Chase (1853–1925) secured a compromise resolution which contained the following typical wording:

> ... the denial of any of the historical facts in the Creeds goes beyond the limits of legitimate interpretation ... At the same time recognizing that our generation is called to face new problems raised by historical criticism, we are anxious not to lay unnecessary burdens upon consciences, nor unduly to limit freedom of thought and enquiry, whether among clergy or among laity: We desire, therefore, to lay stress on the need of consideration in dealing with that which is tentative and provisional in the thought and work of earnest and reverent students.[30]

The historical problem connected with the miracles in the creeds continued to cause controversy for some years. Herbert Hensley Henson (1863–1947) was not himself a biblical scholar, but a historian. Yet he was convinced of the positive religious value of historical criticism of the Bible. While he never explicitly denied the virgin birth and the bodily resurrection of our Lord, he supported the freedom of enquiry of those scholars who did. There was protest when he was nominated Bishop of Hereford in 1917. He was pressured to declare that he accepted the creed *ex animo*, i.e., from the heart, sincerely. But in his autobiography he explained that this did not imply that his acceptance was "nakedly and unintelligently literal."[31] Yet while Henson remained a champion of historical criticism as applied to the Bible and the creeds, he held theologically to a firm orthodoxy on the subject of the divinity of Jesus Christ, and he was alarmed at the famous Modern Churchmen's Conference at Girton College, Cambridge, in 1921. His refusal to countenance theological unorthodoxy as opposed to historical criticism became more pronounced in later years and makes him in my opinion in some ways the forerunner of neo-orthodoxy.

Essays Catholic and Critical

Gore lived until 1932, but long before his death "Liberal Catholicism," which he had founded, advanced well beyond *Lux Mundi*. The newer school refused to follow Gore in making the creeds a limit to the pursuit of historical criticism in the Bible. The creeds were less the doctrinal interpretation of historical facts which the historical criticism of the Bible had to verify, than more properly the crystallization of the spiritual experience of the believing community. E. G. Selwyn, already known as the editor of *Theology*, an organ of Liberal Catholicism, also became editor of *Essays Catholic and Critical*, the more radical Liberal Catholic successor to *Lux Mundi*.[32] Its avowed intention was to bring catholicism, conceived as the living tradition of Christian experience, into synthesis with the results of historical criticism. Most of the contributions dealt with questions of systematic theology in an apologetic key . But one of them, "The Christ of the Synoptic Gospels" by E. C. Hoskyns (1884–1937), was devoted to questions of biblical criticism.[33] Hoskyns attacked liberal protestantism not by falling back on a more conservative estimate of the biblical sources, but by showing that a frank acceptance of the critical method vindicated orthodoxy, both catholic and protestant. Hoskyns taught his pupils never to shrink from radical critical conclusions in the interests of orthodoxy.[34] It was no longer necessary for instance to uphold the traditional authorship of the Fourth Gospel in order to defend the doctrine of the incarnation, nor was it necessary to maintain the Pauline authenticity of the Pastorals in order to defend historic episcopacy.[35]

Gore was not happy with some of these developments. With two other scholars of his generation he edited *A New Commentary on Holy Scripture* to which many of the newer liberal catholics contributed, including Selwyn and Hoskyns.[36] An interesting feature of this volume is the way in which the editors added footnotes dissenting from the opinion of their younger collaborators. There would have been more such footnotes had not Gore himself written the commentary on St. Luke.

By 1930 the historical-critical method had come to be largely accepted in the Church of England. It is true that there was a fundamentalist fringe of conservative evangelicals but they lived at that time in near isolation. Anglo-catholics, liberal evangelicals, modernists all largely agreed on critical method. As a whole, Anglicans continued to be more conservative and cautious than the Germans. They were slow to come to terms with form-criticism and to this day they are still trying to digest redaction criticism (the study of the work of the evangelists as editors and authors). Very few Anglicans would follow completely the positions of the Bultmann school on dates and authorships.[37] But we can take it that after a slow beginning, and after only very cautious and gradual coming to terms with it, the historical criticism of the Bible is now accepted as a legitimate and necessary aspect of Anglicanism.

Biblical Criticism in the Episcopal Church, U.S.A.

In 1844 a committee of bishops was set up to enquire into the teaching of the General Theological Seminary. The main concern was the infiltration of Tractarianism. But one question asked (surprisingly for this early date, sixteen years before

Essays and Reviews) was: "Has it been publicly or privately taught in the Seminary that any portion of the sacred narrative in the book of Genesis is of the nature of myth or principally allegorical."[38] Perhaps the alarm was occasioned by the discoveries of geology which showed the world to be much older than 6,000 years.

The next thing that we hear of in S. T. Addison's history of the Episcopal Church is that in 1865 the House of Bishops approved of the Bishop of Cape Town's excommunication of Colenso (see above), and soon after the evangelical Bishop McIlvaine of Ohio addressed a letter to the clergy and ministerial candidates condemning the teachings of *Essays and Reviews* and that of Colenso. Until this point we hear of no one actually perpetrating such offenses. But the impression at this period is that critical notions were already coming from England. In the 1860s and 1870s the theory of evolutionism was spreading in the States, for the British scientists Tyndall and Huxley had crossed the Atlantic and were delivering popular lectures. It was the Broad Church clergy who first took up the new ideas, and argued that Episcopalians should welcome the truths of modern science. Their guiding principle is summed up by the motto which appears on the library of the Virginia Theological Seminary: "Seek the truth, come whence it may, cost what it will."[39] The Broad Churchmen believed themselves to be reacting in accordance with Anglican principle for they appealed to Hooker and Butler. In 1875, W. R. Huntington, a disciple of F. D. Maurice and best known as the father of the Chicago-Lambeth Quadrilateral, asserted that "the theologians must look upon the naturalists as their allies rather than as their antagonists."[40]

The seminaries, however, were slow to follow this lead. General Seminary was the center of Tractarianism, and Virginia of pietistic evangelicalism and Calvinism in theology.[41] At the dedication of Aspinwall Hall (where these words are being written) in 1859 Bishop Johns of Virginia declared "The Seminary has never slipped the cable of its faith and drifted with the tide of the thought of the day. It has discovered no new truths in Scripture, nor any new way of explaining old truths."[42] It was the Episcopal Theological School in Cambridge, Massachusetts, which pioneered the teaching of the historical criticism of the Bible. Twenty-five years before anything much happened in other seminaries Professors Nash and Steenstra taught the critical approach to the Bible without trouble from the trustees. Some bishops, however, did refuse their ordinands permission to attend the Cambridge seminary.

In 1884 the Rev. R. Heber Newton, Rector of All Soul's Church in New York City, preached a course of sermons which he subsequently published under the title, *The Right and Wrong Uses of the Bible*.[43] In it he initiated his readers to the composite structure of the Pentateuch, treated the early stories of Genesis as "primitive sagas" and the stories of Abraham, Isaac, Jacob and Joseph as "traditions."[44] These lectures created a great sensation, as it was the first time that such views were addressed to a popular audience in America. Charges of heresy were bandied about. The Assistant Bishop of New York, Henry Codman Potter, described by his biographer as "a low churchman by inheritance" but "a broad churchman by temperament," sympathized intellectually with Newton, but as a bishop was concerned to keep the peace, and requested him to discontinue the lectures. Newton loyally complied, but after their discontinuance he stated:

> Nothing has been said here that is not an old story to Biblical scholars, and all that has been said, as you know, has been in the profoundest reverence for the real spiritual revelation, which came to mankind through the historic growth of the 'people of religion.' Whatever has been said here has been said with a view to aiding you in disentangling the overgrowth of legend and myth in the Old Testament tradition from this inner body of truth; that thus you might read these venerable sagas of Genesis, which alone we have covered, without affronting your reason or your conscience by trying to make science out of its myths or history out of its legends, while you listen the more heedfully to their spiritual truths.[45]

Although silenced in his church, Newton, as we have mentioned, proceeded to publish his lectures. The charges of heresy were renewed but the bishop quietly ignored them. His inaction was a major contribution to the acceptance of historical criticism of the Bible in the Episcopal Church.

Some years later Henry Potter made a further contribution to freedom of biblical sholarship by ordaining Charles Augustus Briggs of Union Theological Seminary (see above). Potter's biographer gives the reason why Briggs chose to apply for orders in the Episcopal Church: "Temperamentally orthodox, and holding the fundamental doctrines of religion with an old-fashioned austerity, he sought a communion which was at the same time conservative in theology and progressive in its hospitality to the results of honest scholarship. This he found in the Episcopal Church."[46] Briggs' ordination to the diaconate took place peacefully, but protests were made when he came up for ordination to the priesthood. The Rev. F. W. Clendenin objected to Briggs' work, *A General Introduction to the Study of Holy Scripture*. Briggs' explanation of glossalalia as ecstatic speech rather than the gift of languages threw doubt on the Pentecost narrative as a whole (the domino theory!). He leaves us with "no Bible except that which 'historical criticism' may be able to dig out from the 'rubbish of ecclesiastical institutions, liturgical formulas, priestly ceremonies and casuistic practices.'" In the main the opposition came from the Anglo-Catholic wing. The conclusive answer to them was given to the effect that, if Briggs were excluded, there would then be no place for the *Lux Mundi* school either! Unperturbed by these protests, Potter ordained Briggs to the priesthood on May 14, 1899—a notable victory for the view that the historical criticism of the Bible was compatible with loyalty to the orthodox Christian faith.

As we have noted, the main opposition to Briggs' ordination came from Anglo-Catholics. What happened after 1900 was the gradual victory of *Lux Mundi* principles among Anglo-Catholics and especially at the General Theological Seminary. By the 1930s General had become the leading center of liberal catholicism, exemplified in the publication under the editorship of Frank Gavin, Professor of Ecclesiastical History at General, of the American counterpart to *Essays Catholic and Critical* under the title of *Liberal Catholicism and the Modern World*.[47] The essays on the Old and New Testaments were written respectively by Cuthbert Simpson of General and by Frederick C. Grant, at the time Dean of Seabury-Western Theological Seminary. Since liberal catholicism bases its faith chiefly upon the religious experience of the catholic Church throughout the ages the Bible can be viewed as only *one* of the sources of faith, and therefore, it is easier for catholics to be more open to the historical-critical method than protestants. Another exemplar of liberal catholicism was Burton Scott Easton, whose commentary on the Pastorals frankly recognized their post-Pauline origin.

At the Virginia Theological Seminary the evangelical emphasis on the Bible made it more reluctant to admit critical methods. A significant figure in the introduction of such methods at the Virginia Seminary is Carl E. Grammer, who must have been something of an enfant terrible among the older professors with their strict Calvinist backgrounds.[48] He came to the Seminary in 1887 and approached the Bible critically. Though popular among the student body, the trustees pressured him into resigning in 1898. It was however Cosby Bell (1881–1933) who is looked back upon as one who more than any other contributed to the triumph of liberal evangelicalism at Virginia. He was Professor of Theology from 1906 until his untimely death in 1933.

A surprising feature of the American Church, compared with the Church of England, is that in the Episcopal Church there are no surviving conservative evangelicals of the type of John Stott and J. I. Packer. Until the recent founding of Trinity Seminary near Pittsburg there was no seminary comparable to Tyndale Hall, Bristol, or to St. John's College, Nottingham. Perhaps the group that founded the Reformed Episcopal Church in 1874 siphoned off fundamentalist conservative evangelicalism before it had developed self-consciously as a reaction to biblical criticism. As a result, the Episcopal Church, when compared with the worldwide scene, lacks an important constituent part of Anglicanism. This is both gain and loss. On the one hand the Episcopal Church has been spared some of the battles that still beset its mother church; e.g., the veto the conservative evangelicals have imposed on the contents of *Alternative Services Book* (no prayers for the dead, no clear statement of the eucharistic oblation, and later no private absolution in the form "I absolve you"). But there is also loss: a too frequent substitution of psychologism or mere social activism for a true adherence to the gospel on the part of those who style themselves "evangelicals." Many of the so-called evangelicals in the American Church might more accurately be described as liberal pietists.

Soundings and After

In 1962 a group of Cambridge scholars resorted once more to the typical Anglical genre, and produced a volume of essays entitled *Soundings*.[49] This signaled in Anglicanism a reaction against the prevailing neo-orthodoxy and sought to reopen some of the questions raised by the older liberalism. It was followed by John A. T. Robinson's *Honest to God*.[50] The whole theological mood changed after that. But the changes were in the area of systematic theology rather than of biblical criticism. Both the neo-orthodox and the newer radicals were committed to the historical-critical method, and their difference was on theological rather than on critical issues. The critique leveled at the neo-orthodox by the newer radicals was that their position represented an uneasy combination of liberalsim in critical matters and orthodoxy in theology. Thus the neo-orthodox insisted on talking of the mighty acts of God in history, but under the withering impact of criticism the so-called mighty acts dwindled to practically nothing that could certainly be established. The historical event of the exodus for instance was reduced to an east wind blowing over the Sea of Reeds, and the resurrection (as a historical event) to a handful of subjective visions.

Oddly enough, however, John Robinson himself wrote a book in 1976 in which he sought to revive very conservative and often pre-critical datings to the new Testament works, so that every

New Testament document is dated before the fall of Jerusalem.[51] His basic argument is one from silence. The fall of Jerusalem was such an epoch-making event in the history of the early church that it is, argues Robinson, incredible that it was never mentioned. Accordingly, it cannot have occurred when the New Testament documents were written. A most interesting feature of his work is the way in which the author has ransacked the forgotten scholarly literature of the nineteenth and earlier twentieth centuries and has recovered the work of Anglican and other British scholars who, with typically cautious conservatism, were arguing against the more radical views of the German "higher critics." The most significant example is Robinson's rediscovery of the Bampton Lectures for 1913 by G. Edmundson.[52] This older scholar put forth learned arguments to show that Acts was written in Rome by Luke the companion of Paul not later than 62. It may be that some of Robinson's early datings will reestablish themselves. I am, for instance, open to the possibility that Colossians is genuinely Pauline and that it might have been written during Paul's imprisonment in Caesarea. Philemon would then have been written at the same time. But in his treatment of the Gospels Robinson tends to seize on traditions which were shaped before 70 and to base his argument exclusively upon them, ignoring traditions clearly later than 70.

Wrong-headed as Robinson's conclusions are in many respects, his work is an intellectual feast and a scholar's delight. Yet only among conservative evangelicals have his conclusions been welcomed. There is no real sign of a school of radical theologians emerging with conservative positions on matters of historical criticism.

Conclusion—Where Are We Today?

In 1980 the present writer wrote of a need for a moratorium on historical-critical discussion as far as the New Testament is concerned.[53] A little injudiciously, perhaps, he spoke of the "bankruptcy" of the historical-critical method. What he had in

mind was the ever more minute dissecting of the text that forms
the staple content of Ph.D. theses today. Instead he called for a
shift of emphasis to the theological exegesis of the biblical text,
and for a renewed commitment on the part of the biblical
scholars to seeing their task as a service to the church. He
proposed "that critical scholars, at least those who understand
their vocation as a service to the church, should impose upon
themselves the self-denying ordinance of a moratorium on
historical-critical analysis of the gospels and the Pauline homol-
ogoumena and concentrate upon their theological exegesis."
This was not a call for a fundamentalist abandonment of the
historical-critical method. That method has yielded indispensable tools for the theological exegesis that is needed. But it
does mean that historical criticism supplies us only with the
tools and concerns itself only with the prologomena to our real
task—which is the theological-critical interpretation of the
biblical text.

5

Science and the Bible

by W. Taylor Stevenson, Jr.

The understanding of "science" which informs this chapter is the prevalent one in the English-speaking world in which modern science is epitomized in the natural sciences with their stress upon objectivity, prediction, control, and number. This science derives from the controlled experiment which can be reproduced by members of the scientific community.[1]

I understand the Bible to be the text of the Old and New Testaments as it is presented and interpreted in an ongoing, critical, and redemptive process by the Christian Community. This interpretation takes place as the Bible is read, studied, and above all incorporated into the liturgical life of that community. As the Bible is appropriated in these ways Christians find themselves "drawn into the redemptive drama chartered in the pages of Scripture" and discover their "vision, hope, identity and encounter with God."[2] It is in this sense that "The Holy Scriptures of the Old and new Testaments (are) the revealed Word of God" ("The Chicago Quadrilateral") which "containeth all things necessary to salvation" (Article 6 of the Thirty-Nine Articles). This understanding of the Bible as it lives within the life of the Church is set forth in a most satisfactory way by Frederick Borsch in the final chapter of this book. It is this understanding exactly which informs this chapter.

It is the fundamental thesis of this chapter that there can be no conflict between science and the Bible when each is properly understood. Rather, and more positively, the two are in the modern period necessary to one another and support one another.

This fundamental thesis will be developed in the following stages: (1) A description of the popular misunderstanding of the conflict between science and the Bible which is actually a conflict between scientism and the Bible; (2) a delineation of the characteristics of science: (3) a contrasting of the intention of science, scientism, and the Bible, respectively; (4) a discussion of Darwinism as a case study of the supposed conflict between science and the Bible; and finally (5) a delineation of the ongoing, positive relationships between science and the Bible.

The Conflict Between Scientism and the Bible

The publication in 1841 of Ludwig Feuerbach's *The Essence of Christianity*, was the first "scientific" criticism of biblical religion which was both systematic and influential. For Feuerbach nature was at one and the same time the supernatural reality upon which all of natural and human existence is dependent, and also that empirical (known by sense experience), quantifiable, and increasingly explicable reality which alone must be attended to if we would understand our human stiuation. While Feuerbach's perception of the supernatural dimension of nature gradually fell by the wayside, his insistence upon being attentive to empirical nature in our efforts to understand what it means to be human was highly influential. Among those who reflect the influence of Feuerbach's thought are Kierkegaard, Nietzsche, Marx, Freud, Berdyaev, Heidegger, and Satre.

Feuerbach was not, of course, the first to discover the crucial role of the finite and empirical in understanding nature and human nature. Rather, he recognized an idea whose time had come and he proceeded to develop it in a systematic and provocative way. Feuerbach's goal was to attend to the finite and the empirical in order to turn the "friends of God" into the "friends of man." He was aware of the contribution of the

Christian doctrine of the Incarnation to his goal: "the second person (of the Trinity) being however in reality . . . the sole, true, first person in religion."[3] Or, in other words, it is the Son in his humanity who is the fundamental source of value and human meaning and thus in reality "God." The Christian teaching of the Incarnation has stated this in the past in a disguised way, but in *The Essence of Christianity* Feuerbach would have us see what Christians have unknowingly been saying all along: man is God. So it was that in the 1840s Feuerbach set forth in detail the major ideas of the Death of God theologies in the 1960s.

Christian theology was the fundamental groundwork for Feuerbach's system. The more immediate preparation for Feuerbach, however, had been the philosophical work of René Descartes (1596–1650) with his stress upon the human subject which is incapsulated in his famous phrase, "I think, therefore I am." Descartes' epochal work manifests the "turn to the subjective at the beginning of modern times" (Rahner). This turn is manifested on almost every page of Feuerbach. Thus:

> In the personality of God man clearly celebrates the super-naturalness, immortality, independence, and limitlessness of his own personality. The existence of God? The interest I have in knowing that God is, is one with the interest in knowing that I am immortal . . . God is my hidden, my assured existence: he is the subjectivity of subjects, the personality of persons.[4]

This was the set of ideas or the worldview whose time had come in Western Europe and especially in the northern part of Western Europe. And it was this area, together with North America, which was to be the center of scientific and technological development from the eighteenth century to the present. It is not a scientific worldview, as we will come to see, for a scientific worldview is a contradiction in terms. Feuerbach does articulate, however, the inclusive, quasi-religious worldview which provides *for popular imagination* the framework within which scientific and technological activities take place. This worldview is widely denominated as "scientism." I will utilize this term because its very ambiguity makes it a useful term. The first syllable of the term ("scien-") suggests that it is intimately related to science, although as we will see that relationship is quite marginal. The latter syllable ("-tism") is the clue that scientism is quasi-religious idealogy. In short, scientism is a confused position and the term expresses that very confusion.

Scientism assumes an important role in the following discussion, and therefore its major characterisitcs need to be noted. First, the individual person or personality is the ultimate source and the final judge of all value. There is no appeal beyond the person. Transcendence is excluded, i.e., nothing transcends the person.

Second, it follows by implication that it is the individual, historically embodied person in his or her empirical concreteness who is the source of all value. It is this individual who engages in the empirical perception of things. Insofar as we are "immortal" or "limitless," that immortality and limitlessness or transcendence will be manifested in some empirical and historical way. For example, in that popular form of scientism known as Darwinism, the "immortality" and "limitlessness" of the human self is manifested as it emerges out of the simplest forms of life. These simple forms have been progressively transcended in a series of spontaneous transformations which have resulted in "man" as we have known him in recent millennia, and whose future development will be manifested in his descendents in the millennia to come. This constitutes a disguised eschatology and immortality couched in terms of progressively developing empirical and historical biological exemplars. We will return to this in the next major section of this chapter.

Third, individuals and their perceptions, however complex, are "assured." Anything which might exceed the capacity of human knowing is assumed or declared to be nonexistent. If there are problematic aspects in our humanity and in our perceptions, these are provisional; a cheerful, continued examination of our empirical situation will ultimately resolve what is problematic. This overwhelming optimism arises out of and reinforces the attitude that the meaning of our human existence is at hand and self-explanatory. It must be self-explanatory and self-authenticating by definition, for there is no appeal beyond the self and its perceptions. In its crudest, most popular form, this attitude is expressed by saying that I know a stone is a stone because when I kick it I can feel it. So much for metaphysics!

4 A fourth characteristic of scientism is that it has its own spirituality. This spirituality is marked by an attitude of defiance toward anyone who would suggest that there might be anything more to our human experience than that which is taken to be self-evidently present to sense experience.

We, who live within Western civilization, and especially if we live in one of the countries bordering upon the North Atlantic, have become accustomed to this worldview and its claims. This familiarity should not blind us to the astounding nature of these claims and the ensuing spirituality. The optimism expressed here knows no bounds; neither the optimism about our ability to know and control, nor the tacit confidence that our ability to know and control will issue in our greater well-being. Equally, the preeminence assigned to humanity, and particularly to the human self, is breathtaking. Scientism's worldview is the polar opposite of the worldview manifested in all traditional religions of the past and of the present (for example Islamic, West African, Native American, and so on). This polarity helps to explain the confusion and sometimes bitter conflict which exists between the dominant Western worldview and that of traditional cultures. The distance between the dominant Western worldview and that espoused and lived out by the high religions of the East (Hinduism and Buddhism), is also enormous. In none of these religions is any ultimate confidence expressed in the value of the empirical experience of the historical individual. The fact that we have assumed as self-evident a worldview radically at variance with that of the vast majority of humanity, both historically and geographically, should at least give us pause.

When scientism is compared with the worldviews of spirituality manifested in Judaism and Christianity the differences are also profound. At the same time there are significant positive relationships. This is as we should expect because scientism arose within the Christian culture of Europe, especially northern Europe. The high value assigned to the individual in Judaism and especially Christianity with its doctrine of the Incarnation is the ground out of which arises (with whatever other contributing factors) scientism's insistence upon the ultimate value of the individual.[5] The positive attitude toward the material world expressed in God's good creation (Genesis 1, 2) and in Jewish and Christian sacramentalism is the ground out of which arises scientism's absolutizing of empirical experience. The radical, future-oriented optimism of the eschatological faith of Judaism and Christianity is the ground out of which arises scientism's radical, future-oriented optimism in regard to the course of events within the order of this world. Many similar positive relationships could be given. The difference, and it makes all the difference, is that while scientism arose out of the ground of biblical religion, scientism abandoned the biblical affirmation that the individual, the creature, and the course of the historical world all find their final meaning and source in the trustworthiness of God. In scientism the transcendent reference is totally gone at the explicit and conscious level. Yet, at the same time, the transcendent reference lives on in a hidden or unacknowledged way. It is this hidden transcendence which supplies the assurance in scientism's astounding claims concerning the historical individual, the empirical order, the human future, and so on. It is this situation which gives scientism its great power. The cost of this covertness to scientism is that it does not recognize its own implicit roots and consequently its own inherent confusion.

The supposed conflict between science and the Bible, then, is a conflict between scientism and the Bible with their respective religious claims about the cosmos, human nature and destiny. Scientism's religious claims are covertly religious, the Bible's claims are explicitly religious. Scientism and the Bible both recognize the necessity of transcendence if the human enterprise is to be creative: Scientism locates its source of transcendence covertly in humanity's infinite desire to know, its power to persevere, and its incrementally achieved ability to succeed. The Bible explicitly locates its source of transcendence in—or better, confesses itself to be located by—the transcendent God who is both the ground of and also the call beyond every human desire, power, and achievement. Scientism confesses ultimate reality, the reality which cannot be denied, to be located in our humanity. The Bible confesses our humanity to be located in ultimate reality, the God who cannot be denied. At the conscious and explicit level the God of scientism is declared to be within our humanity. In contrast, the humanity of the biblical person is located explicitly with God. Which comes first, human being or God's being, makes all of the difference.

The conflict between scientism and the Bible, then, is a religious and theological conflict. More specifically, the conflict is a family conflict. As we have seen, scientism arose out of a biblical ground and hence shares much with the Bible in terms of its perception of human nature and history. The intimacy of such family or civil conflicts renders them especially bitter. In family or civil conflicts there is the memory of a common heritage and the judgment that the other side has betrayed that heritage in part. Hence, from a biblical perspective scientism is a heresy because it has betrayed and abandoned a crucial part of our common heritage, the transcendent God of Abraham, Isaac, and Jacob. From the perspective of scientism, the religion and theology grounded in the Bible represent a betrayal of our common heritage, namely, the spirit of truth which always leads us into new ways of perceiving and ordering our world. Such family conflicts are intractable and persistent, and so this conflict has been since the early nineteenth century when it was first fully articulated by Feuerbach.

The Characteristics of Science[6]

Our topic is science and the Bible. We need therefore a definition of science that is focused in such a manner that it will forward our inquiry in three ways. First, our definition should enable us to see the differences and similarities between science and scientism. Second, it needs to be made clear why it is impossible for there to be a conflict between science and the

Bible. Finally, our definition of science should provide a basis for both appropriating science as a part of our biblical heritage and also enabling us to perceive the analogies between the scientific enterprise on the one hand and the religious and theological enterprise of biblical faith on the other hand.

Science is characterized by four qualitites, objectivity, prediction, control and number. This can be visualized with the help of the following diagram provided by Huston Smith:

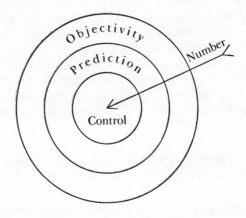

Each of these qualities needs to be discussed in turn.

Objectivity. Objectivity means being able to lay claim to inter-subjective agreement. Concretely, scientific objectivity is present when scientifically trained persons can agree upon, discuss, and use definitions ("facts"), procedures, goals, and so on. There are various kinds of objectivity, for example, historical, economic, theological, and many others. These are the many realms of objectivity. Each realm has it "objectivity facts." Each realm constitutes a discipline in which human subjectivity is laboriously tutored and formed in a particular way.

Scientific objectivity is one such realm. Because of the formal and informal educational structure of the contemporary Western world, many people have been tutored in an elementary way to participate in scientific objectivity. A few people, such as physicists and chemists, have had their subjectivity rigorously tutored in a scientific way. For all practical purposes, scientific objectivity had its beginnings in the sixteenth or seventeeth century. Prior to that time there was no scientific objectivity and hence no scientific facts. In the contemporary world there are many people for whom there are no scientific facts, for example, those who live in the traditional societies of West Africa or Southeast Asia. Such people are not "stupid." Rather, their subjectivity has been tutored in other ways. On the one hand, scientific facts refer to something beyond our human subjectivity; these facts are "out there" and stable. On the other hand, scientific facts are human constructions which are constantly being reformulated. The same is true of the facts in the other realms of objectivity. So, while objectivity is crucial to science, it is not unique to science. The uniqueness of science emerges progressively as we turn to prediction, control, and number.

Prediction, control, and number. A science must be able to make some predictions about its subject matter, for example, the path of an object in space or the medicinal effect of the ingestion of a particular drug. The greater the degree of accuracy of such prediction, the more useful the science. The degree of accuracy of physics and chemistry (the so-called "hard sciences") is high, while the degree of accuracy of such sciences as medicine and meteorology is relatively low. The centrality in science of the controlled experiment is oriented to achieving an ever-greater degree of accuracy. The difficulty of achieving accuracy of prediction is known to anyone who has so much as engaged in an elementary course in physics or quantitative chemical analysis. The necessary disciplines of attentiveness, consistency, and skillful technique are rigorous. Months are sometimes necessary in order to learn to perform satisfactorily one step in an experiment.

The aim of rigorous discipline is to arrive consistently at the predicted outcome of an experiment. Or, the aim is to achieve control over the particular phenomenon with which the experiment is concerned. Ideally all eventualities must be anticipated in a controlled way.

Number plays an increasingly important role as the scientist moves from objectivity to prediction and on to control. Quantity (size, weight, movement, duration, and so on) is all-important, and to quantify is to number. Ideally, all quantities and eventualities should be included within the numerical equation. If a factor cannot be quantified it is not amenable to scientific control. In physics and chemistry it is relatively easy to achieve this situation for all practical purposes. In biology and medicine it is more difficult.

As one moves into studies which focus upon the activities of the human subject, the situation is more difficult yet. In economics, sociology, and psychology prediction and control is reduced to the prediction and control of statistical probabilities and is limited to those dimensions of economic, sociological, and psychological phenomenon which are amenable to quantification. In the discipline of history the quantification and numbering of artifacts are possible, but controlled experiment is not. Hence, it is misleading to speak of scientific history. History has its own objectivity, but it is not scientific history except in an analogical sense.

The progressive loss of relevance of science as one moves from physics to history is most pertinent to our subject— science and the Bible. It is pertinent because this progressive loss of relevance makes manifest that as the human self comes progressively to the center of our attention, science becomes progressively less useful. In history this usefulness is almost gone, while a scientific psychoanalysis or scientific painting would be an absurdity.

This situation is just as it should be and in no way does it constitute a criticism of science. What this situation does manifest is an essential and deliberately chosen limitation of science. Science intends to reduce the human self to one who sees the world as a series of specimens or exemplars, interactions, energy exchanges, and secondary causes.[7] Hence, the scientist as scientist intends that the world be finite, perceptible by the human senses, and quantifiable in terms of number. This is the empirical world of the scientist. It is an intentionally and rigorously restricted world subject to prediction and control.

This very restrictiveness may appear simple to us through long familiarity, but the insight that it is possible to be so restrictive, and to be so consistently, was an act of human imagination which has transformed human life in the realm of number (average income, years of life expectancy, speed of travel, and so on). The magnitude of this transformation should not blind us to the extremely restricted way in which science knows.

Specifically, there are four things in which science has no interest, and cannot and will not yield: (1) intrinsic and normative values, (2) purpose, (3) ultimate and existential meaning, and (4) quality.[8] Huston Smith's characterization of these four things in a masterly fashion deserves to be quoted at length.

Intrinsic and Normative Values: "Science can deal with instrumental values, but not intrinsic ones. It can tell us that smoking damages health, but whether health is better than somatic gratification it cannot adjudicate. Again, it can determine what people do like, but not what they should like."

Ultimate and existential meanings: "Science is meaningful throughout, but there are two kinds of meaning it cannot interpret. One of these is ultimate meaning (what is the meaning of it all?), while the other type is existential (the kind we have in mind when we say something is meaningful). There is no way science can force the human mind to find its discoveries involving; the hearer always has the option to shrug his shoulders and walk away. Unable to deal with these two kinds of meanings, science 'fails in the face of all ultimate questions' (Jaspers) and leaves 'the problems of life... completely untouched' (Wittgenstein)."

Quality: "This is basic to the lot, for it is their qualitative components that make values, meanings, and purposes important. Qualities, however, being subjective, refuse to step into even the initial, 'objective' ring of science's concentric circles as I have diagrammed them; nor do they follow its arrow of number... Science's inability to deal with the qualitatively unmeasurable leaves its dealing with what Lewis Mumford calls a 'disqualified universe.'"

Science, then, neither has nor does it intend to have normative values, purpose, ultimate and existential meanings, or qualitative judgments. Thus science lacks all of the essential components of a worldview or a view of the self. "Science capitalizes on this freedom from context and tries to show us a contextless world ... "[9] It is just this lack of context which constitutes so much of the attractiveness of science. The scientist recognizes no transcendent cause or reality. The scientist, however, is transcendent to the world for "he stands in a position of objectivity over against the world, a world which he sees as a series of specimens or exemplars, and interactions, energy exchanges, secondary causes ... "[10] In this transcendent realm the air is very thin but very pure. It is adequate to support a self which has been reduced almost to the vanishing point. The full self of the scientist, with all of its ambiguities and conflicts, is left behind for the working day. He or she returns to this conflicted self at the end of the working day, or when power struggles within the scientific community arise, and demonstrates then that the scientist is not better or wiser than any of the rest of us. It is this lack of any explicit worldview which enables science to penetrate cultures other than that of the West in which science arose.

Science, however, does have an implicit worldview or view of the self in this severely restricted degree: it is possible and useful in controlled experiments to isolate and to attend to that component of human experience which is amenable to number, prediction, and control. Science does not even argue for or attempt to justify this restricted view of the world and the self. Rather, this restricted view simply is accepted from "somewhere else" and then "justified" instrumentally, that is, "It works." What is assumed from somewhere else is an implicit view of nature which declares simultaneously that nature is desacralized (hence open to analysis and control), orderly (amenable to number), and worthy of investigation (a qualitative judgment). Further, science implicitly assumes that human beings are potentially capable of conducting such investigations successfully (another qualitative judgment). The familiarity in the West of these ideas should not trick us into thinking that they are self-evidently true and universally accepted by all people of good will. They are not accepted, for example, either by the traditional cultures of the past or the present, nor by contemporary nihilistic philosophies. Nor is it possible for anyone to demonstrate conclusively that these implicit ideas of science should be accepted. Certainly science cannot demonstrate them, nor is it interested in any such project. These implicit ideas are simply assumed or borrowed from somewhere else.

In the Bible, however, science's implicit view of the world and the self is in effect made explicit, although in an undifferentiated form. The Bible, like science, is not able to demonstrate in a rational way the validity of this view of the world and the self. Such a demonstration is not possible. What the Bible does do is to confess a view of the world and the self which contains "in a nutshell" (that is in an undifferentiated way) a view which is congruent with the view of the world and the self manifested in science. The Jew and the Christian confess or proclaim a transcendent God: "He is not here." It follows that if God is not in nature pantheism is overcome and nature is desacralized. A desacralized nature is open to analysis and control. It is further confessed and proclaimed in the Bible that the creation is God's; it is ordered by him out of his wisdom and through his word (John 1:1ff). It is a good creation given into our human care (Genesis 1, 2), and hence worthy of our concern, attention, understanding, and so on. Still further, the Bible proclaims a very significant role for humanity with God in respect to the creation. Men and women are capable of hearing and responding to God. There is an interdependent relationship between God and humanity which is developed in terms of the covenants between Yahweh and Israel, and then in terms of the new covenant established in Jesus Christ. There is a very high estimate of human potentiality in Judaism, and this is intensified in Christianity where in one human being God and humanity coinhere. "If Abraham's faith can be defined as 'for God everything is possible,' the faith of Christianity implies that everything is also possible for man."[11]

Such are the very significant similarities between, on the one hand, the implicit and assumed views of science concerning nature and humanity and, on the other hand, the explicitly confessed views of Jews and Christians concerning nature and humanity. In my judgment, this biblical confession was the enabling condition for the eventual development of science in the West. In any case, biblical faith was at least a benign environment for the growth of science. Far from the Jew or Christian having anything to complain about in the implicitly assumed view of nature and humanity manifested in science, there is much for which we should be thankful. We will return to this later.

Science, Scientism, and the Bible: Similarities and Differences

The purpose of the preceding section was (1) to establish the characteristics of science in order to contrast them with the characteristics of scientism; (2) to make clear the impossibility of a conflict between science and the Bible; and (3) to enable us to begin to appropriate science as a discipline which has in part developed out of our biblical heritage. In this section we will be concerned primarily with (1)and (2) and will turn to (3) in a later section.

The contrast between science and scientism. Scientism has what it takes to be a fully rounded view of the world and of what it means to be human. Scientism's view of the world and the self, as we discussed earlier, has three major components. First, the individual is the ultimate source and final judge of all value. Transcendence is denied. Second, it is the historically embodied individual who knows. It is through the empirical knowledge of things, including other persons, that knowledge and value are to be found. Or, "(a) nothing that lacks a material component exists, and (b)...in what does exist the physical component has the final say."[12] Third, there is the optimistic assumption that human knowledge is assured. There are of course problems in our human perceiving and knowing, but our empirical perceptions will finally resolve these problems. The meaning of our human existence is, if only we have eyes to see, at hand and self-explanatory.

Such is scientism's view of the self and the world. Scientism affirms everything which science itself does not and cannot affirm: intrinsic and normative values (only that which has a material component exists), purpose (there is an ultimately self-explanatory process in which material components manifest themselves), ultimate and existential meaning (all value is found in the observation of and reflection upon the material world). There is no controlled experiment which is able to even test, much less confirm, any of these affirmations. For example, how would one conduct a controlled experiment to test "only that which has a material component exists"? Nor can these affirmations be invested with number and expresseed in any equation. These affirmations are useless as means of prediction and control, for we know as a matter of experience that the self (including the self displayed by the most single-minded followers of scientism) goes caroming around the Cosmos like an unguided missle (Percy). Scientism lacks all of the essential qualities possessed by science. Science lacks all of the judgments of normative values and of quality made by scientism. Science has no way of evaluating the claims of scientism, and hence has no interest in them. Scientism, nothing daunted, wishes nevertheless to borrow the aura of science as a means of giving credibility to its claims. Carl Sagan's popular television series *Cosmos* is a good example of a scientistic point of view wrapping itself in the guise of science.

Why the desire of scientism to form this illogical alliance with science?

The most fundamental answer is summed up in an old-fashioned word: idolatry. The purpose of idolatry is to control. By means of my idolatrous activities I wish to participate in the power of my idol, for example, class privilege, political party, wealth, and so on. Scientism is an "idol of the study" (Barfield). This idolatry proceeds in the following manner. Science, as we have noted, is able to control to some greater or less degree a very limited part of our environment. This scientific activity is not idolatry because the scientist recognizes the provisional and non-exhaustive character of all scientific judgments. A scientific judgment about "x" is not *the* truth about "x," and there is more truth about "x" than the scientific judgment will ever comprehend. Scientism attempts to take the approach of science and apply it to the totality of human experience. The provisional character of science proper is abandoned. The controlled experiment now takes place in the head, in the "study," of the follower of scientism. In these mental experiments normative judgments abound. The primary normative judgment is this: that which is not material—not a thing, not an exchange of energy—does not exist. Or, that which scientism does not wish to consider is declared not to exist. Thus, "all" is included and it is intended that all things be controlled. Scientism is totalitarian, and the perversion of science to its own purposes is part of this totalitarianism. Never mind that this totalitarianism, like all totalitarianisms, works only in the most limited and temporary sort of way.

In subverting science to its own purposes, scientism incurs one result which it does not consciously intend: the human subject, the self, moves toward extinction. We have seen in our discussion of the characterisitics of science that in science the self is reduced to that which observes and quantifies things ("exemplars," "energy exchanges"). The scientific self intentionally eschews normative values, meaning, and purpose—all that constitutes a fully human self, a person. Scientism, in attempting to adapt the procedures of science to its own purposes, enters into the following confused enterprise.

Scientism, following the lead of science, wants to see the self in terms of material things. Things, however, as we have seen, are without the normative values, meaning, and purpose which go to make up the self. So it is that scientism attempts to find our humanity in relation to that which is inferior to our humanity: things. The attempt is a failure. Value, meaning, and purpose cannot be derived from that which is without any of those qualities. The valid, carefully circumscribed procedures of science proper become disastrous when scientism attempts to adapt them to yield a comprehensive view of the world and self. In the biblical tradition, the self made in the image of God, has a world. In scientism, the self made in the image of the thing, is had by the world (things, exemplars, energy exchanges). Or, "We become what we worship."

Martin Buber said all of this over a generation ago in his beautiful and highly influential *I and Thou*. According to Buber the world is twofold: there is the open and free world of I-Thou in which I receive myself from another self (Thou) which is finally God (the Eternal Thou). And there is the closed and controlled world of I-It in which I receive myself from things and in so doing discover that I am simply a controlled thing. Scientism lives in the world of I-It. Yet, in spite of Buber, those upon whom he drew, and those whom he influenced, the vain dream of a controlled world continues. Scientism is the dominant expression of this dream at the present. The vain dream is a reenactment of Genesis 3 in which in mythic form there is the expression of the attempt of men and women to control their own destinies. It is difficult to imagine a more misbegotten dream of the world and the self than that of scientism. Through the total misconstrual of science, scientism arrives at a position so vacuous that, as discussed in the opening section of this chapter, it can only continue by misappropriations the values and meanings (a good creation, human value, hope for the future) wrenched from the context of the biblical heritage which it so despises.

The Impossibility of Conflict Between Science and the Bible. The entire preceding discussion has stated by clear implication why there can be no conflict between science and the Bible. It only remains to make explicit what has been implicit.

The intentions of science and the intentions of the Bible are quite distinct. Each is engaged in a thoroughly different enterprise. Science and the Bible share in one aim, objectivity. There are, however, many types or realms of objectivity—as we discussed earlier. The objectivity appropriate to the Bible is demonstrated daily throughout the world in the liturgies, in the prayers, and in the preaching of Jews and Christians. These activities center around the biblical narratives with their symbols and myths in which our individual and corporate salvation is manifested. In these narratives the uppermost concern is with intrinsic and narrative values, ultimate and existential meanings, and quality. The rigorous discipline of biblical objectivity is described at length in the concluding chapter of this book, "All Things Necessary to Salvation." The controlled experiment is totally absent from that discipline.

In contrast, the objectivity appropriate to science is concerned with that very limited portion of human experience which is amenable to prediction, control, and number. Here the controlled experiment is essential. Science is not concerned with intrinsic and normative values, ultimate and existential meanings, or quality.

In brief, the purposes and procedures of science and of the Bible are so totally divergent that they are not and cannot be in competition or conflict with one another. Conflict only arises when the procedures of science are misappropriated by scientism in order to formulate an anti-biblical theology of salvation; or when the procedures of science are misappropriated by biblical literalists ("fundamentalists") in order to transform the Bible into a book of science concerned with prediction, control, and number. Such unnecessary conflicts are best exemplified in the controversies surrounding Darwin's theory of the descent of man, to which we now turn.

Darwinism and the Bible

For a variety of reasons the theory of Charles Darwin (1809–1882) about the descent of man demands the attention of anyone considering the relationship of science and the Bible. For the purposes of our discussion Darwin's evolutionary theory particularly demands our attention because it is at present the exemplification of scientism which is most pervasive and influential. Darwin's theory, as we will see, attempts to use objective scientific facts to found a worldview replete with intrinsic and normative values, purpose, and existential meaning—scientism exactly.[13] The persistence and pervasiveness of the attempts of the "Creationists" to reinstate the biblical account of creation in the curriculum of public schools is an impressive negative testimony to the influence of Darwin's theory. It is to the credit of the Creationists, however inadequate the details of their position, that they recognize and oppose the totalitarian claims of Darwin's theory.

While few Anglicans subscribe to the largely obscurantist arguments of the Creationists or fundamentalists, the negative influence of evolutionary theory is felt by most Anglicans and by Christians generally. Quite apart from the issue of biblical literalism, the claim of Darwinism holds that the natural and human world are simply the products of chance. Few if any of us, regardless of our religious position, are untouched by this claim. As biologist Lewis Thomas puts it: "Evolution is our most powerful story, equivalent in its way to a universal myth."[14] In the judgment of Huston Smith, if this myth were to collapse "The modern age would be over, for the notion is so much its cornerstone that were it to crumble, a new edifice would have to be built."[15] The stakes in this discussion, then, are high.

The appeal of this covert myth, however mistaken it may be, is evident. The appeal of evolution is its founding hope of a collective "future that will upgrade the quality of life by the mere fact that lives are born into it."[16] Life without hope is impossible, and evolution supplies that hope for many. All religions articulate by way of a creation story a basis for human hope of some kind, and the religious quality of scientism is revealed in that it too has a creation myth, evolution. It is this human need for *some* creation story which helps us to understand why it is that on no other scientific (actually scientistic) theory does the modern mind rest so much confidence on so little evidence.[17] Evolution is, as we will argue in the following paragraphs, an idol of the study. In the final section of this essay a way of taking the legitimate insights and hopes of evolutionary theory in a biblical perspective will be suggested.

Another significant reason why a discussion of evolution should be a part of this book is that a major part of the debate centering around Darwin's theory has taken place in an Anglican milieu. Just as Feuerbach's atheistic ideas had long preceded him, so had the idea of evolution long preceded Darwin—for example, by Jean Baptiste Lamarck (1744–1829).

However, just as Feuerbach had suggested a mechanism which supported and gave credence to previous atheistic opinions, so Darwin suggested a mechanism which supported and gave credence to previous evolutionary opinions. The ensuing controversy ran, and often raged, throughout the Victorian period. Darwin's most prominent champion was T. H. Huxley (1825–1895). Huxley was answered by a variety of theologians and scholars: George Rawlinson, Bishop Wilberforce, Edward Pusey, and others.[18] In these controversies bewilderment, confusion, and prejudice were to be found on all sides, but as a whole the opponents of Darwin showed up badly. The terms of the Darwinian controversies have now changed substantially, primarily because we have come to recognize that science (in this case biology) and theology are two distinct realms of inquiry and discourse. The preceding sections of this chapter have sought to establish that distinction, and to show that the two are not antithetical. It is the purpose of this section to show the distinctiveness of these two realms specifically in terms of biology (evolutionary theory) and theology.

Darwin's Theory of Natural Selection. It is crucial to begin by understanding just what Darwin's theory states. I want to describe this theory at some length, for it is important to know just what it is that I wish to reject.

The key to Darwin's theory is "natural selection," the mechanism which gave support and credence to earlier evolutionary opinions. A basic but good definition of natural selection is given by a prominent contemporary biologist, John Tyler Bonner:

> The concept of natural selection is deceptively simple. In modern terms, it says that individuals in a population of a species vary. Furthermore, these variations are genetic, that is inherited. Because certain individuals will be more successful than others in a particular environment, the population will slowly change into a new form, a new species. By success one means reproductive success. A variant is successful if it contributes a large number of offspring for the next generation; in that way it proportionately increases its own genetic characters in the chang-

ing population. For this reason and others, the environment itself changes, which in turn alters the nature of what is selected. This is *natural* selection, where ecological environments impose the conditions of selection.[19]

This evolutionary development of the species was preceded by the evolutionary complication of much simpler compounds. In the words of *The New Encyclopaedia Britannica* ("Evolution"):

> It is not unreasonable to suppose that life originated in a watery "soup" of prebiological organic compounds and that living organisms arose later by surrounding quantities of these compounds by membranes that made them into "cells." This is usually considered the starting point of organic ("Darwinian") evolution.

The New Encyclopaedia Britannica does, of course, represent a semi-popular level of discussion, but the focus of our discussion is precisely that of a popular cultural attitude.

Evolution then, in the careful language of Michael Polanyi, is the sum total of successive accidental hereditary changes, beginning with the simplest organic compounds and extending to the anthropoids and finally man, "which have offered reproductive advantages to their bearers. The sequence of hereditary changes, leading to the replacement of the original types by better equipped variants, is described as 'natural selection,' and the 'force of natural selection' is supposed to have brought forth the successive forms of life that have eventually produced man.... (More generally, the history of nature shows) a cumulative trend of changes tending upward towards higher levels of organization, among which the deepening of sentience and the rise of thought are the most conspicuous."[20]

Finally, there is the less careful but, in terms of the popular cultural understanding which is our subject, very accurate characterization of the sweep of evolutionary theory by the psychiatrist, Karl Stern:

> If we present, for the sake of argument, the theory of evolution in a most scientific formulation, we have to say something like this: "At a certain moment of time the

temperature of the Earth was such that it became most favourable for the aggregation of carbon atoms and oxygen with the nitrogen-hydrogen combination, and that from random occurrences of large clusters molecules occurred which were most favourably structured for the coming about of life, and from that point it went on through vast stretches of time, until through processes of natural selection a being finally occurred which is capable of choosing love over hate and justice over injustice, of writing poetry like that of Dante, composing music like that of Mozart, and making drawings like those of Leonardo."[21]

Stern observes provocatively that these ideas, familiar to most of us from the time of grade school, have much in common with the psychotic thinking of schizophrenics. This is true in the sense that, as we shall see, the successive ideas of evolutionary theory are loosely and fancifully related to one another in a way which cannot be coherently substantiated. This can be correlated with our earlier discussion of scientism (and, again, popular evolutionary theory is a form of scientism) in which we noted that scientism is based upon a severely diminshed human self divorced from most of human experience.

The criticism of Darwinism which I want to make, however, is not psychoanalytic but rather philosophical and theological. Let us begin by stating emphatically what is correct about Darwinism.

What is to be affirmed in evolutionary theory is its specifically scientific component. This component is concerned with objectivity, prediction, control, and number; it is not concerned with normative values, purposes, ultimate meaning, or quality. This scientific component is concerned with the fossil record which issues in a taxonomy which is subtle and wondrous. It is estimated that there are over 1,100,000 known spiecies of animals and at least 350,000 known plant species.[22] Moreover, the fossil record demonstrates that the evolutionary sequence is to be affirmed. Simpler forms of life did precede more complex ones; the amoeba does precede more complex biological forms of life. This has long been intuited, as for example in Genesis 1 and 2, and all of the scientific inquiry which informs evolutionary theory substantiates and expands that intuition in an exciting and wonderful way. While the controlling experiment is obviously not possible in this area, there is an evolutionary script written in fossil remains which is descriptive of one dimension of the good creation, and evolutionary studies have enabled us to read that script. The script in itself says nothing of the purpose or meaning or quality of creation for that is not the interest of science. Nevertheless, not to be thankful for having been enabled to read that script is at best churlish. The appropriate response here for the person whose faith looks to the God of Abraham, Isaac, and Jacob is a eucharistic response: thanksgiving and praise.

Having said that, and without any thought of retracting it, two objections to evolutionary theory must be raised. The first objection is relatively minor although not unimportant. This concerns the details of evolutionary theory. The second objection is philosophical and theological in character and is absolutely crucial for it demonstrates that popular evolutionary theory is a form of scientism. I want to explore each of these objections in turn.

The first objection is perhaps only an observation, namely that the so-called "gaps" in the fossil record are enormous and will probably never be filled. Here we need to distinguish between "micro-evolution" and "macro-evolution." Micro-evolution refers to evolution on a small scale (such as that which gives rise to protective coloration and food-gathering habits) and within narrow limits. Darwin's classical study of the differentiation between types of finches on one of the Galapagos Islands is an example of micro-evolution. No one disputes this form of evolution, or that the principle of natural selection accounts for it in an adequate way. In contrast there is macro-evolution which addresses the problems of major evolutionary changes over a period of millennia. In macro-evolution the problems are serious.

One example of the problems of macro-evolution is to be found in the commonly cited example of evolutionary development of the genealogy of the horses or equine animals. Charles Deperet in *Le Transformations du Monde Animal* observes that

Geological observation establishes in a formal manner that no gradual passage existed between these genera; the last Palaeotherium was extinct long since, without transforming itself, when the first Architherium appeared, and the latter had disappeared in its turn, without modification, before being suddenly replaced by the invasion of Hipparion ... The supposed pedigree of Equidae is a deceitful delusion, which simply gives us the general process by which the tridactyl hoof of an Ungulate can transform itself, in various groups, into a monodactyl hoof, in view of an adaptation for speed; but in no way enlightens us on the palaeontological origin of the horse.[23]

Similarly birds are supposed to have evolved from reptiles, but the geological support for this supposition is very scanty. The distinctive qualities of the bird (feathers, hollow bones, distinctive musculature for flying, and excretory system designed for rapid digestion and excretion) are radically different from the corresponding features of reptiles and would have had to emerge simultaneously in order to enable reproductive success.

Finally, in regard to macro-evolution anyone who has followed the recent widely publicized discussions attendant upon the discovery in Ethiopia of the fossil remains of a female anthropoid dubbed "Lucy" will know that the comment of Loren Eisely made in 1953 still stands: "How the primeval evolved into *Homo sapiens*, what forces precipitated the enormous expansion of the human brain—these problems ironically still baffle the creature who has learned to weigh stars and to tamper with the very fabric of the universe."[24]

Such problems as these are numerous and have been detailed from a scientific perspective by Douglas Dewar in *The Transformist Illusion*[25] and by many others. These observations about the limitations of the properly scientific studies of evolutionary paleontology only become objections when these limitations are ignored or minimized. At the popular level at least these limitations are commonly ignored. What *is* gradually emerging in the reflection upon evolutionary theory is that Darwinian theory is a scientific model or paradigm predicated upon micro-evolutionary studies which become inadequate when that model is extrapolated to explain macro-evolutionary changes. The data from the fossil record have been forced into the inadequate Darwinian paradigm in order to explain macro-evolution. Darwin's nineteenth-century theory is probably on the verge of collapse.[26] Scientific paradigms do change as Thomas Kuhn has set forth in *The Structure of Scientific Revolutions*, [27] and when the change comes it comes quite suddenly. As a result of such a change all of the previously gathered data is seen in a new and very different perspective. In the meantime, however, for all of its problems, Darwinian theory is the most coherent and hence heuristically useful paradigm we have. It is better to think with the help of this paradigm than not to think at all. From a biblical perspective there is nothing to object to in the provisional continued use of Darwin's theory, but only to the absolutizing of that theory whereby it becomes an "idol of the study."

The first objection we discussed to Darwin's theory was raised from a scientific perspective and focused upon the adequacy both of the details and the controlling paradign of evolutionary theory which gives coherence to those details. Now we turn to the second objection. This objection is raised from a philosophical and theological perspective and is focused upon the values, purposes, and ultimate meanings inherent in the worldview of Darwin's theory. The judgment we reached at the end of our exploration of the first objection was that evolutionary theory is to be provisionally accepted in spite of its many problems. The judgment we will reach at the end of our exploration of the second objection is that the worldview of Darwin's theory is scientistic and must be rejected.

The hypothesis of natural selection is crucial to evolutionary theory, and so we turn to that hypothesis as we begin our exploration of the inadequacies of evolutionary theory from a philosophical and theological perspective.

Evolutionary theory is, as we saw in our preceding discussion, a description of the descent of man. Evolutionary theory is also an explanatory theory of that descent. Its claim is that all there is to be known about man, his complete complement of faculties and potentials, can be accounted for by the process of natural selection which works mechanically by way of chance variations. What is the purpose and hence the meaning of this process? The human species as we know it today. What is the source or causative agent of this process and its final fruit? Chance. On what basis do we arrive at the judgment that man is the purpose and culmination of this evolutionary process? On the basis of what has appeared by chance, namely man.

Now the cause of a process extending over millennia and encompassing the entire organic realm cannot be observed. Therefore the cause must be postulated as a hypothesis. The hypothesis is "Chance." Chance, however, is "precisely what a hypothesis is devised to save us from. Chance, in fact, = no hypothesis." Chance as a type of hypothesis is analogous to drowning as a type of swimming—under the supposition that because drowning is "something we can do with ourselves in water, drowning should be included as one of the different ways of swimming."[28]

Evolutionary theory in effect makes the following proposal: out of that which is without value, value arises by chance. More concretely, there are simply things (amino acids, protozoa, reptiles, and so on) which by chance (natural selection) culminate in a valued and valuing being, man.

Whatever else this theory is, it is not science. It is not science because once evolutionary studies move beyond the observing and classifying of the fossil record, they are not based on observation. One cannot observe the progressive emergence of value. Nor is the controlled experiment or prediction possible beyond the mini-evolution effected by the botanist and animal breeder. Nor can the evolutionary process be reduced to number and expressed in an equation.

What evolutionary theory does do is to elaborate under the guise of science a comprehensive worldview with normative values (natural selection), purpose (the descent of man), existential meaning (participation in the evolutionary process), and quality (all that which contributes to the evolutionary process). As a science, evolutionary theory fails on every count; it does not meet the criteria of natural science and it engages in the assertions of value and purpose which are excluded by science.

Evolutionary theory then is clearly scientism, and like all scientism is a hoax.

This hoax, however, is pervasive and approaches being an "unquestioned truth." There are two reasons for the redoubtable status of evolutionary theory. First, it is assumed in the modern period that valid inquiry begins and proceeds without presuppositions, without the importation of values or explanations which beg the question which is being explored. Any factor which transcends what is at hand, all that goes to make up the full human self, is excluded. Darwinian theory does exactly that: "life out of non-life, intelligence out of its absence, explanation out of that which in no way contains that which is to be explained . . . "[29] In this sense the hoax "works."

As our discussion in the earlier portion of this chapter indicated, however, this presuppositionless inquiry by a deracinated self which purports to arise out of nothing is only possible if transcendence is covertly introduced. Without transcendence the human self becomes embalmed in the present as the avenues for personal and intellectual exploration in the future are closed off and hope and courage disappear. Hence, that which evolutionary theory explicitly excluded must be covertly included. Darwinian theory accomplishes this too. Transcendence is introduced by way of natural selection. As Huston Smith puts it:

> To speak plainly, as long as we can believe that there is a principle operative in nature—natural selection—that works to produce the higher from the lower, we can take courage. God is reinstated; a different god to be sure, but akin to the earlier one in that "he" too will see to it that things turn out all right. He does not preclude false starts any more than his predecessor did, but in the long run the victory is assured. We are in good hands.

There are close parallels between Darwin's theory and that of Feuerbach, and that should not surprise us because both arose within the culture of mid-nineteenth-century northern Europe. Both have a very high estimate of humanity (a high anthropology) and look confidently toward a better future.

Further, both Feuerbach's philosophy and Darwinian theory exclude a transcendent God, and then proceed immediately to reintroduce transcendence covertly at the center of their respective systems. Feuerbach, as we saw, does this by hypostatizing nature, giving it both natural and supernatural qualities. Darwin follows a closely parallel path with his idea of natural selection, which has both a natural and empirical quality manifested in the fossil record, and a "supernatural" quality in that it reveals the meaning and purpose of the created order. In theological language, both Feuerbach and Darwin presuppose a good creation, a high anthropology, and a positive eschatology. For Feuerbach and Darwin these three fundamental presuppositions come from "somewhere else."

Surely it is no coincidence that these same three fundamental presuppositions are those manifested uniquely in the Adamic myth (initiated with the First Adam, completed in the Second Adam, Jesus Christ) which undergirds the Old and New Testaments. The Bible is the "somewhere else" of the overtly religious scientism of Feuerbach and Darwin.

This suggests a way in which from a biblical perspective those contributions of Darwinian theory which are valid can be reappropriated and used until such time as there emerges a better paradigm for evolutionary study. This way has been developed at great length by Michael Polanyi in his *Personal Knowledge*. Here it is only possible to make the briefest sketch of his way.

Polyani distinguishes between the *conditions* of evolution and the *action* of evolution. Evolutionary theory explores the conditions of evolutionary change through the examination of the fossil record. Simpler forms do precede the more complex. As we have said before, all of that marvelous record is to be affirmed with gratitude.

What we cannot be grateful for, however, is that "Darwinianism has diverted attention for a century from the descent of man by investigating the *conditions* of evolution and overlooking its *action*. Evolution can only be understood as a feat of emergence."[31]

Darwinianism illegitimately attempts to explain the action or fundamental rationale of evolution in terms of the covertly religious concept of natural selection. The fact that Darwinianism covertly introduces religious ideas (specifically a truncated form of the Adamic myth) into a purportedly scientific argument indicates that something is amiss. What is amiss is that Darwinianism chooses not to recognize that "At each successive stage of this epic process we see arising some novel operations not specifiable in terms of the preceding level."[32] Moreover,

> the consecutive steps of a long-range evolutionary progress—like the rise of consciousness—cannot be determined merely by their adaptive advantage, since these advantages can form part of such progress only in so far as they prove adaptive in a peculiar way, namely on the lines of continuous ascending evolutionary achievement. The action of the ordering principle underlying such a persistent creative trend is necessarily overlooked or denied by the theory of natural selection ... Recognition (of this ordering principle) would ... reduce mutation and selection to their proper status of merely releasing and sustaining the action of evolutionary principles by which all major evolutionary achievements are defined.[33]

The action of evolution, then, is to be understood not in terms of natural selection but as a "feat of emergence." But what is "emergence" with its "ordering and innovative principles"?

That question can only have a religious, and specifically a mythic, answer. After all, as we have seen, even Darwinianism gives a covertly religious answer to that question. Polyanyi would make the answer overt and explicit. He speaks of "a prime cause emergent in time" which has "directed itself at aims that are timeless." This "prime cause" is responsible for the emergence of the "myriad centres" of life which paleontology records. These centres "are all akin to us. For all these centres—those which led up to our own existence and the far more numerous others which produced different lines of which many are extinct—may be seen engaged in the same endeavor towards ultimate liberation. We may envisage then a cosmic field which called forth all these centres by offering them a short-lived, limited, hazardous opportunity for making some progress of their own towards an unthinkable consummation. And that is also, I believe, how a Christian is placed when worshipping God,"[34]

Conclusion: God, Who is All in All is Likewise One

It is the fundamental thesis of this chapter that there can be no conflict between science and the Bible when each is properly understood; and, further, that in the modern period the two support one another and are necesary to one another.

I have attempted to substantiate this thesis first in general terms, and then in the specific terms pertaining to evolutionary theory. In both cases the conclusion was the same. Science and the Bible are two distinctly different operations of human consciousness and imagination which ask different questions, proceed by different methods, and arrive at different conclusions. They both aim at truth, but their respective truths are of a different order. They cannot be in conflict.

If, however, science and the Bible are distinctly different, they are not separate. At the very least they arose together historically. Whatever the contributions of Greek philosophy and Arabic mathematics, science arose not in ancient Greece or within medieval Islam but in early modern Europe whose culture and inhabitants were permeated by the religion and theology of the Bible. It is no surprise then, as our discussions have shown, that science and the Bible share the most fundamental presuppositions concerning the creation, our humanity, and our orientation to a positive future. It is to just these three elements (creation, anthropology, and eschatology) that Owen Barfield alludes when he observes: "I believe that the blind-spot which posterity will find most startling in the last hundred years or so of Western civilization, is, that it had, on the one hand, a religion which differed from all others in its acceptance of time, and of a particular point in time, as a cardinal element in its faith; that it had, on the other hand, a picture in its mind of the history of the earth and man as an evolutionary process; and that it neither saw nor supposed any connection whatever between the two."[35]

These common presuppositions of science and the Bible are so fundamental that the two can only properly be considered partners in the divine-human enterprise of history. The respective roles of science and the Bible, however, are distinctly different.

The common presuppositions are *established* in the only way fundamental presuppositions can be established, through symbols and the mythic narratives about those symbols. In the Bible the narratives about these symbols and myths constitute the redemptive drama of the First and Second Adam and their relationship to their creator God and his kingdom. It is this narrative which is appropriated by the Christian community as that narrative is read, studied, and above all incorporated into the liturgical life of that community. It is this narrative which expresses, and is unthinkable apart from, the presuppositions of the good creation established in the covenants between Israel and its God, a high anthropology which culminates in the appearance of the Second Adam, and a positive orientation toward the future manifested in the yearning of Israel and the Church for the kingdom which is to come. These presuppositions delineate the cosmos of the Bible and the God who created that cosmos. As we have seen, science is unable to contradict that cosmos, nor does it have any interest in doing so. Moreover, the end of that cosmos would be the end of science sa we know it.

If, however, this is the way these fundamental presuppositions are *established*, it is not the only way in which they are explored. These presuppositions are explored in the Bible itself as succeeding generations of Jews and later Christians take up and rearticulate the biblical cosmos. The goodness of the creation, for example, appears one way in Genesis, and another way in Job, and yet another way in Romans.

There are, however, other inevitable ways in which Jews and Christians have come to explore the cosmos given to them in the biblical narrative. This exploration proceeds through a specialization or differentiation of our human thought. This specialization or differentiation takes many forms, for example, philosophical, historical, literary, scientific, and many others. Each of these ways of exploring our human situation is distinctive, having its own portion of experience to which it restricts its attention and its own way of proceeding. And each way has its own independence and integrity. Thus literary problems and exploration cannot receive philosophical answers, and historical explorations are conducted in historical and not literary ways. So they are distinct. Each way may possibly inform the others, but none may infringe upon the others. All proceed, however, upon the basis of certain fundamental, non-demonstrable presuppositions about what it means to be human in the world. This is true of all cultures.

The focus of this essay is our own Western culture and that specialized or differentiated form of thought within our culture called science. Here, we have argued, the fundamental presuppositions are supplied by the biblical narrative of the First and Second Adam. Science is dependent upon that narrative but at the same time has its own integrity and independence: no biblical answers to scientific questions; no scientific answers to biblical questions.

It is out of this perspective that I have argued that in the modern period science and the Bible need each other. They are partners in a common enterprise. Positively, the Bible gives to science the presuppositions it must have; and science utilizes and explores those presuppositions in important ways which are impossible to the Bible.

There are no conclusions to arguments which are not already implicit in the presuppositions of the arguments. Science and the Bible share the most fundamental presuppositions. We would suspect, therefore, that finally the results of the scientific and the biblical explorations would arrive at the same place. It is just this possibility that philosophers of science suggest from time to time:

> If, instead of rummaging through science for direct, literal clues to the nature of reality, we could outgrow this fundamentalism and read science allegorically, we would find

sermons in cloud-chambers. That the deeper science advances into nature the more integrated it finds it, lends resonance to (though it does not prove) the faith-claim that the same holds for being as a whole: God, who is all in all, is likewise One. Or again, that science has found reality in its physical aspect to be incomparably more majestic and awesome than we had supposed suggests—it does not prove—that if we could see the full picture we would find its qualitative depths to be as much beyond what we normally suppose as science has shown its quantitative ones to be.

And remember, we are speaking of lightyears.[36]

6

All Things Necessary to Salvation

by Frederick Houk Borsch

The history of the Bible's place in the Anglican tradition
during the nineteenth and twentieth centuries may be read as a
story of retreat and loss. While one can now see some of the
unresolved tensions and signs of the weakening of foundations
in previous centuries, by comparison the Bible seemed then to
have an assured place as the primary and unique authority for
Anglican Christians. Gradually, and then with increasing
momentum, the challenges of the scientific and historic consciousness and the awareness of the claims of other religions
have induced qualifications and modifications into official and
semi-official Anglican statements on the authority and inspiration of Scripture.[1] While some Anglicans have attempted to
reassert a doctrine of scriptural supremacy and forms of literal
inspiration, most have accepted a more circumscribed role,
even if the implications have not always been thought through.

This present state of affairs may be viewed as a development
from within a history of Anglican latitudinarianism. We have
recognized historical and political reasons, reaching back at
least into the sixteenth century, for degrees of ambivalence and
measures of wide tolerance in understanding the character of
the Bible's authority and inspiration. As long as Anglicans
could agree that the Bible had a central and at least in some way
crucial role for faith and practice (especially in worship), perhaps that was the most that could be expected. "There is no
exact dogma about inspiration which we are required as

Churchmen to receive," Charles Gore rather proudly maintained. "Certainly no one has a right to impose on his followers any particular belief about inspiration, its nature and limits."[2] Necessity was in some sense turned into a virtue as the Bible became more widely available in English and more people learned to read. The capacity of most individuals to hear and read the Bible and to make spiritually guided decisions for themselves with only a minimum of guidance from Church leaders was seen, at least in some quarters, as a basis for the Anglican Communion's strength—a sign of the maturity it expected from its members. "The dispersal of authority in Anglicanism is rooted in the conviction that Christians to whom the scriptures are read in their own language [especially within the context of worship] are able to judge of the essentials of faith."[3]

There are, however, obvious dangers involved in making a particular set of writings so central to the life of a community of believers and then leaving its interpretation quite so open. The centrality may give to many the understanding that the Bible can and should be used with an authoritative, almost legalistic decisiveness that others are not willing to accept. Or some parts of the Bible are used in this manner and others are not without much forethought and a resultant confusion of argument and lack of integrity. The Scriptures may become a cause of divisiveness rather than a source of unity within the community and communties of the Church.

An opposite danger is that the Bible will be highly honored but not taken seriously, quoted but not applied to faith and practice with any rigor or consistency. As the tides of relativism, the scientific method, and historical criticism make more problematic the ways in which the Bible is to be heard, the Bible then comes to be revered more than read. The translations grow more varied, the bindings fancier, but the book remains on the shelf. Passages of Scripture are more venerated in Church services than listened to or expounded. How then can the Bible have an authoritative place in the life of the Church and of individuals other than in terms of lip service?

There is no doubt that the Churches of the Anglican Communion live today with most of these dangers and often experience them, sometimes acutely. There are even times when the dangers combine and one feels dogmatically batted over the head with unread Bibles. Scripture can be used to attack or support almost any idea by those who know only snippets of its content and give little heed to any principles of interpretation.

It is nonetheless the argument of this chapter that there is much in the contemporary Anglican approach to the Bible that may be understood affirmatively as being rightly oriented by Scripture itself, by the experience of its use, and by thoughtful and prayerful reflection on its role for Christian faith and life. The dangers that are involved in accepting the central and unique role of the Bible for faith, while yet making its authority relative to other aspects of Christian experience, are risks that must be run. If, however, the Bible is to play its proper role, measures must be sought to counteract or at least minimize the risks. Let us proceed by reminding ourselves of certain historical aspects and characteristics of the Bible, then consider how Scripture can best be regarded as an inspired source of revelation for the Church, how it can be viewed as authoritative, and, finally, reflect on the understandings and measures the Church might use today to insure the Bible's proper role.

In Communities of Faith

The Bible emerged from the experience of communities who believed that God had been and was mysteriously but decisively present and active among them. It is of critical importance to remember that the communities of faith preceded the composition of the Bible and then were the context for its development and writing. During the stages when the Bible was composed (a period over one thousand years) the communities were in interaction with the parts of the Bible that already had been written, further commenting on them and then adding to them.

As the Christian Churches emerged after the life, death and resurrection of Jesus, the only Scriptures they knew were those of Judaism. The writings of the New Testament were in many ways a commentary on the earlier Scriptures in the light of the Christ event, but they also changed the interpretation of the story of Israel for Christians. Then, of course, there was still a period of several hundred years before the Church came to an approximate agreement on which books were to be regarded as authoritative for the Christian faith. Throughout this period, most especially in its earlier stages, there remained a strong sense that what makes a person a Christian was personal contact with the risen Christ through the continuing community of disciples and knowledge through them of the basic stories and teachings of the faith.[4] Among the first generations of Christians it was in spoken not written words that the living Christ was best met and one gained a sense of God's presence in the world. The God who could not be seen nor captured in the fixed form of written statements could yet mysteriously be overheard in the dynamic of the community's ongoing preaching and telling of its stories.[5] Only gradually did the Scriptures come to occupy a place as a source for inspiration and witness to the faith which could be said to be on a par with the community's continuing oral teaching and which could be used not only as a guide but also a corrective to that teaching. Since that era, within most Christian traditions, there has been at least a measure of awareness that the Bible is the community's book and must be in some form of dialectic with the continuing community of faith for its proper understanding and interpretation.[6] Perhaps, above all, it is to be remembered that Christianity's best means of continuity and propagation (for theological as well as practical reasons) is from persons to persons. It is in that context that the Bible finds its most traditional role.

Diversity in the Bible

We have noted that the Bible was composed over a period of hundreds of years. It comes from many different cultures and several languages. Even in the relatively brief New Testament period we now recognize that diverse communities and perspectives strongly influenced what was written and how it was presented. Certainly the group to which the Letter to the Hebrews was written sounds quite distinctive from the community that received the Letter of James. The Christian community in Corinth must have varied widely from the one which first heard the Gospel according to Matthew. The four Gospels are the transformation into written texts of a history of several decades of teaching, controversy and persecution, of retelling and shaping, resulting in quite particular emphases. The different New Testament authors also had their distinctive attitudes toward the Jewish Scriptures and applied different methods of interpretation to them.

Awareness of this diversity has at times caused anguish to believers who expect or hope to find in the Bible a more univocal witness to the shape and character of the faith. Yet this same awareness has been an enlightenment and help to others trying to understand constructively the diversity of emphases throughout Christianity today and even just within the Anglican Communion. If Christianity had something of this character from its beginning stages, maybe such pluralism can be viewed as of theological and historical benefit—a given which is not a later development but somehow of the essence of the Christian experience.[7] Regardless of our reaction to diversity and pluralism in the Bible, however, it must be dealt with as one of the historical realities for biblical interpretation.

Sometimes this diversity can be welcomed rather easily: different perspectives on Jesus deepen one's understanding of all he can mean for humanity. Yet at other times Scripture seems to speak in such different voices as to be at least ambiguous if not paradoxical or even contradictory. God and his human creatures have some form of kinship and relationship; he may be spoken of anthropomorphically. Yet God and his ways are utterly different, virtually unknowable apart from revelation from beyond any source of natural human knowing. God is a stern, implacable judge; but his mercy is abundant and beyond human measure. Human beings, their actions and choices are almost wholly in divine control. Still individuals and a people are responsible for what they do. The kingdom of God is already begun, yet is in the future. It can be spoken of as a place and as an inner experience. Jesus is fully human and also of God.

One can try to turn seeming contradictions into paradoxes and then seek to resolve them, but one may also begin to recognize that the very dialectic character of so much of the Bible can have its purpose.[8] It seems deliberately to force one away from easy answers or set solutions to religious concerns and questions. Perhaps especially in the teaching of Jesus there sometimes appears to be a studied ambiguity of response, parable telling and even riddling which initially interrupt those who ask for a direct answer to their questions: What is the kingdom of God like? What must I do to inherit eternal life? How often shall my brother sin against me and I forgive him? Why do you eat with tax gatherers and sinners?

Jesus' responses are words and actions which tell of the blind seeing and deaf hearing, while those who seemed to have good sight and well-trained hearing are blind and deaf to him. Those formerly regarded as unacceptable now sit down and enjoy the great dinner party. Calamity is to be seen as new opportunity. There is sudden, mysterious abundance and amazing grace. His parables often begin amid the circumstances of everyday life: in farms and fields, with two brothers, a meal, the time of sowing and reaping. But then, as the tales proceed, they often take surprising twists and turns. As the story becomes less plausible on its surface, cracks appear in what one has regarded as apparent reality, and the hearer is asked to look for some deeper truth. One is invited to play the parts of various characters in the story and share in their experience. The metaphorical movement at the heart of the parable lures one further in to see if there one may perceive new possibilities regarding God's mysterious presence and activity in the world—what Jesus spoke of as the kingdom of God. It is as if to say that if one only looks on the surface of things one may not have eyes to see or ears to hear how God is present to his creation. The process has been described as one of "reorientation by disorientation."[9] If one is to become aware of the kingdom, a new way of hearing, seeing and hoping (what the Gospels call *metanoia*, repentance—a change of heart and mind)—is necessary.

Often the parables work by reversal, pointing to the awareness that the kingdom's activity is surprising and unexpected.[10] Its suddenness also demands a response. New kinds of relationships between masters and servants, brothers, parents and children allude to the new order of the kingdom. A repeated theme of the parables involves having, losing and finding, or hiding and finding. One must search, though discovery may then come as a gift. This process is not only a theme but also the structure of many of these stories: the hearer must search for their meaning. The stories more than suggest that the most essential and fundamental truths of life cannot be easily expressed or readily apprehended. One must explore.

Participation through Narrative

One must also invest oneself—participate in order to understand. Genuine knowledge and understanding come only through participation. Narrative and the allied use of symbol and metaphor continually invite that sharing. One can well believe that this is among the reasons that so much of the Bible is in story form, and that all of it is placed in the frame of the biblical drama of a people being lost and found, of life lost and raised up again. This is, of course, as true of the Old Testament as the New, and various recent commentators have helped readers to see how the little gaps in the stories, the ambiguities involved in dialogue and the presentation of character, the shifting narrative perspective and other aspects of story-telling draw hearers into the tales and allude to truths and mysteries about life which can be expressed in no other form.[11]

These interpreters are helping readers to hear inflections of the Bible which were more available to earlier generations. During the past two centuries various cultural and intellectual movements have strongly inclined many Christians to believe that there are only two important questions one can ask of a biblical passage: did it happen (or how did it happen?) and what does it mean? Given the potential benefits and the challenges of the new historical methods, the first question became the predominant focus for both the more liberal and conservative biblical critics. Then as other disciplines and areas of human inquiry became more oriented to producing answers to questions and offering statements of meaning in propositional language, it also seemed of importance to be able to state biblical truths in a similar fashion. Narrative came to be seen as secondary.[12] The task of the expositor was to draw the meaning out of the narrative after which the story could be discarded or used only for illustrative purposes. This was something like saying that one could exhaust the value of *King Lear* by investigating its roots in historical antecedents and then drawing out the message that true love will not advertise itself for its own advantage and may be seen too late. The story would be retained only to illustrate the major points.

Fortunately, there have always beeen forces at work which have helped Anglican Christians to retain some awareness of the primacy of narrative for a biblically-based theology—a recognition that the stories of the Bible are not the illustrations for God's word; they are that word. Here the general conservatism of many English scholars and Church people has not been without its benefits. They were less quick to believe that the newer approaches to biblical study were all-sufficient—that there were not other ways of knowing. Here, too, the strong narrative and poetic gifts of the people aided in the awareness that story and metaphor offered ways of understanding that could not be fully comprehended by the languages of logic, science or efforts at historical accuracy. Apocalyptic description and stories of creation, for example, sounded richer chords of significance when people had heard their deeper poetic and symbolic characters. Appreciation for the capacity of metaphor to say what otherwise oculd not be said or even thought helped keep religious language from becoming either idolatrous or irrelevant.[13] God is father, but he is not to be literally identified with human ideas of father. God's activity and presence are a kingdom and a banquet but in ways that are at once like and not like what the metaphors connote. The metaphors live only when one participates in their tensive creativity. The heritage or presence among Anglicans of Shakespeare, Donne, Herbert, Milton, Carew, Blake, Keble, Trollope, Austen, Eliot, Auden, Lewis and Paton keeps bright these awarenesses.

Probably the greatest value in this regard has been the central role of the Bible in liturgy. The regular reading and hearing of Scripture in the dramatic setting of corporate worship, along with the use of biblical motifs and images in the words of the liturgy throughout the cycle of the Church year, can bring about new hearing for the narrative power of the Bible. This *knowing* of the Bible by the individual worshiper and the congregation helps them to interpret present opportunities for service, their sufferings, the absence of God yet a sense of his mysterious nearness, all in the light of the biblical drama. The themes, metaphors, and plots of the stories of Scripture (not just their surface *meanings* but this deeper level of hearing) are then catalysts for the telling of new stories of faith and grace in their own lives. Scripture thus forms the character of the community and of the individuals within it, framing their understanding of good and evil and informing the way they live and the choices they make.[14]

History and Story

This approach to Scripture as narrative and as forms of parable and poetry in narrative context does not answer all our questions. Most late twentieth-century people have concerns about the Bible's relationship to history and its claims upon their lives which require historical study, forms of exegesis, and analysis in the light of experience and the use of reason. In some instances, such as the story of Job or the parable of the prodigal son, any relationship of the story to historical event may be unimportant. In other cases, such as the stories of the virgin birth of Jesus, readers may recognize, along with William Temple, that historical questions, while not irrelevant could cause us to miss the major theological purpose of the narratives.[15] When, however, it comes to the manner in which

Jesus met his death and the nature of the resurreciton, most people feel the press of historical concerns more acutely.[16]

In all of these instances modern disciples can find great value in information assembled by archaeologists, sociologists, historians of literature and other students of the Bible and its settings. The information may, first of all, help one to recognize how great the distances sometimes are between contemporary ways of viewing the world and those of the past. The informed reader of the Bible then recognizes how easily some of the original concerns and attitudes of the biblical writers can be misconstrued. In many ways they lived in one world while present-day disciples live in quite another. The vision of both is limited within their particualr horizons.

This awareness can help in gaining perspective on our ways of *seeing* the world—reminding that our viewpoint is itself relative and highly conditioned by many temporary customs and conventions of education and culture. The Bible has the advantage of belonging to no comtemporary culture and so challenging every people not to be bound just by the present *grasp* of life. This challenge can then lead to constructive efforts to see how the horizons of the present and past might touch, bringing about some sharing. Through better understanding of the *world* of the early disciples—their circumstances and ways of seeing and interpreting—their lives may take on greater depth and color. Given the belief that there are some enduring aspects of human nature that are shared over the generations and eras, one may come to see and hear and feel somthing of their world.[17]

We remind ourselves, however, that historical data and analyses cannot by themselves create this vision. Imaginative effort is also needed, and the vehicle for the imagination—the time-machine between the two eras—is participation in narrative. Both historical understanding and direct engagement with the text are necessary for a full and balanced reading of the Bible.[18]

Even this balanced approach will not, however, definitively answer all the hard questions which the inquiring mind brings to the Scriptures regarding the relationship of biblical story to historical event. In addition to large gaps in understanding created by the distance of the centuries, one recognizes that the biblical writers were not thinking in terms of questions asked by the historically trained mind of today. Many of their stories might better be called "history-like" than history in our terms.[19] Most of the biblical narratives could better be described as stories that use historical elements rather than history in story-form. Events which happened in history served as the catalysts for the stories which were then passed on and further shaped by the faith experiences of the community. Every human effort to report and understand is, of course, involved in such an interpretive process to a greater or lesser extent. Even what is being seen and heard in the present moment is largely determined by what one is looking for and how one is trained to perceive it by means of memory and intellect. In this sense we realize that all knowing is the result of interpretation, but this interpretive effort seems to have been especially important in the forming of biblical insights and stories. When one asks how the Bible may be thought to be inspired, it may be most helpful to focus on this interpretative process.[20]

Inspiration

A variety of views have been put forward as ways of understanding the inspiration of the Bible.[21] Sometimes the emphasis falls on the words themselves as being inspired and carrying revelation in themselves. Perhaps at the other end of the spectrum the stress is on God's presence in specific events which the people of God then reported as best they could. A more common Anglican view is an intermediary stress on the Scriptures being the word of God "because God inspired their human authors."[22] This leaves more open such problems as how one would know that God had acted in a particular historical circumstance and whether that event must be accurately reported to be a source of further inspiration. It also does not require a belief in the verbal inerrancy of Scripture.

Pressing more closely, one may suggest that it is the very process of interpretation—that distinctively human capacity to tell a story about what happens—which is most particularly the realm of God's revelatory activity. Indeed, from the human perspective there are many ways in which the interpretation *is* what happens as the mind seeks to give connectedness and significance to the present experience by aligning it with the past through memory and with the future by imagination. It may be in our story-shaping ability and related ways of interpreting that the inspiration of the Spirit of God (in whose *image* the human spirit is made) should be most recognized. Perhaps more particularly one might conceive of the Spirit as that "go-between" activity of God which makes possible the human interaction with the events of the material world and brings about the opportunity to give them significance and meaning.[23]

Clearly the emphasis here would fall on a more subjective rather than objective view of inspiration, but since it tends to locate the activity of God between what happens in the material world and the human interpretation, it is at least related to both. A more important advantage may lie in the clues it can give present-day disciples, suggesting how they can align their expectations for inspiration from the Bible with God's activity among those who composed the Bible. It is through the interpretive process itself that inspiration is realized. There in the interplay between story and event disciples search, probing between narrative (and other interpretive efforts) and *what happens* for motive, purpose and significance. In this struggle to use words and stories in order to understand Christians believe they hear God.

Viewed in this light, not only is the work of interpretation seen to be unavoidable, but it is also prized as the chief arena for the activity of the Holy Spirit. Those who would today regard the Bible as inspired can confirm that sense of inspiration in their own experience. Indeed, the only way a claim for the inspiration of the Bible could legitimately be made is if there is some such correspondence in present experience of the interpretation of the Bible and of life.[24]

Again, one realizes how and why participation is required and narrative structure is so important. As one becomes part of the interpretive process, what has been mere observation can be deepened to the point that insight is gained for one's own life. If that insight then seems a gift and to share in truth that is essential to all life, it will be called revelation. But there is no such revelation through mere reading or hearing. It does not sit on a printed page. One must both enter and be drawn in. It is this kind of experience which might most accurately be called a *fundamental* hearing of the Bible. This is what the Bible is meant to do for Christians—to help them discover, to see and hear and to find perspective on matters of fundamental importance to life.

Not all our questions about relationship with historical event, interpretation and inspiration are thus answered or can be answered. We may still wish for a closer correlation between the history-like story of the Bible and what we may regard as actual history. We must remember, however, that what the biblical authors seek to relate is what can be called "effective history"[25]—that is what they regard as the full significance of events in the interrelationship with how they believed themselves guided by God to interpret them and with how their understanding of God's purposes has led them to perceive the world about them. Any other kind of reporting would but glide on the surface of events and overlook their potential to become part of the process of revelation.

With Bishop Gore we remind ourselves that no one doctrine or theory of inspiration is required of any Anglican.[26] Probably no single viewpoint can be adequate for such a large topic dealing with how humans come to know (and think about knowing) and the possibility of divine presence in the world and interaction with human experience. It is probably also true that our whole approach to the question of inspiration must alter as our ways of viewing our world change—as, in this sense, we live in different worlds. Our discussion to this point, however, does allow for a comprehensive attitude toward inspiration that is focused on the relationship between the interpretive process and experience and on God active in that living encounter. It allows scope for a sense of divine presence in relation to events and among those who composed the Bible and through their recorded words. The discussion has also, we believe, rightly emphasized the manner in which participation in the interpretive process is necessary for revelation to be said to happen. On the one hand, Scripture invites this participation and can lure its hearers in through its narratives. But it is also essential that the hearers commit themselves at least to the expectation that revelation can then take place. A readiness and willingness to hear God are requisite. On these terms the Bible speaks from faith to faith.

Hearing in Community Today

As part of this commitment the individual will participate in a community of faith. It was in community that the traditions were first formed. From the beginning the understanding and interpretation of the traditions depended in large measure upon their being heard and reflected upon in community. It was here especially that the narratives were known as the model or master stories of faith, through which, when retold and reheard, it was expected that revelation would happen.

The chief example of these master stories for the worship of the community is the last supper. Through its liturgical reenactment Christians experience again the presence of their Lord, remember his passion, death and resurrection, and anticipate the fellowship of the new age. Although in different ways, other stories too (and the teachings, oracles, hymns and laws which come with them) are to be reexperienced as word or speech *events* in community. The community gives them their living setting and significance. It is through human speech and relationship that the word of God is best heard.

These stories, prophesies, sayings and songs reciprocally make and shape the community and help give it its character and continuing identity.[27] The remembrance of exodus and exile, of Moses and David, Jeremiah and Jonah, the narrative of a child's humble birth, of shared meals, the bread and wine, the cross, and the vibrant new hope which followed—on the roads to Emmaeus and Damascus: without the knowledge and sharing of these stories there would be no community. Even when individuals read the Bible privately, they are doing so as participants in this community of stories. Their reading is informed by their community experience, and the influence of their reading in the contexts of their particular lives is then carried back into their common life with other Christians.

Again it must be emphasized that the stories most come alive, not when they are merely seen on a page, but when living voices give them new life. As the words and score of a song can only be narrowly appreciated through the reading of the eye and must be heard if one is to *know* the song, so must the biblical narratives, songs and poems be *played* if people are to participate in them. Through that experience of telling and hearing they are meant to become the sacraments of the voice of the Spirit of Jesus carried on in the community. It is through the community helped by the Bible that the living Jesus is heard—not the other way round. Through human meeting and sharing the stories of biblical faith can then also kindle new parables of faith and hope.

Scripture, Reason and Tradition

Obviously, tensions in the interpretation of the Bible are going to continue to be experienced. There will be differences between individuals and the community, between communities, between the traditional understandings and those of the present day. These are not new. We have seen that such tensions are already present in the Bible. They can be creative, making individuals and communities dissatisfied with all too comfortable understandings and causing them to probe more deeply. What is vital is dialogue—a readiness to listen and to expect to hear afresh.

Human reason will be part of the interpretive dialogue—just as it was important to the formation of the Bible. Contemporary Christian experience—the challenges and opportunities of the ongoing Christian community—will affect interpretation, as they left their imprint on the composition of the biblical mate-

rials. The past experience of the Church in its use of the Bible
and in the forming of liturgies, creeds and doctrinal positions
will all influence the course of contemporary biblical understanding. This is what has been called the *consensus fidelium*, and
it is a work of the whole people of God guided by the Spirit,
men and women of prayer, scholars, preachers, saints, those
engaged in works of charity and pastoral care, and everyone
faithfully involved with the world in labor, study and daily
living and loving.[28] In our generation we are learning again
that those who are poor among us and who experience disad-
vantage and oppression are especially important in the work of
hearing and interpreting the Bible. The bishops (with their
assistants) are the visible continuity of this teaching and interpreting office. The Bible is also in dialogue with them—
provoking and exhorting, acting as a critic for the present-day
Church. In this process the Church is engaged not just in the
recitation of truths but in a voyage of discovery. This is how
Leonard Hodgson described the adventure of biblical faith:

> The New Testament shows [the early Christians] trying to
> make head or tail of what had happened on the basis of
> their Jewish understanding of God and the universe. So
> far from having given us a full and final explanation of the
> meaning of our faith they were taking the first steps
> towards its discovery, initiating a process which under the
> guidance of the Holy Spirit has been continuing since and
> is still going on... we have to take into account how the
> understanding of it by the New Testament Christians has
> been deepened and enriched in the experience of their
> successors and is still being deepened and enriched by our
> experience of life in the world today.[29]

Our thirst for some more certain form of authority is likely
not answered in this dialogue. What, we still wish to know, is to
happen when we are in the midst of controversy about an article
of belief, Church practice or a matter of ethics? Which then is
primary and takes precedence in coming to decision: the Bible,
tradition or reason together with experience? And who is to
decide?

In a contemporary evaluation of the heritage of the Anglican and Episcopal Churches one of my colleagues in the writing of this series of essays set forth these priorities:

> Scripture and the Tradition aligned to it possess priority over reason and experience.... We must, however, acknowledge another priority, the priority of perception. We are first of all reasoning, experiencing people.... Human development, too, holds a priority.... Tradition, understood in terms of the Church's authority, comes first, conveying the Scripture to us, convincing us of its nature until by experience we affirm its truth....[30]

The author was quite aware of what he was doing. In the dialogue of our experience and reason with tradition and Scripture it would be a mistake to grant to one an absolute primacy. They function best and best foster maturity of Christian discipleship when they are dancing with one another in "creative interplay."

There are, however, reasons why the Bible may be said to have certain forms of primacy. Reason and tradition change; experience varies; but Scripture is formed into a *canon*, a kind of measuring rod, a rule or standard of faith. It is what Christians continually return to in order to measure discipleship. The Bible now contains the master stories shared in common by all Christians of different cultures and times which provide identity and present examples of faithful living. They offer the community its basic message of hope and challenge, of judgment and grace. They provide the common language of faith for all Christians.

The Bible also has a primacy because of its essentially narrative character. Through its *life-likeness* narrative continually reminds Christians that it is in the experience of life itself that God is most likely to be known. Generalizations and analytic efforts to state more abstract truths have their important place, but they are secondary reflections on the particularities of life where—biblical narrative suggests—God is to be experienced. This life-likeness is, moreover, meant to help *ground* disciples in everyday particularities as part of their effort to respond to God and serve others. The Bible's emphases upon loving neighbors, doing justice, speaking the truth in love, hungering and thirsting for righteousness and making peace are meant not to be lived in theory, but amid the frustrations and hopes of passing minutes and pocket change in daily history.

With its ambiguities and ironies, uncertainties and paradoxes, narrative is also continually reminding that there is much about God and his presence in the world which humans do not understand. This is not the only thing but it may be the most important thing that the Bible can lead those who would otherwise too readily *domesticate* God for their own purposes to understand about God.

Yet, as soon as these forms of primacy have been granted, it must also again be recognized that the Bible has always to be interpreted through reason and Christian experience before it can be known as revelation. It is not a question of whether this should be done. We all do. The questions have to do with how consciously and faithfully it will be done.

So the intricate dance goes on—full of curtsies and bows—within the community of faith which alone can make decisions about its belief and practice. Led in teaching by its bishops as the visible representatives of the tradition's continuity and unity of the Church, using experience and reason, and with the Bible as its canon of model stories, the community of disciples seeks to know and to do God's will. Though Christians might think they would prefer it otherwise (that they would be given some more absolute form of authority), this is evidently the way God wants authority to be experienced by his followers. Guided by the Bible, led by the Spirit, the authority develops from within.

Facing in God's Direction

Tensions regarding the authority and use of the Bible can, however, still become destructive if the Bible is used in the wrong ways. When during the reformation period, the Bible was heard and proclaimed as a counterbalance to certan aspects of what was regarded as wrongful tradition, a proclivity was unfortunately strengthened—a tendency to use the Bible as a kind of proof-texting answer book with respect to issues of Church life and practice. Often unaware or hiding from the fact that they too had to use reason and their own experience and understanding of their traditions to interpret the Bible, many of the inheritors of the reformation employed the Scriptures to try to settle arguments both great and small. The understandable result was a process which splintered reformed Christianity into literally hundreds of Church denominations, each claiming to be more rightly based on the Bible.

The Bible is not, however, an answer book. It can speak powerfully to any number of contemporary issues and concerns, but its voice is distorted when asked to give specific answers to matters that its human authors would not even have understood. Moreover, it was not primarily intended as an answer book in its own times. If it had been, one can only imagine that it would have been written very differently. Certainly there are passages (especially in the earlier parts of the Old Testament) which speak specifically to particular issues, but more often than not the teaching is of a more general character. In the Gospels one may even hear a deliberate effort on Jesus' part to deflect the concerns of those who wanted him to pronounce a new law or set of ethics. By the use of questions and story he asks those who would learn from him to think of authority and responsibility in a new and different way.

A master story in this regard is the parable of the good Samaritan, set in the dialogue between Jesus and a lawyer who is a type of the religious individual seeking to use the law as the absolute arbiter for his life (Luke 10:25-37).[31] Jesus hears the lawyer's initial testing question ("What shall I do to inherit eternal life?") as an invitation to dispute about the law and which of its commands takes precedence. The lawyer knows that the commands of love are paramount but then feels the need to find some manner of legalistic application. Jesus would seem to have listened to him and his need very carefully. He recognizes that the lawyer is really asking the opposite of what he may think he is asking. His primary concern is not to know who are all the neighbors he can love. Instead he wants to know whom he must love and whom he can disregard as neighbor and set outside his ethical concern. He really wants to know "Who is *not* my neighbor?" Confronted with all those who might make demands upon his charity and goodness, the lawyer wants religious law to tell him who he can put outside of his concern while still regarding himself as an ethical person.

Jesus responds with the story of an injured man who was helped by someone who didn't need to ask the lawyer's question. The parable dramatically shifts the whole focus of the discussion from a negatively oriented concern with being ethical to the possibility of genuine goodness. Hearers become aware that their real problem is not so much that they don't know what to do or how they are supposed to behave. Their difficulty is that they lack the power to try to love their neighbors as themselves.

Jesus evidently did not intend to offer a new set of laws or ethical system. His stories and teachings offer not so much answers as the direction in which one is to face to discover the true character of eternal life—the life of the kingdom of God. We have seen that he called for a *metanoia*—a repentance which led to a new way of seeing life and of living, a righteousness that exceeded that of scribes and pharisees (Matthew 5:20), not in more written law but in power for caring, forgiveness, acceptance and healing.

"The Bible," wrote Phillips Brooks, "is like a telescope. If a man looks *through* his telescope, then he sees worlds beyond; but if he looks *at* his telescope, then he does not see anything but that. The Bible is a thing to be looked through, to see that which is beyond, but most people only look at it; and so they see only the dead letter."[31] Indeed, to imagine and worship a God that could somehow be defined by human words would be a form of idolatry leading not to human growth and maturity but to narrowness and death. The Bible is not meant to be a written code that kills but a vehicle of the Spirit that gives life. (See II Corinthians 3:6.) The Bible points beyond itself just as does the story of the good Samaritan to the injured man and to the one who has the power to heal. The injured man is the Christ in all who are hungry, thirsty, strangers, naked, sick and in prison whom disciples are to help (Matthew 25:35-36). Jesus also stands in and behind the parable as the one who reaches out in compassion. He did not just tell such stories, but in the disciples' memory he was a good Samaritan to Bartimaeus and Zacchaeus, the paralytic and the man with many demons, the Syrophoenecian woman and Mary Magdalene, and so many others.

The lawyer is asked if he would like to *do* as the good Samaritan. (The word is repeated four times in the dialogue. This is not meant as a theoretical discussion. The parable is about the power to *do* love.) The law can then be his guide, but, rightly interpreted, it is also his source of freedom and power for the life of the new age. Contemporary disciples may well hear themselves being challenged as to how they will use the Bible.

The Risk of Biblical Freedom

Such freedom is full of risks. The Bible is to be central and essential to the life of Christian witness and discipleship, but it is not absolute in its authority. The freedom to hear the Spirit guiding the whole Bible so that one does not "so expound one place of Scripture that it be repugnant to another"[33] can present challenges just as daunting as the Judean lawyer must have felt when asked whether he was able to emulate a Samaritan. Contemporary disciples are called to be more honest and forthright with respect to the fact that all Christian traditions, in practice if not in theory, "recognize that some parts of the Bible are more authoritative than other parts."[34] Probably it is here also important to stress the obverse corollary: some parts are of less significance for contemporary Christian life than others. Faithfully accepted, this recognition can lead to much new freedom for the Church to worship the living God and to try to be God's people in this generation rather than fighting battles or continuing arguments which belong to the past.

This does not mean, however, that those parts of the Bible regarded as less significant for life today are no longer to be heard and reflected upon. In fact, what this recognition gives to the Church is a freedom to ponder such portions of the Bible in a historical and faith perspective which permits them no longer to be covertly ignored but to have a genuine place in the community's regular hearing of the Bible. In this perspective it may also happen that such passages and books will one day take on a different and new significance for the community. One sees this happening even in this age as, for instance, apocalyptic imagery (with its inherent optimism regarding God's power to renew his purposes in creation)[35] and the profound humanism of wisdom literature (with its appreciation of human strengths more than weaknesses in the relationship with God) have gained a new hearing and power for revelation.[36]

Many contemporary Christians have been made aware of the importance of this biblically inspired freedom in interpretation and use of the Scriptures because of the frequently patriarchal cast of large sections of the Bible. Reason and developing Christian experience help disciples to see that this cast of language does not dictate what God requires or wants of his people today.[37] The spirit which guides this freedom should not be inhibited by the Bible but can be heard speaking through the Bible, just as the Spirit which led earlier disciples to seek to overcome slavery came from a Bible which otherwise only passively addresses the issue.

One thus takes seriously the teaching that "Holy Scripture containeth all things necessary to salvation." The stories and allied material of the Bible provide the sense of direction—the signposts—which enables disciples to experience God's presence in the world and to learn of his purposes. They offer the source of power to begin to do his will. At the same time they free Christians from being bound to any absolute authority other than the Spirit of God made best known in Christ to whom the Bible points.[38] Nothing else can be required as necessary for belief and faithful living.

The Bible is then both judge and critic as well as guide and source of strength and comfort. When rightly heard it is God's word—not just of judgment or just of grace, but of challenge and hope at once. Perhaps above all, it judges the community when it tries to use the Bible to avoid the responsibilities of Christian freedom even as it also offers the grace and power so to live.

Central and Fundamental

One can look back on the history of Anglicanism and see—as with all Churches—a checkered response to God in its use of the Bible. Often Scripture has been used divisively and as the basis for a new legalism. At other times it has been reverenced but given little heed. Perhaps more often it has been used inconsistently mainly to seek to legitimate the status quo polity, economic position, and mores of the dominant religious party.

Yet one may also see times and places where Christian communities, finding themselves addressed as the body of Christ, have been drawn into the redemptive drama charted on the pages of Scripture and have there discovered vision, hope, identity and encounter with God. The fabled tolerance of Anglicanism (when it has not been mere indifference) has been part of its *genius*, enabling Anglican Christians to use the Bible both seriously and with the responsible freedom it inspires. In a reciprocal manner the diversity and dialectical character of the Bible has had its effects upon Anglican theology and its willingness to tolerate wide differences in matters not considered essential to faith and even in the interpretation of those that are. There has been a recognition that as central and essential as the Bible is, it is not an absolute authority but points the Church instead to the discernment of the Spirit of God working within the community.

That central role of the Bible has been safeguarded—not so much in doctrine or law—but by its place in the liturgy of the Church and the devotional life of its people. Since it is through the life of the community that the Bible is to be heard and interpreted, then obviously it is important that it be regularly read, pondered and commented upon. In this way also the basic narrative character of the Bible has continually reminded the people that it is in the human interpretation of daily life that God offers to be found.

As it has been in the past, this use of the Bible as a fundamental guide and source of truth is again threatened. In a time of high relativism, of economic distress and global fears, a part of all of us wants an absolute authority. The security of an answer book understandably seems attractive. Even among those aware of the dangers and false blandishments of such an approach, a covert, selective neo-literalism may substitute for gospel candor and freedom.

Perhaps a more obvious threat today is posed by lack of familiarity with the Bible. Our cultures offer so many other attractions—so many other stories and information presented so entertainingly. Fewer people read their Bibles as we quickly pass from the Gutenberg age to an audio-visual era.

There is no easy answer to this problem but it is well worth remembering that the biblical stories were orally and (through personal contact) visually communicated before they became established in a book to be read. The Bible's power, we remember, is most known when its stories come alive through retelling. There may now, therefore, be opportunities for Scripture to be heard and *seen* in better ways than in the recent past.

There can be little doubt, however, that much of the *genius* of Anglicanism depends on a community which knows and reflects on the Bible—so that it becomes, in Stephen Bayne's apt phrase, "the architecture of our thoughts." It is at least as important as it ever was that the community ask for leaders carefully trained in the fundamental knowledge of Scripture, and its history and principles of interpretation—leaders who will know the temptations to a false biblicism and know how to resist them. The community must then ask of its leaders and of itself that the Bible be read, heard by its children, pondered, interpreted and enacted so that it may be (as Gregory the Great who helped bring the Gospel to England expressed it) a river of faith "both shallow and deep, in which the lamb can find footing and the elephant can float."[39] Guided and supported by that stream, the community finds the strength to venture on.

Through this book, both simple and profound, the people gain a vision of the age that now comes—a promised realm of new opportunities for justice and the making of peace.

Notes

Introduction

[1]From what is known as "The Chicago Quadrilateral" of 1886. This and a number of related documents are conveniently set out in *A Communion of Communions: One Eucharistic Fellowship*, edited by J. R. Wright (New York: Seabury Press, 1979). See p. 232.

[2]From the "Statement of Faith and Order" of the 1949 General Convention of the Episcopal Church.

[3]See Article VI of "The Articles of Religion" ("The Thirty-Nine Articles") and "The Lambeth Quadrilateral" of 1888.

[4]"The Lambeth Quadrilateral."

[5]See the *Treatise on the Laws of Ecclesiastical Polity*, Books I–III. There are any number of restatements of the theme. Cf. the section "Scripture and Reason" (pp. 97–117) in *Anglicanism: The Thought and Practice of the Church of England, Illustrated from the Religious Literature of the Seventeenth Century*, ed. P. E. Moore and F. L. Cross (London: SPCK, 1957). See the classical treatment by Charles Gore, *The Holy Spirit and the Church* (New York: Scribners, 1924), especially pp. 244–279.

[6]Article VII of "The Articles of Religion."

[7]Article XX.

Chapter 1. The Bible in the Anglican Reformation

[1]*The Complete Works of St. Thomas More* (New Haven: Yale University Press, 1963–) [hereafter, "More, *Works*"], vol. 4, pp. 218–219.

[2]*The Advancement of Learning and New Atlantis*, ed. Arthur Johnston (Oxford: Clarendon Press, 1974), pp. 220, 222–223. G. P. Marc'hadour and T. M. C. Lawler (More, *Works*, vol. 6.2, p. 494) call attention to the contrast described by R. W. Chambers in his biography of More: "whilst More does not make his Utopians Christian [before the visit of More and his friends], and does

not give them any sacred book, Bacon invents an outrageous piece of 'miraculous evangelism'" (London: Jonathan Cape, 1948, p. 362).

[3]STC 2216, sig. A4ᵛ (preliminaries) [hereafter STC = Pollard and Redgrave, *A Short-Title Catalogue of Books... 1475–1640;* London, 1926; see *note* 68]. The text of the preface, usually omitted from modern editions of the King James Bible is available in Geddes MacGregor's *A Literary History of the Bible* (Nashville: Abingdon Press, 1968), pp. 220–242; quotation, apparently from a different edition, on p. 225.

[4]Miles Coverdale, *Remains,* ed. George Pearson, Parker Society [hereafter abbreviated "P.S."] (Cambridge, 1846), p. 13.

[5]If Marshall McLuhan overstates his thesis when he declares that Gutenberg's invention created "a totally new human environment," he nonetheless has proved his case for the revolutionary character of the change that printing introduced into civilized society. See his *Understanding Media: the Extension of Man* (New York: McGraw-Hill, 1968), p. vi, and his basic statement in *The Gutenberg Galaxy: The Making of Typographic Man* (Toronto: University Press, 1962).

[6]Martin Luther, "Open Letter to the Councillors of the German Cities," 1524, *Works,* ed. Pelikan and Lehmann (Philadelphia and St. Louis: Muhlenberg and Concordia Presses, 1955–   ) 45:363; *D. Martin Luthers Werke, Kritische Gesamtausgabe* (Weimar: H. Bohlau, 1883–   ) 15:40.

[7]Dom Jean LeClercq, "The Exposition and Exegesis of Scripture from Gregory the Great to Saint Bernard," in *The Cambridge History of the Bible,* vol. 2, *The West from the Fathers to the Reformation,* ed. G. W. H. Lampe (Cambridge: the University Press, 1969) [hereafter *CHB,* 2], p. 197.

[8]Gardiner to Edward Vaughan, 3 May 1547, *The Letters of Stephen Gardiner,* ed. J. M. Muller (New York: Macmillan, 1933), p. 274. Injunction 7 of the 1538 Royal Injunctions of Henry VIII, W. H. Frere and W. M. Kennedy, Visitation Articles and Injunctions of the Reformation, 3 vols., Alcuin Club Collections, 14–16, 2:38.

[9]Quoted by Margaret Deanesly, *The Lollard Bible and Other Medieval Biblical Versions* (Cambridge: the University Press, 1920, repr. 1966), p. 163, from *Opus Minor,* Brewer, RS, 328. This study of the medieval popular use of the Bible draws its conclusion from a large assortment of diverse sources. Luther reported the verse that students memorized:

Littera gesta docet; quid credas allegoria;
Moralis quid agas; sed quid speres anagoge.

The writing as it stands teaches the events; allegory, what you are to believe;
The moral sense, what you are to do, and the anagoge, what you are to
hope.

This is from Luther's commentary on Galatians (Weimar ed., 95:24).

[10]*Obedience of a Christian Man,* in the Parker Society edition of *Doctrinal Treatises and Introductions to... Holy Scriptures,* ed. H. Walter (Cambridge, 1848), p. 303; pp. 303–331 expound on this theme at length.

[11]An excellent discussion of the subtleties of medieval exposition is found in Beryl Smalley's article "The Bible in the Medieval Schools" in *CHB* 2:197–220.

[12]June, 1530, Thomas Berthelet as in A. W. Pollard, *Records of the English Bible* (London, 1530), p. 167.

[13]Deanesly, *Lollard Bible*, p. 204; pp. 156–204 describe the evidence discussed in this paragraph.

[14]Arundel to John XIII, 1411; in Henry Hargreaves, "The Wycliffite Versions" in *CHB*, 2:388.

[15]Deanesly, *Lollard Bible*, p. 296.

[16]*A Dialogue concerning Heresies*, 1.25 in More, *Works*, 6:153.12–17; for reading restrictions, see 3.16 at 6:341.9–27.

[17]The editions at Venice were printed by Daniel Bomberg, the first of 1516/17 edited by a Christian Jew, Felix Pratensis and the second of 1514/25 by Jacob ben Chayim. Pagnini's Old Testament appeared in 1518 and Munster's, which also contained the Hebrew text, in 1535.

[18]1516 and 1519; Erasmus produced three more editions before his death in 1536. The second edition contained the more drastic changes in the Latin translation.

[19]Letter to Henry Bullock, *The Epistles of Erasmus*, tr. Francis M. Nichols, vol. 2 (New York: Longmans, Green, 1962), p. 328.

[20]Text given in Appendix I in Deanesly, *Lollard Bible*, p. 386, from *An Exhortation to the diligent studye of scripture made by Erasmus Rotterdamus*, 1529, STC 10493. The "Exhortation" was translated from the first edition of Erasmus' Greek New Testament.

[21]*Apologia adversus debacchationes Sutoris* in *Desiderii Erasmi Roterodami Opera Omnia* (Leiden, 1706; republished, London: Gregg Press, 1962) 9:786C. Erasmus wrote his defense of free will against Luther in 1524. This *Apologia* was published in 1529 in response to Peter Sutor's pamphlet of 1525.

[22]Ulrich Zwingli, *Hauptschriften*, ed. Fritz Blanke, Oskar Furner, and Rudolf Pfister, vol. 1 (Zurich: Zwingli-Verlag, 1940), p. 113. An English translation is available G. W. Bromily, ed., *Zwingli and Bullinger*, Library of Christian Classics, vol. 24 (Philadelphia: Westminster Press, 1953), pp. 90–91; "Scriptures and Word of God" ("*Gschrifft und Wort Gottes*") is there translated as "Word and Spirit of God."

[23]*D. Martin Luthers Werke. Kritische Gesamtausgabe* (Weimar: H. Bohlau, 1883–   ) 31.1:425. An English translation is available in *Luther's Works*, ed. Jaroslav Pelikan and Helmut T. Lehmann (Philadelphia and St. Louis: Fortress and Concordia Presses, 1955–   ) 13:385.

[24]John Calvin, *Institutes of the Christian Religion*, 1.6.2., as in Library of Christian Classics, 2 vols., ed. John T. McNeill, tr. Ford Lewis Battles, 1:72.

[25]Martin Luther, Commentary on Psalm 82:4, written in 1530, in *Luther's Works*, 13:68.

[26]To the Christian Nobility of the German Nation, 1520, *Luther's Works*, 44:204–205.

[27]Commentary on Ephesians 4:11, *Opera quae supersunt omnia*, Corpus Reformatorum (Brunswick, 1863–1900) 51:198. An English translation is available in the set of *Commentaries* published by the Calvin Translation Society (Edinburgh, 1847–1855) 41:280.

[28]*Luther's Works*, 53:316.

[29]John Calvin, *Institutes*, 4.10.30; ed. McNeill, 2:1207.

[30]"Decree concerning the Canonical Scriptures," fourth session, April,

1546, in H. J. Schroeder, *Canons and Decrees of the Council of Trent* (St. Louis and London: Herder, 1955), pp. 17–19.

[31]Much speculation has arisen in the sixteenth century and since over the extent to which Henry himself actually wrote the work; historical evidence suggests that, whatever may have been the contributions of those whose advice he solicited and employed, the king had a major role in the composition of the treatise.

[32]As applied to the Church Fathers, see W. P. Haugaard, "Renaissance Patristic Scholarship and Theology in Sixteenth-Century England," *The Sixteenth Century Journal*, 10.3(1979):37–60.

[33]The story has often been told of the development and character of the English Bible, with accounts of those who contributed to it and analyses of the interdependence of various translations in vocabulary and style. Recent studies, all of which have contributed in various ways to this chapter include S. L. Greenslade, "English Versions of the Bible, 1525–1611," *CHB*, 2:141–175; Greenslade, *The Work of William Tyndale* (London and Glasgow: Blackie and Son, 1938); J. F. Mozley, *William Tyndale* (London: SPCK, 1937); Mozley, *Coverdale and his Bibles* (London: Lutterworth Press, 1953); Charles C. Butterworth, *The Literary Lineage of the King James Bible, 1340–1611* (Philadelphia: University of Pennsylvania Press, 1941); Butterworth, *The English Primers (1519–1545): Their Publication and Connection with the English Bible and the Reformation in England* (same press, 1953); Charles C. Butterworth and Allan G. Chester, *George Joye 1495?–1553: A Chapter in the History of the English Bible and the English Reformation* (same press, 1953); F. F. Bruce, *History of the Bible in English, from the Earliest Versions* (Oxford University Press, 1978); Geddes MacGregor, *The Literary History of the Bible* (Nashville: Abingdon Press, 1968).

[34]Pollard, *Records*, p. 80.

[35]*The Acts and Monuments of John Foxe*, ed. Stephen Reed Cattley (London, 1838), 7 vols., 5:127.

[36]Mozley, *Tyndale*, pp. 98–101; *CHB*, 2:143.

[37]*Enchiridion of Erasmus*, tr. and ed. Raymond Himelick (Gloucester, Massachusetts: Peter Smith, 1970), pp. 49–50.

[38]From Tyndale's preface to the 1530 English Pentateuch, in *Doctrinal Treatises*, ed. H. Walter (Parker Society, Cambridge, 1848), p. 396.

[39]The printing of the first edition (4to) begun in Cologne was stopped by city authorities; Tyndale carried these printed pages with full sets of notes and introductions to Worms where he proceeded to have printed hastily an edition (8vo) bereft of most of this supplementary material. Copies of both the Cologne fragment and the full but unglossed New Testament found their way to England.

[40]William A. Clebsch, *England's Earliest Protestants, 1526–1535* (New Haven: Yale University Press, 1964), p. 314. Even those who feel that Clebsch may have read too much of later English Puritanism into Tyndale's teaching must admit the strong case which he presents for an emphasis in the later writings which is not found so emphasized in Luther's writings.

[41]More, *Works*, 6.1:288–289. I have modified punctuation and changed to modern usage of "u" and "v," and substituted "the" for "ye."

[42]More, *Works*, 8.1:177.

[43]Proclamation of June, 1530; Pollard, *Records*, p. 168.

[44]Tyndale included Old Testament lessons appointed for two Sundays and for thirty-seven other days, including the Wednesdays and Fridays in Lent (Butterworth and Chester, *Joye*, p. 183).

[45]See note 39, above.

[46]From the preface to the 1527 *Parable of the Wicked Mammon* in *Doctrinal Treatises*, p. 38.

[47]No copies of Joye's first Primer of 1529 have survived, but the British Library has a copy of the 1530 *Ortulus Anime*. Butterworth has tabulated the scriptural passages in various early English primers (*Primers*, Appendix II, pp. 288–290).

[48]Isaiah (1531) and Jeremiah (1534) from Zwingli's 1529 work; Psalms (1534) from his posthumous 1532 edition; Proverbs (probably 1533) from Melanchthon's 1525 edition. Mozley suggests that Ecclesiastes is based on Luther's German Bible (*Coverdale*, p. 50), but Butterworth and Chester doubt Joye's competency in German (*Joye*, p. 142). The only extant copies of Proverbs and Ecclesiastes are from an English edition which may have been published early 1535; circumstantial evidence suggests Antwerp editions of both in 1533 (pp. 136–138).

[49]Tyndale's words are from the preface to his revision of the New Testament published in November, 1534, three months after Joye's anonymously corrected edition had appeared; quoted from Mozley, *Tyndale*, pp. 274, 276. Joye's words are from the *Apology*, published in February, 1535, in which he defended his actions in response to Tyndale's accusations; quoted from Butterworth and Chester, *Joye*, p. 150.

[50]Joye's new revision appeared on 9 January and Tyndale's final edition with the publisher's initials "G.H." in its completed form sometime in 1535. I follow Butterworth and Chester (*Joye*, pp. 185–186) rather than Mozley in this sequence of borrowings (*Coverdale*, pp. 51–52).

[51]Joye's *Psalter* appeared on 16 January 1530, and Tyndale's *Genesis* on the 17th.

[52]*Acts and Monuments*, 5:120. Mozley brings a wealth of supporting evidence to this account of Foxe in refutation of the doubts of some modern historians (*Tyndale*, pp. 146–152).

[53]*Remains*, p. 12. Coverdale continues this theme later in the preface in the passage quoted above on p. 15.

[54]After considerable debate over the place of printing, a 1935 article in *The Library* (4.16) as modified by Mozely (*Coverdale*, pp. 74–77) establishes the strong probability of Cologne. Two extant copies of the first edition carry the date of 1535; two others, 1536 (*Mozley*, p. 115n).

[55]*Remains*, pp. 10–11.

[56]Much of this work is a revised version of Luther in the Swiss dialect, but the prophets, poetical books of the Old Testament, and the Apocrypha are distinct translations to which Reformed, and even anabaptist scholars had contributed.

[57]Stylistic studies show that in the Old Testament, Coverdale principally relied on the two German translations for the post-Pentateuchal historical books, largely on the Zurich Bible for the poetical and prophetic books, and on both Zurich and the Vulgate for the Apocrypha. Yet everywhere, he draws freely from all his sources. See Mozley, *Coverdale*, ch. 5 and *CHB*, 3:148–149.

58Jeremiah 3:11; Joye had used the word consistently (Butterworth and Chester, *Joye*, pp. 120–121).

59Butterworth, *Lineage*, p. 97.

60*Remains*, p. 11.

6119 December 1534 from Pollard, *Records*, pp. 176–177.

62Printed in Mozley, *Coverdale*, p. 111; dating and occasion discussed, pp. 110–112.

63*De Antiquitate* (1572), p. 385, as translated and printed in Mozley, *Coverdale*, p. 120.

64Injunction No. 7 in Walter Howard Frere and William M. Kennedy, *Visitation Articles and Injunctions of the Period of the Reformation*, 3 vols., Alcuin Club Collection, XIV–XVI (London, 1910) 2:9. The injunction is not in Cranmer's register, evidence of its withdrawal, but it appears in a printed copy in the library of Corpus Christi College, Cambridge, as well as in Bonner's register in London (see 2:1n).

654 August 1537 from Pollard, *Records*, p. 215.

66Mozley describes the character of the Bible in detail (*Coverdale*, ch. 8).

67Injunctions for St. Mary's, Worcester, and for Worcester Diocese, both in 1537, Frere and Kennedy, *Articles and Injunctions*, 2:12–15.

68The first published in England was Marshall's Primer which appeared in 1535. The Rouen Primer of 1536 had a translation of the Psalms which was independent of Joye's and Coverdale's work (Butterworth, *Lineage*, pp. 103–107); also *Primers*, *passim*.; STC 15988–95 and 15997–16008 as in A. W. Pollard and G. R. Redgrave, *A Short-Title Catalogue of Books...1475–1640* (London, 1926).

69STC 2965, 15999, and 16008 (Butterworth, *Primers*, pp. 162–163).

70Injunctions 2 and 3 of 1538, Frere and Kennedy, *Injunctions*, pp. 35–36.

71All these were published by Grafton and Whitchurch; another edition of the text of the first 1539 edition was published by another printer in April 1540, apparently for private rather than for church use (Mozley, *Coverdale*, pp. 218–219).

72Coverdale, *Remains*, p. 497.

73Thomas Cranmer to Cromwell, 14 November 1539; *Miscellaneous Writings and Letters of Thomas Cranmer*, Parker Society, ed. Edmund Cox, Cambridge, 1846, p. 396.

74Cranmer, *Writings*, pp. 118 and 122.

75Great Bible, 1539 (STC 2068), sig.*v^v.

76"To the Reader" from Gardiner's *A Declaration of such articles as George Joye hath gone about to confute as false*, in J. M. Muller, ed., *Letters*, p. 164.

77This wording is Lee's; he also required heads of religious houses to do the same. Shaxton specified Sundays as well as holy days and qualified the reading of both lessons "if there be time thereto," insisting only on "one of them at the least." Injunctions 11 of Lee and 2 of Shaxton; Frere and Kennedy, *Articles and Injunctions*, pp. 46–47 and 54.

78Injunction 1; Frere and Kennedy, *Articles and Injunctions*, p. 61.

79Injunction 18; Frere and Kennedy, *Articles and Injunctions*, p. 88.

806 May 1541; Pollard, *Records*, p. 264.

81See discussion below in Hatchett, "The Bible in Worship," ch. 2, pp. 81ff.

[82]The biblical texts were primarily based on the translations in the Rouen Primers rather than on those in the Great Bible.

[83]Richard Taverner, a London lawyer, produced a revision of Matthew's Bible which was published in 1539, but it was, of course, superseded by the Great Bible and left few marks on English biblical history.

[84]The Convocation record is printed in D. Wilkins, *Concilia Magnae Britanniae et Hiberniae* (London, 1737) 3:860–862. For Gardiner's 1547 letter to Cranmer, see Muller, ed., *Letters*, p. 313.

[85]"An Act for the Advancement of true Religion and for the abolishment of the Contrary," as in Mozley, *Coverdale*, p. 283.

[86]*The King's Book or A Necessary Doctrine and Erudition for any Christian Man,* ed. T. A. Lacey (London: SPCK, 1932), p. 6.

[87]Coverdale, *Remains*, p. 11.

[88]Katherine Parr, *The Lamentacion of a Synner*, 2nd edition (London, 1548) STC 4828, sig. Ei.

[89]Injunction 7; Frere and Kennedy, *Articles and Injunctions*, 2:118.

[90]Injunctions 20 and 32; Frere and Kennedy, *Articles and Injunctions*, 2:122–123. Injunction 20 implied Erasmus' *Paraphrase* on the whole New Testament, not just on the Gospels required by injunction 7, but the second volume had not been published; when it appeared, it included Tyndale's preface to Romans. This volume never had the sale of the first which *parishes* were required to purchase; see E. G. Devereux, "The English *Paraphrases* of Erasmus," *Bulletin of the John Rylands Library*, vol. 51 (1968–69), pp. 359–361).

[91]Injunction 32; Frere and Kennedy, *Articles and Injunctions*, 2:128–129.

[92]*Certain Sermons or Homilies appointed to be read in Churches in the time of the late Queen Elizabeth* (Oxford, 1840), pp. 1, 2, 3, and 7.

[93]"Against Contention and Brawling," *Certain Sermons*, p. 126.

[94]"Of the Salvation of Mankind," *Certain Sermons*, p. 19.

[95]See below, pp. 81ff; 91–93.

[96]*The First and Second Prayer Books of Edward VI* (New York: E. P. Dutton [Everyman edition], 1949), p. 34. Collect for the 2nd Sunday in Advent (Proper 28 in the Season after Pentecost in the 1979 *Book of Common Prayer* of the Episcopal Church in the United States). As a consequence of this collect, for many years the 2nd Sunday in Advent was observed as "Bible Sunday" in much of the English-speaking world.

[97]*First and Second Prayer Books*, pp. 300, 301, 308–309, 312, 315, 317, 446, 447, 454–455, 457, 461, and 463.

[98]Butterworth, *Lineage*, p. 153–156.

[99]Charles Hardwick, *A History of the Articles of Religion* (London: George Bell) in appendix III.II, pp. 289 and 294–298.

[100]Injunction 22 for York Minster; Frere and Kennedy, *Articles and Injunctions*, 2:320.

[101]Injunction 105 of the 1554 Articles for the Diocese of London; Frere and Kennedy, *Articles and Injunctions*, 2:354–355 and note.

[102]James Brooks' Injunctions for Gloucester, 1556, No. 4; Frere and Kennedy, *Articles and Injunctions*, 2:402. Brooks was bishop of the diocese from 1554 to 1558.

[103]John Standish, *A discourse wherein is debated whether it be expedient that the*

scripture should be in English for all men to read that will, December, 1554, sig. E5 and F8, as quoted in Mozley, *Coverdale,* p. 293.

[104]*A Brief Discourse of the Troubles Begun at Frankfort in the Year 1554,* reprinted from the 1575 edition (London, 1846), p. 49.

[105]Estienne had published a Greek New Testament with verse divisions at Geneva in 1551, and in 1555 published a Latin Bible with these divisions. The scholarly printer Estienne often used the Latin form of his name, "Stephanus," and the two designations are used interchangeably in referring to the publishing house.

[106]Calvin and Beza collaborated on a French revision published in 1560; the first complete protestant Italian Bible was published in Geneva in 1562, based on earlier translations; Spanish versions of the Psalms and New Testament appeared in Geneva in 1556 and 1557; see *CHB,* 2:110–111, 119, and 125–127.

[107]A sixteenth-century biography of William Whittingham mentions as collaborators Miles Coverdale, Christopher Goodman, Anthony Gilby, Thomas Sampson, and William Cole; Gilby and Cole, together with three others not on this list, remained with Whittingham. Cf. Lloyd E. Berry, introduction to facsimile edition of *The Geneva Bible,* 1560 ed. (Madison: University of Wisconsin Press, 1969), p. 8. All of these were in Geneva and were later identified with various degrees of reforming militancy under Elizabeth. The extent of the participation, if any, of Goodman and Sampson is open to debate.

[108]STC 2093, 1560, 4o; STC 2095, 1562, folio; STC 2106, 1570, 4o; STC 2117, 1576, folio (Christopher Barker, London).

[109]*Geneva Bible* (1969), p. 29.

[110]Proclamation of 27 December 1557; John Strype, *Annals of the Reformation... during Queen Elizabeth's Happy Reign,* 4 vols. (Oxford, 1824) 1.2:391–392.

[111]Article 55; Frere and Kennedy, *Articles and Injunctions,* 3:7.

[112]Roger Ascham, *The Schoolmaster,* in *Works,* ed. J. A. Giles, 3 vols. (London, 1864–1865) 3:143.

[113]"State Papers relating to the Custody of the Princess Elizabeth at Woodstock in 1554," ed. C. R. Manning, *Norfolk Archaeology* (Norfolk and Norwich Archaeological Society, 4:1855) 161, 172, and 175.

[114]John E. Neale, *Elizabeth I and her Parliaments,* 2 vols. (London, 1953–1957) 2:100.

[115]William P. Haugaard, *Elizabeth and the English Reformation* (Cambridge: University Press, 1968), pp. 129–130.

[116]Injunctions 6, 16, and 27; Frere and Kennedy, *Articles and Injunctions,* 3:10, 13–14, and 18. Whereas the Edwardian injunction had required studies of all clergy under the degree of bachelor of divinity, the Elizabethan order lowered the requirement to those under the degree of master of arts; a far smaller percentage of the clergy held the more advanced divinity degree.

[117]Injunctions 31 and 42; Frere and Kennedy, *Articles and Injunctions,* 3:20–21.

[118]No. 22, 1571 Provincial Injunctions, and No. 8, 1572 York Cathedral Injunctions; Frere and Kennedy, *Articles and Injunctions,* 3:280 and 348.

[119]Article [11], 1598; W. P. M. Kennedy, *Elizabethan Episcopal Administration,*

3 vols., Alcuin Club Collections, Nos. 25–27 (London, 1924) 3:308. A set of injunctions for cathedrals issued at the beginning of Edward's reign had called for "some part of the holy Scripture read in English" at meals; no. 11, 1547; Frere and Kennedy, *Articles and Injunctions*, 2:137.

[120]Harwick, *Articles*, pp. 295–299. The Thirty-Nine Articles of Religion, adopted in 1563 were reaffirmed in 1571, when they received the full royal assent. In that same year both Convocation and Parliament laid down regulations requiring subscription to the articles before ordination and before entering on a church cure.

[121]*De Regno Christi*, 2.60; *Melanchthon and Bucer*, ed. Wilhelm Pauck (Philadelphia: Westminster Press, 1969), pp. 378–379.

[122]*A Catechism Written in Latin by Alexander Nowell*, ed. G. E. Corrie (Cambridge, 1853), p. 226.

[123]Letter to William Cecil, 19 January 1561[2]; Pollard, *Records*, p. 287. The reference in the letter to Jewel's *Apology*, published 1 January 1562, makes it clear that the letter is dated "1561," old style, thus 1562, new style.

[124]9 March 1565; Pollard, *Records*, p. 286. Elizabeth had granted a printer a license to print the Geneva Bible, subject to being "ordered...as may seme expedient" by these bishops of Canterbury and London. Having made the review, the bishops propose that the queen extend the length of the printer's exclusive license.

[125]26 November 1566, Pollard, *Records*, p. 287.

[126]Parker to Cecil and Parker to Elizabeth, 5 October 1568; *Correspondence of Matthew Parker*, J. B. Bruce and T. T. Perowne, eds. (Cambridge, 1853), pp. 334–338. In a letter of 22 September to Cecil, Parker had remarked that the Bible lacked only "some ornaments" (p. 334). It is possible that when Parker and Grindal wrote in 1566 in support of the publication of the Geneva Bible, they had used the authority given to them of overseeing the proposed edition to excise the "prejudicial notes."

[127]Parker to Cecil, 5 October 1568; Parker, *Correspondence*, p. 335.

[128]Parker enclosed a list of the translators in his 5 October letter to Cecil, and the same initials were included in the printed text. The bishops include, in addition to Parker, Alley of Exeter, Davies of St. David's, Sandys of Worcester, Parkhurst of Norwich, Barlow of Chichester, Horne of Winchester, Bentham of Lichfield and Coventry, Grindal of London, Scambler of Peterborough, Cox of Ely, Bullingham of Lincoln, and, if a scholarly conjecture is right, Jones of Landaff. Other clerics include Canon Andrew Pierson of Canterbury, a chaplain to the archbishop, Dean Andrew Perne of Ely, Dean Gabriel Goodman of Westminster, and, probably, Thomas Bickley of Canterbury who may have taken over from Bishop Guest of Rochester when Parker disapproved of his work on the Psalms (Parker, *Correspondence*, pp. 334n–336n; Pollard, *Records*, pp. 30–32).

[129]Parker, *Correspondence*, pp. 336n–337n.

[130]Butterworth, *Lineage*, p. 178.

[131]The Great Bible had a much less controversial summary of the chapter: "He sheweth what preferment the Jewes have, and that both the Jewes and Gentyles are under synne, and are justifyed only by the grace of God in Christ."

[132]Parker to Cecil. 5 October 1568; Parker, *Correspondence*, p. 337.

[133]The folio edition of 1585 returned to the original Bishops' Bible text (Butterworth, *Lineage*, p. 185).

[134]From 1572 to 1578: STC Nos. 2107–2113, 2113a, 2114–2116, 2121, 2122, and 2124; after 1578: Nos. 2141 (1584), 2149 (1588), 2156 (1591), 2167 (1595), and 2188 (1602). The Bishops' version of the New Testament, however, remained more popular than has generally been noticed; versions were printed even after the 1611 Authorized Bible appeared: STC Nos. 2883 (1582), 2896 (1598), 2897 (1600), 2904 (1605), 2912 (1613), 2916 (1617). At the beginning of the reign of James I, new canons, which in many cases regularized the royal and episcopal regulations of Elizabeth's reign, called upon parishes if they be "yet unfurnished" to supply "the Bible of the largest volume" (Canon 80, in appendix to *Certain Sermons or Homilies*, p. 569). No editions of the Bishops' Bible appear in James' reign.

[135]*A brieff discours off the troubles begonne at Franckford, A. D. 1554*, 1575, pp. 192 and 193–194.

[136]STC No. 2117; the previous year two editions of the New Testament with the 1560 Genevan text were published (STC Nos. 2876–2877).

[137]STC 4441 (1579); Sir Francis Walsingham was the councillor whom Tomson served.

[138]The Tomson text consulted was that printed in a 1602 Bible (STC 2185). The Bishops' Bible has no note at either Matthew 18:17 or I Timothy 5:17.

[139]The Rheims New Testament was published again in 1600 (STC Nos. 2884 [1582] and 2898 [1600]). Fulke's work also appeared in a new edition in 1601 (STC Nos. 2888 [1589] and 2900 [1601]).

[140]A. L. Rowse, *The Expansion of Elizabethan England* (London: Macmillan, 1555), p. 74. For general background of Welsh volumes, see *CHB*, 3:170–172, and Haugaard, *Elizabeth*, pp. 44, 74, and 126.

Evelyn Philip Shirley, ed., *Original Letters and Papers in Illustration of the Church of Ireland, during the Reigns of Edward VI, Mary and Elizabeth* (London: 1851), p. 317.

[142]August, 1587; John Roche Dasent, ed., *Acts of the Privy Council of England*, N. S., vol. 7 (London, 1893), pp. 201–202.

[143]*CHB*, 3:172–173.

[144]From "A View of popish Abuses," attached to the second edition of the 1572 "Admonition to Parliament"; H. C. Porter, ed., *Puritanism in Tudor England* (London: Macmillan, 1970), pp. 124–125.

[145]*Of the Lawes of Ecclesiasticall Politie*, V.22.10; *The Folger Library Edition of the Works of Richard Hooker*, vols. 1–3 (Cambridge: Harvard University Press, 1977–1981) 2:99.

[146]"A Treatise of the Vocations of Callings of Men," in *The Work of William Perkins*, ed. I. Breward (Appleford: Sutton Courtenay Press, 1970), pp. 448 and 454.

[147]Thomas Rogers, *The Catholic Doctrine of the Church of England*, ed. J. J. S. Perowne (Cambridge, 1854), p. 90.

[148]*Lawes*, III.11.6; *Works*, 1:251.

[149]*Lawes*, I.14.1; *Works*, 1:125–136.

[150]*Lawes*, II.8.5; *Works*, 1:189.

[151]*Lawes*, VI.2.2; *Works*, 3:5; punctuation altered.

[152]*Lawes*, III.4.1; *Works*, 1:213.

[153]*Lawes*, II.8.7.; *Works*, 1:191.

[154]"The Millenary Petition," H. Gee and W. J. Hardy, *Documents Illustrative of English Church History (New York: Kraus Reprint, 1966), pp. 511 and 509.*

[155]*STC 2216, sig. A6ᵛ (preliminaries); MacGregor, Literary History,* p. 233.

[156]From a contemporary pamphlet by William Barlow describing the conference (STC 1456), quoted in Pollard, *Records,* p. 46.

[157]James' letter to Bancroft, 22 July 1504; Bancroft's circular letter, 31 July; Pollard, *Records,* pp. 331–333.

[158]Pollard, *Records,* pp. 53–55.

[159]These are a description which the English delegation presented at the 1618 Synod of Dort (Pollard, *Records,* pp. 336–339) and a biography of one of the translators, John Boys, by Anthony Walker (pp. 55–56). Walker's account suggests "six in all, two out of every company," which may indicate that the Hebrew and Greek teams worked somewhat independently of one another.

[160]The French Protestant Bible had reached its perfection in the edition by the Genevan pastors of 1588 with a preface by Beza. In Spanish, Cipriano de Valera published a New Testament in London in 1596, followed by the full Bible, printed in Amsterdam in 1602. Geneva was the home of the Italian Giovanni Diodati who there published a full Bible in 1607, possibly in time for the English translators to consult it.

[161]STC 2216, sig. B2ʳ (preliminaries); MacGregor, *Literary History,* p. 239.

[162]Butterworth, *Lineage,* p. 231.

[163]Butterworth, *Lineage,* appendix 2, pp. 355–358.

[164]*CHB,* 3:168.

Chapter 2. The Bible in Worship

[1]The Edwardian Injunctions of 1547 called for a homily every Sunday (Edward Cardwell, *Documentary Annals of the Reformed Church of England* [Oxford: University Press, 1839], Vol. I, p. 19); the 1549 Prayer Book called for a sermon or homily at every Eucharist.

[2]D. Wilkins, *Concilia Magnae Britannae et Hiberniae ab Anno MCCCL ad Annum MCXLV* (London: Sumner A. Gosling, 1737), Vol. III, p. 863.

[3]*Cranmer's Liturgical Projects,* edited by J. Wickham Legg (London: Harrison and Sons, 1915).

[4]*Breviarium Romanum a Francisco Cardinali Quignonio,* ed. by J. Wickham Legg (Cambridge: University Press, 1888); *The Second Recension of the Quignon Breviary,* ed. by J. Wickham Legg (London: Printed for the Society [Henry Bradshaw Society] by Harrison and Sons, 1908).

[5]A. L. Richter, *Die evangelischen Kirchenordnungen des sechszehnten Jahrhunderts* (Weimar, 1864).

[6]*Cranmer's Liturgical Projects,* pp. 143–153.

[7]Ibid., pp. 154–165.

[8]Ibid., pp. 3–14.

[9]Ibid., pp. 15–17, 167–197.

[10]For the English Prayer Books see F. E. Brightman, *The English Rite* (London: Rivingtons, 1915).

[11]Proper Psalms were appointed only for Christmas (19, 45, 85 and 89, 132), Easter (2, 57, 111 and 113, 114, 118), Ascension (8, 15, 21 and 24, 68, 148), and Pentecost (48, 67 and 104, 145).

[12]The following books and chapters were omitted: Genesis 10 (a geneological table), Exodus 25–31, 36–39 (regulations regarding the tabernacle), Leviticus 1–17, 21–27 (ceremonial law), Numbers 1–9 (levitical regulations), 1 and 2 Chronicles (duplicatory), Song of Solomon, Ezekiel 1, 4–5, 8–12, 15–17, 19–32, 35–48 (obscure or apocalyptic), 3 and 4 Esdras [1 and 2 Esdras], Esther 10–16 ("the rest of the book of Esther"), Song of the Three Children (mostly contained in the Benedicite), the Prayer of Manasseh, and 1 and 2 Maccabees.

[13]January 1 (Genesis 17, Romans 2, Deuteronomy 10:12-22, Colossians 2), January 6 (Isaiah 60, Luke 3:21-38, Isaiah 49, John 2:1-11), January 25 (Acts 22:1-21 and 26), May 1 (Acts 8:1-13), June 11 (Acts 14 and 15:1-35), June 24 (Malachi 3, Matthew 3, Malachi 4, and Matthew 14:1-12), June 29 (Acts 3 and 4), November 1 (Wisdom 3:1-13a, Hebrews 11:33–12:6, Wisdom 5:1-16, Revelation 19:1-16), December 25 (Isaiah 9, Matthew 1, Isaiah 7:10-25, Titus 3:4-8), December 26 (Acts 6:8–7:29 and 7:30-54), December 27 (Revelation 1 and 22), and December 28 (Jeremiah 31:1-17).

[14]Lamentations was to be read on Wednesday, Thursday, and Saturday before Easter; Genesis 22 and Isaiah 53 on Good Friday; Exodus 12, Romans 6 and Acts 2 on Easter Day; Matthew 28 and Acts 3 on Monday after Easter; Luke 24:1-12 and 1 Corinthians 15 on Tuesday; John 14 and Ephesians 4 on Ascension Day; Acts 10:34-48 and 19:1-20 on Pentecost; Genesis 18 and Matthew 3 on Trinity Sunday.

[15]For the Elizabethan Prayer Book see *The Book of Common Prayer 1559*, edited by John E. Booty (Charlottesville: University Press of Virginia for The Folger Shakespeare Library, 1976).

[16]Isaiah 1, 2, 5, 24, 25, 26, 30, 32, 37, 38, 41, 43, 44, 46, 51, 53, 55, 56, 57, 58, 59, 64.

[17]Genesis 1, 2, 3, 6, 9, 12, 19, 22, 27, 34, 39, 42, 43, 45; Exodus 2, 5, 9, 10, 12, 14; Numbers 16, 22, 23, 25; Deuteronomy 4, 5, 6, 7, 8, 9, 12, 13, 17, 18; Genesis 18; Joshua 1, 10, 23; Judges 4, 5; 1 Samuel 2, 3, 12, 13, 15, 16; 2 Samuel 12, 21, 22, 24; 1 Kings 13, 17, 18, 19, 21, 22; 2 Kings 5, 9, 10, 18, 19, 23.

[18]The calendar revision of 1561 substituted Deuteronomy 16 and Wisdom 1 on Pentecost.

[19]Ezekiel 2, 14, 16, 18, 20, 24; Daniel 3, 6; Joel 2; Micah 6; Habakkuk 5.

[20]Proverbs 1, 2, 3, 11, 12, 13, 14, 15, 16, 17, 19.

[21]Romans 6 and Acts 2 (Easter), Acts 10:34-48 and 19:1-20 (Pentecost), Matthew 3 (Trinity Sunday).

[22]Proverbs 20, 21, 23, 24, 28; Ecclesiastes 4, 5, 6; Wisdom 1, 5, 6, 9, 12, 19; Ecclesiasticus 1, 2, 3, 4, 5, 7, 9, 10, 12, 15, 19, 21, 23, 25, 29, 35, 38, 39, 44, 51; Job 1, 24–25, 42.

[23]For the 1561 calendar see *Liturgies and Occasional Forms of Prayer Set Forth in the Reign of Queen Elizabeth*, edited by W. K. Clay (Cambridge: University Press, 1847), pp. 435–455.

[24]The 1552 revision substituted Luke 2:1-14 for Matthew 1 on Christmas Day and a new series of lections for the readings from Lamentations in Holy Week: Hosea 13 and 14, Daniel 9, Jeremiah 31, and Zechariah 9. The 1559 revision omitted Nehemiah 12; 1561 omitted Genesis 11 and 36, Exodus 6, 35, and 40, Numbers 10, 15, 18–19, 26, 28–29, and 33–34, Deuteronomy 13–14 and 23, Joshua 11–22, Ezra 2, 8, and 10, and Nehemiah 3, 7, and 11; 1604 omitted Daniel 14 (Bel and the Dragon), Tobit 5–6 and 8, and Ecclesiasticus 25:13–26:29 and 46:20.

[25]For this revision see Gordon Donaldson, *The Making of the Scottish Prayer Book of 1637* (Edinburgh: University Press, 1954).

[26]January 25, February 2, July 25, August 24, September 21, November 1.

[27]1 Chronicles 10:1–11:26, 13–22, 28–29, 2 Chronicles 1–2, 5–36 .

[28]It restores Exodus 6, Deuteronomy 13–14, Lamentations 5, Tobit 6 and 8, and Bel and the Dragon, and omits Ecclesiasticus 30:18-25. The Sunday table appoints Isaiah 65 and 66 for the Sixth Sunday after Epiphany, abbreviates several readings (Genesis 9:1-19 and 19:1-29, Acts 2:22-47, Deuteronomy 16:1-17), lengthens one reading (Numbers 23–24), makes several substitutions (Genesis 1 and 18 for Genesis 18 and Joshua 1 on Trinity Sunday; 1 Kings 17 for 16, 2 Kings 19 for 22, Ezekiel 13 for 16), and appoints proper New Testament lessons for Palm Sunday (Matthew 26, which had been part of the Gospel of the Day, and Hebrews 5:1-11) and for Evening Prayer on Trinity Sunday (1 John 5). Psalms 6, 32, 38 and 102, 130, 143 were appointed for Ash Wednesday, so that, with Psalm 51 in the Commination rite, the seven Penitential Psalms would be read on that day. Proper Psalms were also appointed for Good Friday (22, 40, 54 and 69, 88).

[29]See paragraph above and Notes 24 and 28 (above).

[30]For example, proposals for revision in the interest of comprehension in 1668 and 1681 (Edward Cardwell, *A History of Conferences* [Oxford: University Press, 1849], pp. 394–396); the revision attempt of 1689 (Timothy J. Fawcett, *The Liturgy of Comprehension 1689* [Southend-on-Sea: Mayhew-McCrimmon, 1973]); the Non-juror Thomas Deacon's *A Compleat Collection of Devotions* (London, 1734); *Free and Candid Disquisitions* (London: A. Millar, 1749); *A New Form of Common Prayer* (London: R. Griffiths, 1753); *Queries Relating to the Book of Common-Prayer* (London: J. Wilkie, 1774); John Wesley's *The Sunday Service of the Methodists of North America* (London, 1784).

[31]For the American Prayer Books of 1789 and 1892 see William McGarvey, *Liturgiae Americanae* (Philadelphia: Philadelphia Church Publishing Company, 1907).

[32]Isaiah 1, 2, 5, 24, 25, 28:1-22, 30, 32, 35, 40, 41, 42, 44, 45, 51, 52:1-12, 54, 55, 57, 59, 61, 62; Jeremiah 5, 22, 35, 36; Lamentations 1, 3:1-36; Jeremiah 7, 9; Ezekiel 14, 18, 20:1-26, 20:27-49; Micah 6; Habakkuk 3; Haggai 2:1-9; Zechariah 13; Daniel 9; Malachi 3–4; Exodus 12 (Easter); Isaiah 43, 48; Hosea 13, 14; Joel 3:9-21; Micah 4, 5; Nahum 1; Zechariah 8, 10; Joel 2; Zephaniah 3; Deuteronomy 16:1-17 and Isaiah 11 (Pentecost); Genesis 1, 2, 3, 6, 9:1-19, 15:1-19, 37, 42, 43, 45, 49, 50; Exodus 3, 5, 9, 10, 14, 15; Numbers 16, 22, 23, 24; Deuteronomy 4:1-40, 5, 6, 7, 8, 9, 33, 34; Joshua 23, 24; Judges 4, 5; 1 Samuel 12, 17; 2 Samuel 12, 19; 1 Kings 8:1-21, 8:22-62, 17, 18; 2 Kings 5, 19; Daniel 6, 7; Proverbs 1, 2, 3, 8, 11, 12, 13, 14, 15, 16.

33Isaiah 59; Luke 6:20-49; Jonah 3; 2 Peter 3.

34Luke 1:1-38, 1:39-80, 3:1-18; Matthew 3:1-12; Luke 2:25-52; Mark 1:1-16; Matthew 2:13-23; John 1:29-51; Matthew 4:12-25; Luke 4:14-33; Matthew 5, 6, 7; Luke 7:19-50; Mark 6:1-29; Matthew 10; Luke 10:1-22; Mark 9:1-29; Luke 19:28-48; Luke 21; Matthew 26; Romans 6 (Easter); Acts 1, 3, 5, 6, 8:5-40; John 17 (Sunday after Ascension); Acts 4:1-35 (Pentecost); Matthew 3 (Trinity Sunday); Acts 9:1-31, 10, 11, 14, 15, 17, 20, 24, 26, 28; Matthew 18, 20, 23, 25; Mark 4, 13; Luke 13, 15, 20; John 3, 7, 8, 9, 10, 11, 13, 15.

35Romans 10, 12, 14; 1 Corinthians 1,2; Hebrews 2; 1 Corinthians 3,13; 2 Corinthians 4, 5; Galatians 2, 3; Ephesians 1, 2, 3, 4, 5, 6; Philippians 1, 3; Hebrews 5:1-10; Acts 2:22-47 (Easter); 1 Corinthians 15; Colossians 1, 3; 1 Thessalonians 3, 4; 2 Thessalonians 3:1-16; Acts 19:1-20 (Pentecost); 1 John 5 (Trinity Sunday); 1 Timothy 6; 2 Timothy 2, 3:1–4:8; Titus 2:1–3:9; Hebrews 10, 11, 12, 13; James 1, 2, 3, 4, 5; 1 Peter 1, 2, 3, 4, 5; 2 Peter 1, 2, 3; 1 John 1, 2, 3, 4; Jude; 2 John.

36Daniel 10, 11:1-29, 11:30-45, 12; Genesis 22: 1-19, Zechariah 9, and John 14, 15, 11:45-47, 13, 18, and Luke 23:50-56 for Morning Prayer, and Hosea 11, 12, 13, Jeremiah 31, Isaiah 52:13–53:12, and Exodus 13 for Old Testament lessons at Evening Prayer, with Philippians 2 on Good Friday and Hebrews 4 on Easter Even. Other changes in the lessons for Holy Days included shortening several (Genesis 17:1-14, Acts 26:1-23, Numbers 11:16-30), lengthening one (1 Thessalonians 5), and making several substitutions (Romans 11 for Luke 3:1-22 on Epiphany, Job 19 for Exodus 17 on the Monday after Easter, Isaiah 26:1-19, Job 19, and 2 Corinthians 5 for Exodus 20 and 32 and 1 Corinthians 15 on the Tuesday after Easter, and Galatians 5 for John 4:1-13 on the Tuesday after Pentecost).

37The translation was questioned by the 1689 revisers and by *Free and Candid Disquisitions* (1749); more selective use is recommended by *An Essay for a Review* (London: T. Cooper, 1734), *The Expediency and Necessity of Revising and Improving the Publick Liturgy* (London: R. Griffiths, 1749), *A Form of Prayer* (London: A. Millar, 1751), *The Beauty of Holiness* (London: R. Baldwin, 1752); *A New Form of Common-Prayer* (1753), *The Liturgy of the Church of England, In Its Ordinary Service, Reduced Nearer to the Standard of Scripture* (London: A. Millar, 1763), *Queries Relating to The Book of Common-Prayer* (1774), Theophilus Lindsey's *The Book of Common Prayer Reformed according to the Plan of the Late Dr. Samuel Clarke* (London: J. Johnson, 1774), Benjamin Franklin's *Abridgement of the Book of Common Prayer* (London, 1773), John Wesley's *Sunday Service* (1784), and the King's Chapel *A Liturgy, Collected Principally from the Book of Common Prayer* (Boston: Peter Edes, 1785).

38*The Book of Common Prayer, and Administration of the Sacraments, and Other Rites and Ceremonies, As Revised and Proposed to the Use of the Protestant Episcopal Church* (Philadelphia: Hall and Sellers, 1786).

39Psalms 19 (omitting the last clause of verse 13), 24, 103; 139 (omitting verses 19-22), 145; 51 (omitting verses 18-19), 42 (omitting verses 8-9 and 12); 37; 1, 15, 91; 32 (omitting verses 3-4 and 10), 130, 121; 23, 34, 65; 84 (omitting verse 9), 85, 93, 97; 8, 33 (omitting verses 10-21), 147 (omitting verse 10), 57 (omitting verses 1-5 and 7); 96 (omitting verses 5-13), 148, 149 (omitting verses 5-9), 150.

40The only readings from Revelation in previous Prayer Books had been

4:1-11 and 7:2-12 as the Epistles on Trinity Sunday and All Saints' Day respectively, 19:1-16 at Evening Prayer on All Saints' Day, and Chapters 1 and 22 at the Daily Offices on St. John's Day.

[41]Chapters 1–8, 10–12, 14–16, 18–22.

[42]Revelation 21:1-8 and 21:9–22:5 for Septuagesima (new); Luke 19:28-48 or 20:9-20 in place of Hebrews 5:1-10 on Palm Sunday; Revelation 1:10-18 in place of Romans 6 and John 20:11-18 or Revelation 5 in place of Acts 2 on Easter Day; 1 Corinthians 15:1-28 and John 20:24-29 on the First Sunday after Easter (new); Romans 8:1-17 in place of Acts 10:34-48 and Galatians 5:16-26 or Acts 18:24–19:20 in place of Acts 19:1-20 on Pentecost; Revelation 1:1-8 in place of Matthew 3 and Ephesians 4:1-16 or Matthew 3 in place of 1 John 5 on Trinity Sunday.

[43]Among the Old Testament lessons about twenty are shortened; five are lengthened to take in a portion of the preceding or following chapter. Isaiah 56:1-8 is substituted for Isaiah 57 on the Fourth Sunday after Epiphany, Exodus 15:1-21 for Exodus 12:37-51 on Easter, Deuteronomy 5 for Deuteronomy 16:1-17 on Pentecost, and Deuteronomy 9:9-29 for Deuteronomy 8 on the Thirteenth Sunday after Trinity. The lectionary for the Second through the Sixth Sundays of Lent is revised: Ezekiel 14, Ezekiel 18:20-32, Micah 6, Zechariah 13, and Zechariah 9:9-17 are to be read in the morning, and Daniel 3, 5, 6, 7:1-18, and 9 in the evening. Near the end of the year, the Eighteenth Sunday after Trinity and following, 1 Chronicles 17, 1 Kings 3:1-15, 2 Chronicles 6, 1 Kings 19, and 2 Chronicles 36 are brought into the series, displacing 2 Samuel 19, 1 Kings 8, and Daniel 6 and 7 (which had been moved to Lent). In the series of readings from Proverbs Chapter 9 is added and 12, 13, and 14 deleted, making way for Malachi 3 and 4 (from Lent) and Ecclesiastes 11 and 12 (on the Sunday before Advent). Among the New Testament lessons several were lengthened,, shortened, or linked together, resulting in the dropping of Matthew 3:1-12 and Acts 28. Hebrews 12:14-29 was inserted for Pentecost, John 5:24-47 replaced Luke 19:28-48 on the Fourth Sunday in Lent, and Luke 19:1-27 replaced Luke 20 on the Nineteenth Sunday after Trinity. Revelation 1, 2, 3, and 22 were appointed for Evening Prayer on the Sundays of Advent, causing Romans 14 and 1 Corinthians 1 and 13 to be dropped. John 11:47–12:50 replaced Hebrews 5:1-10 on the last Sunday in Lent, and Hebrews 4:14–5:10 replaced 2 Thessalonians 3:1-16 on the Sunday after the Ascension. The table of proper lessons for Holy Days was influenced by the 1871 English lectionary, but many changes were made and proper New Testament lessons provided for each Holy Day, including Transfiguration which was new to this calendar.

[44]Old Testament lessons for the first week and a half of Lent were taken from the Prophets, half from Ezekiel, and selected chapters from Job were appointed for mornings from the Second to the Fifth Sundays in Lent, with lessons from the Pentateuch and historical writings in the evenings until the Sixth Sunday in Lent. Selections from the Gospels in course were read in the mornings and from the Epistles in the evenings from the Thursday after Ash Wednesday until the Sixth Sunday in Lent.

[45]Christmas, Circumcision, Epiphany, Purification, Ash Wednesday, Annunciation, Good Friday, Easter, Ascension, Whitsunday, Trinity Sunday, Transfiguration, St. Michael and All Angels, and All Saints' Day.

[46]Psalms 1, 15, 91; 4, 31:1-6, 91, 134; 19, 24, 103; 23, 34, 65; 26, 43, 141;

32, 130, 121; 37; 51, 42; 72, 96; 77; 80, 81; 84, 122, 134; 85, 93, 97; 102; 107; 118; 123, 124, 125; 139, 145; 147; 148, 149, 150.

[47]G. J. Cuming, *A History of Anglican Liturgy* (revised edition; London: Macmillan Press, 1982), pp. 183–184.

[48]Psalms 14:5-7, 55:16, 58, 68:21-23, 69:23-29, 109:5-19, 137:7-9, 140:9-10, 141:7-8 (The South African book, however, did not bracket Psalms 14:5-7, 55:16, 140:9-10, or 141:7-8).

[49]See Bayard Hale Jones, *The American Lectionary* (New York: Morehouse-Gorham Co., 1944).

[50]Psalms 35, 38, 58, 59, 70, 83, 109; also omitted were the following portions of other Psalms: Psalms 18:37-51, 37:25, 40:17-21, 60:6-12, 69:23-29, 89:31-51, 108:7-13, 137:7-9.

[51]Psalms 14:5-7, 55:16, 58, 68:21-23, 69:23-29, 104:35a, 109:5-19, 136:27, 137:7-9, 140:9-10, 141:7-8.

[52]*The Daily Office by the Joint Liturgical Group*, edited by Ronald C. D. Jasper (London: S.P.C.K. and The Epworth Press, 1968).

[53]Psalms 14 and 108 were omitted as duplicatory, and Psalms 58, 59, 60, 79, 83, 109, and 120 as "generally unsuitable."

[54]Psalms 53, 58, 59, 60, 63:9-11, 68:21-23, 69:24-30, 70, 79, 83, 108:7-13, 110:6-7, 120, 127, 133, 137:7-9, 139:18-33 (1979 versification).

[55]Psalms 16, 17, 22, 31, 35, 40, 51, 54, 69, 73, 88, 91, 92, 102, 107:1-32, 140, 141, 142, and 143 are appointed on Fridays, and Psalms 8, 19, 23, 24, 27, 29, 33, 34, 42, 43, 46, 63, 66, 67, 84, 93, 96, 98, 103, 104, 110, 111, 112, 113, 114, 115, 116, 117, 118, 136, 138, 139, 145, 146, 147, 148, 149, and 150 on Saturday evenings and Sundays.

[56]Other Psalms are substituted in Lent for Psalms 105, 106, 140, and 142 and in Easter Season for Psalms 22, 31, 35, 69, 73, 88, 102, and 107:1-32.

[57]Psalms 17:14, 54:5, 55:16-17, 58, 59:6 and 14, 68:21-23, 69:24-30, 79:10 and 12, 83:17, 101:6 and 9, 109:5-19, 137:7-9, 139:19-22, 140:9-11, 143:12.

[58]Cardwell, *Documentary Annals*, Vol. I, pp. 13, 19.

[59]Psalms 8 and 98 on Christmas, 96 on Epiphany, 6 on Ash Wednesday, 32, 130, and 43 on the first Sundays in Lent, 22 on Good Friday, 88 on Easter Even, 3 and 16 on Easter, 47 on Ascension, 93 on the Sunday after Ascension, 33 on Pentecost, 149 on All Saints' Day.

[60]The synoptic accounts of the passion, rather than being read on Sunday, Tuesday, and Wednesday of Holy Week, were spread over five days; an Epistle and Gospel were provided for Easter Even; proper Epistles were provided for the days of St. Barnabas, St. James, and St. Bartholomew when Ephesians 2:19-22, read on St. Thomas' Day, was to be repeated; a different Gospel was substituted on the Sunday after Christmas. and different Epistles on Circumcision, Epiphany, and the week days of Holy Week as well as the feast days of St. John, St. Philip and St. James, St. John the Baptist, St. Matthew, St. Michael and All Angels, St. Luke, and St. Simon and St. Jude; a number of lessons were lengthened slightly and a few abbreviated; a proper Epistle for Purification was dropped.

[61]In 1552 the introits and the provisions for a second Eucharist on Christmas and Easter were dropped, as well as propers for St. Mary Magdalene, and the Gospel for Pentecost was lengthened. In 1662 eschatological propers were appointed for the Sixth Sunday after Epiphany, and an Epistle was appointed

for Purification; Matthew 26, formerly the beginning of the Palm Sunday Gospel, was shifted to Morning Prayer, and the King James Version was substituted for the Great Bible translation. The 1892 book (following the 1877 Irish book) restored propers for a second Eucharist on Christmas and Easter, and also provided propers for Transfiguration. The 1928 American book provided propers for the Second Sunday after Christmas and for Ember Days and Rogation Days, and a second set of propers for Pentecost. It appointed Mark's account of the baptism of Jesus as the Gospel for the Second Sunday after Epiphany, pushing two Gospels back one Sunday and displacing the story of the Gergesene demoniac. It also appointed a different Epistle for Circumcision (Philippians 2:9-13 for Romans 4:8-14) and a different Gospel for Ascension (Luke 24:49-53 for Mark 16:14-20) and for the Ninth Sunday after Trinity (Luke 15:11-32 [the prodigal son] for Luke 16:1-9 [the wise steward]) and restored as an alternative for Maundy Thursday the account of the footwashing (John 13:1-15). It shifted Ephesians 2:19-22 from St. Thomas' Day to the feast of St. Simon and St. Jude, where it replaced Jude 1–8, and appointed Hebrews 10:35–11:1 for St. Thomas' Day.

[62]Cuming, op. cit., pp. 319–320.

[63]*The Lambeth Conference 1958* (London: S.P.C.K.; Greenwich: Seabury Press, 1958), pp. 2.82-3 [sic].

[64]*Ordo Lectionum Pro Dominicis Feriis et Festis Sanctorum* (Vatican City: Typis Polyglottis Vaticanis, 1967).

[65]For a list of readings included in the 1979 Prayer Book lectionary, arranged in biblical order, see *Lectionary Texts for Various Occasions and Occasional Services* (New York: Church Hymnal Corporation, 1983), pp. 278-320.

[66]Here the American and Canadian versions of the lectionary depart from the Roman Catholic which celebrates the Transfiguration on the Second Sunday in Lent.

[67]The 1928 American book provided one proper for "A Saint's Day"; other revisions, for example, the 1929 Scottish, the 1954 South African, and the 1959 Canadian, made more ample provisions for Black Letter Days and other occasions.

[68]John 11:25-26, Job 19:25-27, 1 Timothy 6:7, Job 1:21.

[69]Job 14:1-2, Revelation 14:13.

[70]For an English translation of this document, see E. C. Whitaker, *Martin Bucer and The Book of Common Prayer* (Great Wakering: Mayhew-McCrimmon, 1974), pp. 176-183.

[71]John Strype, *Memorials of the Most Reverend Father in God Thomas Cranmer* (Oxford: Clarendon Press, 1812), Vol. I, p. 277.

[72]H. Gee and W. J. Hardy, *Documents Illustrative of English Church History* (London: Macmillan and Co., 1910), p. 369.

[73]Other feasts devoted to angels were omitted and the phrase "and All Angels" was added to the title of this day.

[74]The 1552 revision restored four Black Letter Days, the 1561 calendar listed more than sixty, the 1604 revision added one, the 1662 two. The first American revision abolished Black Letter Days; the 1979 book restored them, listing more than one hundred.

[75]The prefaces for Christmas Day, Easter Day, Ascension Day, Pentecost, and Trinity Sunday. Omitted were prefaces for Epiphany, Ash Wednesday

("who by fasting...bestowest virtue and its rewards"), feasts of apostles and evangelists ("that through your apostles you would protect your flock"), feasts of the Holy Cross, and feasts of the Blessed Virgin Mary.

[76]The Ave Maria, antiphons, hymns, responsories, nonbiblical readings, and memorials of Mary and of the dead were stripped from the Daily Offices. The giving of salt, all but one of the exorcisms (and that was deleted in 1552), the litany of the saints, the old form for the blessing of the font and many other prayers, and the giving of the candle were omitted from the baptismal rite, and almost every form that was retained was revised. The anointing was stripped from the confirmation rite and every text revised. The blessing and sprinkling of the ring, the use of the pall, the blessing and partaking of non-eucharistic bread and wine, and many of the texts were omitted from the marriage rite. The adoration of a crucifix, the asperges, and many of the prayers were omitted from the Visitation of the Sick, and the one optional anointing retained in 1549 was dropped in 1552. The censings of the corpse, the provisions for Masses on the anniversaries of the death, special forms for particular orders or classes of people, the Dies irae, and many other forms were dropped from the burial rites.

[77]See the revision proposals of 1668 and 1689, William Whiston's *The Liturgy of the Church of England, Reduc'd Nearer to the Primitive Standard* (London, 1713), Thomas Deacon's *A Compleat Collection of Devotions, The Expediency and Necessity of Revising and Improving the Publick Liturgy* (1749), *A New Form of Common-Prayer* (1753), *A New and Correct Edition of the Book of Common Prayer* (London: J. Fletcher, 1768), *Queries Relating to the Book of Common Prayer* (1774), the revisions of Samuel Clarke, Theophilus Lindsey, and the King's Chapel, Benjamin Franklin's *Abridgement*, and John Wesley's *Sunday Service*.

[78]For twentieth-century Anglican Eucharistic rites see B. Wigan, *The Liturgy in English*, 2d ed. (London: Oxford University Press, 1964), C. O. Buchanan, *Modern Anglican Liturgies 1958–1968* (London: Oxford University Press, 1968), C. O. Buchanan, *Further Anglican Liturgies 1968–1975* (Bramcote, Nottingham: Grove Books, 1975).

[79]For example, the Communion verse at the daybreak Mass for Christmas is an expanded version of Zechariah 9:9 "Rejoice greatly,...your king comes unto you holy and the savior of the world,"

[80]For example, in the cockcrow Mass for Christmas Day the Old Testament lesson, Isaiah 9:2, 6-7, begins, "The people who walked in darkness, whom you have created, whom the enemy expelled from paradise by subtle fraud, and led captive with him to hell, have seen a great light."

[81]See E. M. Goulburn, *The Collects of the Day: An Exposition Critical and Devotional of the Collects Appointed at the Communion*, 2 vols. (London: Longmans, Green and Co., 1880); J. A. Devereaux, "Reformed Doctrine in the Collects of the First Book of Common Prayer," *Harvard Theological Review*, LVIII (January, 1965), 49-68.

[82]The Collect for Purity and the Collects for the Sixth Sunday in Lent and Fourteenth after Trinity.

[83]Collect for the Fifteenth Sunday after Trinity.

[84]Collects for Epiphany, the Second Sunday after Epiphany, Sexagesima, the Fifth and Sixth Sundays in Lent, the First after Trinity, and the feast of St. Michael and All Angels.

[85]The Third Collect at Evensong.

[86]Collect for the Fourth Sunday in Advent.

[87]Collect for the Fifth Sunday after Easter.

[88]Collect for the Fourth Sunday in Lent.

[89]Collect for the First Sunday after Trinity.

[90]Collect for the Conversion of St. Paul.

[91]Collects for the First and Fourth Sundays after Trinity.

[92]Collect for the Fourth Sunday in Advent.

[93]Collect for the First Sunday after the Epiphany.

[94]Collect for Septuagesima.

[95]Collect for the Seventh Sunday after Trinity.

[96]Collect for the Thirteenth Sunday after Trinity.

[97]Collect for the First Sunday after Trinity.

[98]Collect for the First Communion on Easter Day.

[99]Collect for the Ninth Sunday after Trinity.

[100]A prayer printed after the Litany in 1544 which entered the Prayer Book in 1559.

[101]See Collects for St. John's Day, Good Friday, the Fifteenth and Twenty-third Sundays after Trinity, and St. Bartholomew's Day.

[102]See Collects for the Fifth and Sixteenth Sundays after Trinity; "congregation" was changed to "Church" in both in 1662.

[103]See, for example, the second collects in both Matins and Evensong and the third in Evensong, the Collects for the Fifth Sunday after Epiphany and the Twentieth after Trinity, and the prayer, "O God, merciful Father," in the Litany.

[104]In the second collect at Matins "whom to know is to live" becomes "in knowledge of whom standeth our eternal life"; in the Collect for the Thirteenth Sunday after Trinity "heavenly" is inserted in "that we may so run to thy heavenly promises"; in that for Ascension Day "so we may in mind dwell in heavenly places" becomes "so that we may also in hearts and minds thither ascend, and with him continually dwell"; and in the Epiphany collect *usque ad contemplandam speciem tue celsitudinis perducamur* is translated "may after this life have the fruition of thy glorious Godhead."

[105]Collect for the Fourth Sunday after Trinity.

[106]Collects for Epiphany, Easter (First Communion), Ascension, the Conversion of St. Paul, and St. Bartholomew's Day; it is translated in the collects for Holy Innnocents' Day, Pentecost, and Purification.

[107]See, for example, the new collects for the Third Sunday in Advent, the Sixth after the Epiphany, and Easter Even (based on a 1637 collect), and the amplification of that for St. Stephen's Day in the 1662 book, or the new collect for the Transfiguration in the 1892 book, or new collects for the feast days of St. Andrew, Holy Innocents, Confession of St. Peter, St. James, Holy Cross, and St. James of Jerusalem in the 1979 book. See also the additional Prayers and Thanksgivings, and the prayers appended to the rites for Visitation of the Sick and Burial of the Dead, in the various revisions.

[108]Compare 1 Corinthians 10:3-4, 12:27, Titus 3:7, Ephesians 2:10.

[109]M. J. Hatchett, "Thomas Cranmer and the Rites of Christian Initiation" (unpublished S.T.M. thesis, General Theological Seminary, 1967), pp. 112–118.

110See the proposals of 1668 and 1689, Whiston's *Liturgy*, Deacon's *A Compleat Collection of Devotions, The Expediency and Necessity of Revising* (1749), *The Beauty of Holiness* (1752), *A New Form of Common-Prayer* (1753), *The Christian Common Prayer Book* (London: A. Millar and W. Johnston, 1761), *Queries Relating to the Book of Common Prayer* (1774), Lindsey's *The Book of Common Prayer Reformed*, Benjamin Franklin's *Abridgement*, the King's Chapel *Liturgy*, and John Wesley's *Sunday Service*.

111Louis F. Benson, *The English Hymn: Its Development and Use in Worship* (Richmond: John Knox Press, 1915), pp. 37–45.

112Reprinted in *Remains of Myles Coverdale*, ed. by George Pearson (Cambridge: University Press, 1846), pp. 533–590.

113See Nicholas Temperley, *The Music of the English Parish Church*, 2 vols. (Cambridge: University Press, 1979).

114Gee and Hardy, op. cit., p. 435.

115"Give peace in these our days" is a translation by E. Grindal of "Gieb Fried zu unser Zeit, O Herr," and "Preserve us, Lord," a translation by R. Wisdom of Luther's "Erhalt uns, Herr."

116See Edna Parks, *The Hymns and Hymn Tunes Found in the English Metrical Psalters* (New York: Coleman-Ross Company, Inc., 1966).

117See Peter Le Huray, *Music and the Reformation in England 1549–1660* (New York: Oxford University Press, 1967).

118See George Wither, *Hymns and Songs of the Church*, with an introduction by Edward Farr (London: Reeves&Turner, 1895).

119London: Thomas Harper, 1636.

120*The Psalmes of David in Meeter* [*sic*] (Edinburgh: Robert Bryson, 1641).

121*The Book of Psalms in Metre Close and Proper to the Hebrew* (London: M. Simmons, 1644).

122London: J. Humpreys, 1707.

123London: J. Clark, 1719.

124*Hymns Founded on Various Texts in the Holy Scriptures. By the Late Reverend P. Doddridge, D. D.*, ed. by Job Orton (London: J. Buckland, 1755).

125See *John Wesley's First Hymn-book*, edited by Frank Baker and George Walton Williams (Charleston: Dalcho Historical Society; London: Wesley Historical Society, 1964).

126London: W. Oliver, 1779.

127London: Henry Thorowgood. This colllection went through over a dozen editions, beginning about 1760.

128Marion J. Hatchett, "The Making of the First American Prayer Book" (Th.D. dissertation, General Theological Seminary, 1972), pp. 190–192, 356–364.

129Ibid., pp. 275–276, 300–301.

130London: John Murray, 1827.

131Benson, op. cit., pp. 349–357.

132Ibid., pp. 435–564.

Chapter 3. Reformers and Missionaries: The Bible in Eighteenth and Early Nineteeth Century England

1W. Neil, "The Criticism and Theological Use of the Bible, 1700–1950," in

The Cambridge History of the Bible, ed. S. L. Greenslade (Cambridge: Cambridge University Press, 1963), p. 247.

[2]Norman Sykes, "The Religion of Protestants," *Cambridge History*, pp. 195–196.

[3]Neil, "The Criticism and Theological Use of the Bible," p. 243.

[4]Norman Sykes, *Church and State in England in the XVIIIth Century* (Cambridge: At the University Press, 1934), pp. 257–258.

[5]Ibid., pp. 258–261.

[6]Ibid., p. 258.

[7]Cited by John D. Walsh, "Origins of the Evangelical Revival," in *Essays in Modern Church History*, ed. G. V. Bennett and J. D. Walsh (London: Black, 1961), p. 143.

[8]Sykes, *Church and State*, pp. 239–240.

[9]Ibid., p. 240.

[10]Cited by Ian Bradley, *The Call to Seriousness* (London: Jonathan Cape, 1975), p. 23.

[11]Sykes, "Religion of Protestants," p. 198.

[12]William Wilberforce, *Practical View of the Prevailing Religious Conceptions of Professed Christians in the High and Middle Classes in This Country Contrasted with Real Christianity* (Boston: Crocker and Brewater, 1829), p. 138.

[13]William Romaine, *The Life, Walk, and Triumph of Faith*, intro. by Peter Toon (Cambridge and London: James Clarke and Co., 1970), p. 263.

[14]Charles Simeon, *Horae Homileticae*, 8th ed. (London: Henry G. Bohn, 1847) 9:136–137.

[15]John Wesley, *Works*, 1st Am. ed. (New York, 1839) 2:126–127.

[16]Ibid., p. 128.

[17]Ibid., p. 129.

[18]Thomas Scott, *The Holy Bible, containing the Old and New Testaments, with original notes, practical observations, and copious references*, 6 vols. (New York: Williams and Whiting, 1810) 1:iii.

[19]Ibid., p. iv.

[20]Ibid., p. v.

[21]Ibid., p. x.

[22]Ibid., p. xv.

[23]Ibid.

[24]Ibid., p. xvi.

[25]Wesley, *Works*, 2:128.

[26]Hugh Evan Hopkins, *Charles Evan Hopkins, Charles Simeon of Cambridge* (Grand Rapids, Michigan: William B. Eerdmans Publishing Co., 1977), p. 173.

[27]Ibid., p. 177.

[28]C. M. Chavasse, "Simeon and His Love for the Bible," in *Charles Simeon. An Interpretation* (London: Lutterworth Press, 1936), p. 68. On Simeon, as well as Scott, see also Stanley Brown-Serman, "The Evangelicals and the Bible," in *Anglican Evangelicalism*, A. C. Zabriskie, ed. (Philadelphia: The Church Historical Society, 1943), pp. 87–93.

[29]Simeon, *Horae Homileticae*, 6:251–252.

[30]Wesley, *Works*, 6:555.

[31]Simeon, *Horae Homileticae*, 1:vi–vii.

[32]Hopkins, *Simeon*, p. 59.

[33] Chavasse, "Simeon," p. 50.

[34]John Newton, *Works* (New York: Daniel Fanshaw, 1823) 6:418.

[35]Chavasse, "Simeon," p. 65, quoting sermons 520, 20, 205, 520.

[36] Ibid., pp. 63–67. The interpretation here is based upon that of Chavasse.

[37]William Meade, *The True Churchman* (Charlottesville, Va.: James Alexander, 1851), pp. 20–21.

[38]Charles Smyth, *Simeon and Church Order* (Cambridge: At the University Press, 1940), p. 23.

[39]See my essay, "Joseph Hall, *The Arte of Divine Meditation*, and Anglican Spirituality," forthcoming in *The Spirituality of Western Christendom III*, from Cistercian Publications.

[40]Romaine, *The Life, Walk, and Triumph of Faith*, p. 265.

[41]Henry Venn, *To Apply the Gospel. Selections from the Writings of Henry Venn* (Grand Rapids, Michigan: William B. Eerdmans Publishing Co., 1971), p. 74.

[42]Simeon, *Horae Homileticae*, 1:xxiv.

[43]*Brief View of the Plan and Operations of the British and Foreign Bible Society* (London: British and Foreign Bible Soc., 1875), p. 1.

[44]Eric Fenn, "The Bible and the Missionary," *Cambridge History of the Bible*, p. 407. This valuable essay has been useful in retelling the story here.

[45]Venn, *To Apply the Gospel*, p. 127.

[46]Fenn, "The Bible and the Missionary," p. 399.

[47]*Brief View*, p. 10.

[48]Venn, *To Apply the Gospel*, p. 171.

[49]In Eugene Fairweather, ed., *The Oxford Movement* (New York: Oxford University Press, 1964), p. 44.

[50]Charles Daubeny, *A Guide to the Church, in Several Discourses*, 3rd ed. (London: F. C. and J. Rivington, 1830), Discourse 1, p. 5.

[51]See Vernon F. Storr, *The Development of English Theology in the Nineteenth Century, 1800–1860* (London: Longmans, Green and Co., 1913), pp. 83–84.

[52]Daubeny, *A Guide to the Church*, Discourse 2, p. 20.

[53]Owen Chadwick, *The Mind of the Oxford Movement* (Stanford, Calif.: Stanford University Press, 1961), p. 38.

[54] Ibid., p. 127.

[55]Bernard M. G. Reardon, *From Coleridge to Gore. A Century of Religious Thought in Britain (London: Longman Group Ltd., 1971), pp. 286–287.*

Chapter 4. Historical Criticism and the Bible

[1]See George Bernard Shaw, "The Monstrous Imposition Upon Jesus," repr. in *The Writings of St. Paul*, ed. Wayne A. Meeks (New York: Norton, 1972), pp. 296–302.

[2]E. C. Hoskyns and F. N. Davey, *The Riddle of the New Testament* (London: Faber, 1931), p. 10.

[3]The classic statement of historical-critical methodology is that of Ernst Troeltsch in an essay which first appeared in 1898 under the title "Über

historische und dogmatische Methode in der Theologie." Repr. E. Troeltsch, *Theologie als Wissenschaft*, ed. G. Sauter *ThB* 43 (1971), pp. 105–127. See the discussion in P. Stuhlmacher, *Historical Criticism and Theological Interpretation of Scripture*, Tr. R. A. Harrisville (Philadelphia: Fortress, 1977), pp. 44–46.

[4]J. S. Semler, *Abhandlung vom freien Gebrauch des Kanons* (1771–74), repr. and ed. H. Scheible (Gutersloh: Mohn, 1967); J. D. Michaelis, *Einleitung in die göttlichen Schriften des Neuen Bundes* (4th ed., 1788)—introducing the historical approach to the New Testament writings. This approach had already been anticipated by a French Roman Catholic scholar, Richard Simon (1638–1712), in his *Histoire critique du vieux Testament* (1673). Simon rejected the Mosaic authorship of the Pentateuch and recognized "doublets," i.e., duplicate accounts of the same events.

[5]J. J. Griesbach, *Commentatio* (Jena, 1789). It should be noted that Griesbach's theory was anticipated by a London Welsh Anglican clergyman, Henry Owen, in *Observations on the Four Gospels* (London, 1766).

[6]The Eliot translation (4th ed.) was reissued with an Introduction by Peter C. Hodgson, *The Life of Jesus Critically Examined* (Philadelphia: Fortress, 1972).

[7]*Essays and Reviews*, Frederick Temple and others (London: Longmans, 1861).

[8]J. Percival, quoted in S. C. Carpenter, *Church and People 1789–1889* (London: SPCK, 1933), p. 505.

[9]A copy of Augustus Hare's *Life and Letters of Baroness Bunsen* (2 vols.; London: Daldys, 1879) came into my possession when the Harford family finally vacated Falcondale House, Lampeter, in 1954.

[10]Cited by Alan Richardson, *Preface to Bible Study* (London:SCM, 1943), p. 25 from J. Estlin Carpenter, *The Bible in the Nineteenth Century* (London: Longmans, 1903).

[11]Urban T. Holmes III in a companion volume in this series, *What is Anglicanism?* (Wilton, Ct.: Morehouse-Barlow, 1982), p. 19, credits the Cambridge trio with "initiating the Anglican tradition of biblical criticism." If by that tradition we mean a sober corrective to German speculation, the same claim might be made for H. Marsh (see above),

[12]"Die Christuspartei in der korinthischen Gemeinde," repr. in F. C. Baur, *Ausgewählte Werke in Einzelausgaben*, ed. K. Scholder (Stuttgart-Bad Canstatt: Fromann, 1963) I:1–76.

[13]Baur followed Griesbach's solution to the synoptic problem. See R. H. Fuller, "Baur Versus Hilgenfeld: A Forgotten Chapter in the Debate on the Synoptic Problem," *NTS* 24 (1978), pp. 355–370.

[14]This startingly late date was triumphantly and objectively refuted by the discovery of the "Roberts fragment" in 1935. See C. H. Roberts, *An Unpublished Fragment of the Fourth Gospel* (Manchester: University Press, 1935). This papyrus fragment emanates from Egypt, 125–40, so we know that John's Gospel was actually circulating there at that time!

[15]Quoted from I. H. Marshall, ed., *New Testament Interpretation* (Grand Rapids, Mich.: Eerdmans, 1977). A full account of the work of the Cambridge trio will be found in S. Neill, *The Interpretation of the New Testament* (Oxford: University Press, 1964), pp. 61–97.

[16]B. M. Metzger, "The Westcott and Hort Greek New Testament, Yesterday and Today," *The Cambridge Review* (20 November 1981), pp. 71–76, esp. 76.

[17]Such is the judgment of S. C. Carpenter, *Church and People* (note 8), p. 536.

[18]*Lux Mundi*, ed. C. Gore (London: Murray, 15th ed., 1899),p. 252.

[19]Ibid.

[20]Ibid., p. 254.

[21]Ibid., p. 256.

[22]Ibid., p. 158.

[23]Ibid.

[24]A. M. Ramsey, *An Era in Anglican Theology: From Gore to Temple* (New York: Scribner's, 1960), pp. 8–9.

[25]*Studies in the Synoptic Problem*, By members of the University of Oxford. Ed. W. Sanday (Oxford: Clarendon, 1911). The two document hypothesis is the view that Mark was the earliest gospel and was used by Matthew and Luke, who also had access to a hypothetical non-Marcan source commonly designated Q (a siglum usually said to be derived from the German word *Quelle = source*, *though this has been disputed*).

[26]*See* V. H. Stanton, *The Gospels as Historical Documents*, Parts I and II (Cambridge: University Press, 1903–1910); F. C. Burkitt, *The Gospel History and Its Transmission* (Edinburgh: T. & T. Clark, 1906). Burkitt was C. H. Dodd's predecessor in the Norrisian chair. An Anglican layman, he established his right to wear a black scarf (tippet) with his D.D. gown.

[27]On Thompson see W. N. Pittenger, "James Matthew Thompson, the Martyr of English Modernism," *ATR* XXXIX (1957), pp. 291–297.

[28]G. L. Prestige, *The Life of Charles Gore* (London: Heinemann, 1935), pp. 343–344.

[29]*Foundations: A Statement of Christian Belief in Terms of Modern Thought*, ed. B. H. Streeter (London: Macmillan, 1912, repr. 1920).

[30]Convocation of Canterbury, April 29, 1914. Quoted by A. M. Ramsey, *An Era* (n. 24), p. 82.

[31]H. H. Henson, *Retrospect of an Unimportant Life* (Oxford: University Press, 1944) I:214.

[32]*Essays Catholic and Critical*, ed. E. G. Selwyn (London: SPCK, 1926, repr. 1929).

[33]The present writer had the good fortune to have Sir Edwyn Hoskyns as his supervisor during the last year of Hoskyns' life (1936–37).

[34]One day when I reported to Hoskyns that J. N. Sanders, another of his pupils, was toying with the idea that the Beloved Disciple was Lazarus, and that form criticism, having destroyed the historicity of the Marcan framework, justified a more historical view of the Fourth Gospel, Hoskyns said to me: "I hope Sanders is not going obscurantist like so many young German students now-a-days." That was of course before the (post-war) ascendency of Bultmann.

[35]Hoskyns' position on critical matters and his caution in allowing "assured results" is discernable in an appendix to *The Riddle* (note 2), pp. 265–288.

[36]C. Gore, H. L. Gouge and A. Guillaume, eds., *A New Commentary on Holy Scripture* (London: SPCK, 1928). All the contributors were Anglicans.

[37]Contrast, e.g., A. H. McNeile, *Introduction to the New Testament*, rev. C. H. S.

Williams (Oxford: Clarendon, 1952) with W. Marxsen, *Introduction to the New Testament* (Philadelphia: Fortress, 1964).

[38]J. T. Addison, *The Episcopal Church in the United States 1789–1931* (New York: Scribner's, 1951), p. 247. Of the various histories of the Episcopal Church (Manross, Chorley), Addison devotes the most space to the rise of historical criticism of the Bible and creeds.

[39]This motto is attributed to Dr. Sparrow of the Virginia Seminary but its precise origin is uncertain.

[40]Addison (note 38), p. 249.

[41]Very instructive for this Calvinistic Anglicanism is W. H. Wilmer, *An Episcopal Manual* (Philadelphia: George, 1841).

[42]A. R. Goodwin, *History of the Theological Seminary in Virginia*, 2 vols. (New York: Gorham, 1923) I:351.

[43]Cf. also R. H. Newton, *The Book of the Beginnings: A Study of Genesis with an Introduction to the Pentateuch* (New York: Putnam, 1884). Both works are protests against the prevailing conservatism of their day.

[44]A full accocunt of the Newton case will be found in G. Hodges, *Henry Codman Potter* (New York: Macmillan, 1915), pp. 135–145.

[45]Hodges, *Potter* (note 44), p. 139.

[46]Hodges, *Potter*, p. 303. This combination of criticism with orthodoxy is a striking anticipation of the later neo-orthodoxy. Cf. our remark on Hensley Henson above.

[47]F. Gavin, ed., *Liberal Catholicism on the Modern World*, vol. 1 (Milwaukee, Wis.: Morehouse, 1934).

[48]On Grammer see Goodwin, *History* (note 42) I:661–663.

[49]A. R. Vidler, ed., *Soundings: Essays Concerning Christian Understanding* (Cambridge: University Press, 1962). This volume elicited replies whose titles drew further on nautical metaphors from Acts 27; E. Mascall, *Up and Down in Adria* (London: Faith Press, 1963) and Alan Richardson, *Four Anchors from the Stern* (London: SCM, 1963). The latter work also responds to A. R. Vidler's *Objections to Christian Belief* and to *Honest to God* (see below).

[50]J. A. T. Robinson, *Honest to God* (London: SCM, 1963). Reactions to this work were collected in *The Honest to God Debate*, ed. D. E. Edwards (London: SCM, 1963),

[51]J. A. T. Robinson, *Redating the New Testament* (London: SCM, 1976). When the author gave the present writer a copy before its publication in the United States he said, "You won't believe any of this."

[52]G. Edmundson, *The Church of Rome in the First Century* (London: Longmans, Green, 1913). J. Fitzmyer has commented on Robinson's book, "It is difficult to respond to a writer who likes to shift the burden of proof to others and characterizes as "dogmatic" (an adjective very dear to Robinson) any view that he opposes." *The Gospel according to Luke*, Anchor Bible 28 (Garden City, N.Y.: Doubleday, 1981), p. 55.

[53]*St. Luke's Journal of Theology* 23 (1980), pp. 90–100.

Chapter 5. Science and the Bible

[1]See Huston Smith, "Science and Theology: The Unstable Detente," in *Anglican Theological Review* LXIII (1981):367. Hereafter cited as "Science." The

methodological aspect of this chapter is heavily indebted to Smith's short article.

[2]Frederick H. Borsch, "All Things Necessary to Salvation," p. 225.

[3]Ludwig Feuerbach, *The Essence of Christianity*, trans. George Elliot (New York: Harper and Brothers, 1957), p. 51. This statement is repeated with many variations in *The Essence of Christianity*.

[4]Feuerbach, *The Essence of Christianity*, as quoted by K. Barth, "An Intorductory Essay," *The Essence of Christianity*, p. xvii.

[5]Cf. Mircea Eliade, *Cosmos and History*, trans. Willard R. Trask (Princeton: Princeton University Press, 1954), especially chap. 4.

[6]The following discussion is indebted to Huston Smith's "Science," *Anglican Theological Review* LXIII:367.

[7]Cf. Walker Percy, *Lost in the Cosmos* (New York: Farrar, Straus, and Giroux, 1983), p. 115.

[8]Cf. Smith, "Science," *Anglican Theological Review* LXIII:370.

[9]Smith, "Science," *Anglican Theological Review* LXIII:374.

[10]Percy, op. cit., p. 115.

[11]Eliade, op. cit., p. 160.

[12]Smith, "Science," *Anglican Theological Review*LXIII:372.

[13]Darwin himself had a more modest estimate of the scope of his theory. By "Darwin's theory" I understand the pervasive contemporary understanding of that theory.

[14]Quoted by Huston Smith, *Forgotten Truth: The Primordial Tradition* (New York: Harper and Row, 1976), p. 126.

[15]Smith, ibid., p. 122.

[16]Smith, ibid., pp. 130–131.

[17]Cf. Smith, ibid., p. 132.

[18]Cf. W. Neil, "The Criticism and Theological Use of the Bible," in *The Cambridge History of the Bible*, ed. S. L. Greenslade (Cambridge: Cambridge University Press, 1963), pp. 255–265. For a fuller account of the controversies surrounding Darwin see C. E. Raven, *Science and Religion* (Cambridge: Cambridge University Press, 1953), Chap. IX. For a review of the direction the more recent debates have taken, particularly within the scientific community, see Stanley L. Jaki, *Cosmos and Creator* (Chicago: Regnery Gateway, Inc., 1980), Chap. 1.

[19]John Tyler Bonner, "Evolution and Darwinism," a reading guide published by Princeton University Press, 1975. No pagination.

[20]Micahel Polanyi, *Personal Knowledge* (Chicago: University of Chicago Press, 1978), pp. 382–383, 384.

[21]Karl Stern, *The Flight from Woman*, quoted by E. F. Schumaker, *A Guide for the Perplexed* (New York: Harper and Row, 1977), p. 113.

[22]Cf. Polanyi, op. cit., p. 350. Polanyi supplies the relevant technical data as available in the early 1950s. Whether or not these figures are still precise is not relevant to our argument.

[23]Cited by Smith, *Forgotten Truth*, pp. 131–132.

[24]Loren Eiseley, "Fossil man," in *Scientific American* CLXXXIX (Dec. 1953): 65.

[25]Douglas Dewar, *The Transformist Illusion (Murfeesboro, Tennessee: Dehoff Publication, 1957).*

[26]*Cf. Smith, Forgotten Truth,* p. 134 *et passim.* Smith cites a variety of sources to support his position.

[27]Chicago: Uniiversity of Chicago Press; 2nd ed., 1970.

[28]Owen Barfield, *Saving the Appearances: A Study in Idolatry* (New York: Harcourt, Brace, & World, n.d.), p. 64.

[29] Smith, *Forgotten Truth,* p. 138.

[30]Smith, *Forgotten Truth,* p. 131.

[31] Polanyi, op. cit., p. 390.

[32]Polanyi, ibid., p. 389.

[33]Polanyi, ibid., p. 385.

[34]Polanyi, ibid., p. 408.

[35]Barfield, op. cit., p. 167.

[36]Smith, "Science," *Anglican Theological Review* LXIII:379.

Chapter 6. All Things Necessary to Salvation

[1]The shift in emphasis on the role of Scripture is helpfully delineated through official Anglican statements by R. H. Fuller in "The Authority of the Scriptures in Anglicanism," in *The Report of the Lutheran-Episcopal Dialogue,* Second Series, 1976–80 (Cincinnati: Forward Movement Press, 1981), pp. 87–113.

[2]Charles Gore, *The Creed of Christians* (London: Wells, Gardner, Darton and Co. Ltd., 1895), pp. 63 and 66. See also his important and at one time controversial essay, "The Holy Spirit and Inspiration" in *Lux Mundi: A Series of Studies in the Religion of the Incarnation,* ed. Gore (London: John Murray, 1890), pp. 315–362. For Gore's mature views cf. *The Holy Spirit and the Church,* pp. 244–279.

[3]S. W. Sykes, *The Integrity of Anglicanism* (New York: Seabury Press, 1978), p. 99.

[4]See André Benoit, "The Transmission of the Gospels in the First Centuries" in the *Gospel as History,* ed. V. Vajta (Philadelphia: Fortress Press, 1975), pp. 145–168.

[5]On the participatory character of oral presence and the radical transformation that took place when the gospel was given the form of a written text, see W. H. Kelber, *The Oral and the Written Gospel: the Hermeneutics of Speaking and Writing in the Synoptic Tradition, Mark, Paul, and Q* (Philadelphia: Fortress Press, 1983).

[6]The importance of the community context is frequently restated in the Anglican tradition. "The Report of the Commission on Christian Doctrine appointed by the Archbishops of Canterbury and York in 1922," which reported in 1937, *Doctrine in the Church of England* (New York: Macmillan, 1938) begins: "The faith and doctrine of Christianity are handed down to us in the context of a living fellowship," p. 27. See also William Countryman, *Biblical Authority or Biblical Tyranny? Scripture and the Christian Pilgrimage* (Philadelphia: Fortress Press, 1981), pp. 59–75. The theme recurs throughout the essays in

Believing in the Church: The Corporate Nature of Faith, A Report by the Doctrine Commission of the Church of England (Wilton, Conn.: Morehouse-Barlow, 1982).

[7]See James Barr, "The Bible as a Document of Believing Communities," in *The Scope and Authority of the Bible* (Philadelphia: Westminster, 1980), pp. 111–113, also p. 109.

[8]See the discussion of conflicts and polarities in the Bible (especially those of visionary/pragmatic and form/reform) by P. D. Hanson, *The Diversity of Scripture: A Theological Interpretation* (Philadelphia: Fortress Press, 1982).

[9]Paul Ricoeur in his essay "Biblical Hermeneutics" in *Semeia* 4 (1975), *Paul Ricoeur on Biblical Hermeneutics,* ed. J. D. Crossan, p. 114. Ricoeur uses the phrase in connection with proverbial statements, but it can also apply to parables. Cf. his discussion of the extravagance of the parables and the extraordinary in the ordinary, op. cit., p. 115.

[10]Cf. J. D. Crossan, *In Parables: The Challenge of the Historical Jesus* (New York, etc.: Harper & Row, 1973) and *Finding Is the First Act: Trove Folktales and Jesus' Treasure Parable* (Philadelphia: Fortress Press, 1979).

[11]See Robert Alter, *The Art of Biblical Narrative* (New York: Basic Books, 1981) and more generally Northrop Frye, *The Great Code: The Bible and Literature* (New York: Harcourt Brace Jovanovich, 1981). For further references dealing with the role of narrative in the Bible and the relationship to theology, see n. 27, pp. 27–28 in F. H. Borsch, "Ears That Hear and Do Not Hear" in *Scripture Today: Handling the Word Rightly,* ed. D. R. McDonald (Wilton, Conn.: Morehouse-Barlow, 1980).

[12]See Hans Frei, *The Eclipse of Biblical Narrative: A Study in Eighteenth and Nineteenth Century Hermeneutics* (New Haven: Yale University, 1974).

[13]Cf. Sallie McFague, *Metaphorical Theology: Models of God in Religious Language* (Philadelphia: Fortress Press, 1983), especially pp. 31–66.

[14]See Stanley Hauerwas, "Casuistry as a Narrative Art," *Interpretation* XXXVII/4 (Oct. 1983), pp. 377–388.

[15]On the place this issue played in Temple's life and thought see F. A. Iremonger, *William Temple, Archbiship of Canterbury: His Life and Letters* (London: Oxford University Press, 1948), pp. 163, 461. Temple's mature view is probably fairly represented in *Doctrine in the Church of England,* pp. 81–83.

[16]For a discussion of the resurrection in the light of historical critical interpretation, see F. H. Borsch, *God's Parable* (Philadelphia: Westminster, 1976), pp. 1–26.

[17]In his *The Use and Abuse of the Bible: A Study of the Bible in an Age of Rapid Change* (New York: Harper & Row, 1976) Dennis Nineham emphasizes the gap in the world views that has become particularly pronounced in recent generations. More optimistic about the hermeneutical task and the possibility of understanding across the ages is A. C. Thiselton, *The Two Horizons: New Testament Hermeneutics and Philosophical Description* (Grand Rapids, Mich.: Eerdmans, 1980). See especially pp. 51–63.

[18]Cf. my discussion in "Ears That Hear and Do Not Hear" in *Scripture Today,* pp. 23–49.

[19]The phrase is Frei's (see n. 12). See also "Story and History in Biblical Theology" in James Barr's *The Scope and Authority of the Bible,* pp. 1–17.

[20]On this process and the so-called hermeneutical circle and the problem of

pre-understanding, see Thiselton, *The Two Horizons*, pp. 103–114 and *passim* and also D. H. Kelsey, *the Uses of Scripture in Recent Theology* (Philadelphia: Fortress Press, 1975) who particularly stresses the community context in preforming ways of understanding and using the Bible.

[21]See, e.g., David Stacey, *Interpreting the Bible* (New York: Hawthorn Books, 1977), especially pp. 43–49 and Bruce Vawter, *Biblical Inspiration* (Philadelphia: Westminster, 1972).

[22]See in the *Catechism* or "An Outline of Faith" in *The Book of Common Prayer* (1979) of The Episcopal Church, p. 853. A. E. Harvey thoughtfully draws the familiar parallel by maintaining that the Bible "is inspired by the same God who accepted the constraints of the incarnation." "Attending to Scripture" in *Believing in the Church*, pp. 25–44. Quote from p. 36.

[23]See J. V. Taylor, *The Go-Between God: The Holy Spirit and the Mission of the Church* (Philadelpia: Fortress Press, 1973).

[24]Cf. again Thiselton, *The Two Horizons*. See Edward Schillebeeckx, *Christ, The Experience of Jesus as Lord* (New York: Seabury Press, 1980), pp. 30–79.

[25]The phrase is H. G. Gadamer's *(Wirkungsgeschichte)*. See his *Truth and Method* (New York: Seabury Press, 1975), p. 268.

[26]See above, pp. 203-204.

[27]Cf. my description of this process in *Introducing the Lessons of the Church Year: A Guide for Lay Readers and Congregations* (New York: Seabury Press, 1978), pp. 4–7.

[28]This understanding of the *consensus fidelium* comes across particularly strongly in the report of the Lambeth Conference of 1948 dealing with the Anglican view of authority.

[29]Leonard Hodgson, *Sex and Christian Freedom* (London: SCM Press, 1967), p. 42.

[30]J. E. Booty, *What Makes Us Episcopalians?* (Wilton, Conn.: Morehouse-Barlow, 1982), p. 32.

[31]Cf. my fuller discussion of Luke 10:25-37 in *Power in Weakness: New Hearing for Gospel Stories of Healing and Discipleship* (Philadelphia: Fortress Press, 1983), pp. 85–98.

[32]I copied these words of Brooks some years ago and now cannot find their place in his works. I would be pleased to know where they can be found.

[33]Article XX of "The Articles of Religion."

[34]See R. P. C. Hanson in *The Continuity of Christian Doctrine* (New York: Seabury Press, 1981), p. 78. Hanson goes on to stress the dangers involved in not making these judgments and in building whole doctrines based on one verse of Scripture.

[35]See A. N. Wilder, *Jesus' Parables and the War of Myths: Essays on Imagination in the Scriptures*, ed. James Breech (Philadelphia: Fortress Press, 1982).

[36]Cf. Walter Brueggemann, *In Man We Trust: The Neglected Side of Biblical Faith* (Atlanta: John Knox, 1972).

[37]See *The Liberating Word: A Guide to Nonsexist Interpretation of the Bible*, ed. L. M. Russell (Philadelphia: Westminster, 1976) and McFague, *Metaphorical Theology*, pp. 145–192.

[38]See the passionate statement on the significance of this freedom by Ernst Käsemann, *Jesus Means Freedom* (Philadelphia: Fortress Press, 1972).

[39]Gregory I in a letter written in 595 as a dedication of his book on Job to Leander, Archbishop of Seville. *Gregorii I Papae Registrum Epistolarum*, Vol. I, ed. Paul Ewald and L. M. Hartmann (Monumenta Germaniae Historica: Epistolarum) Berlin, 1891, p. 357.

Contributors

FREDERICK HOUK BORSCH is Dean of the Chapel and Lecturer with the rank of Professor in the Department of Religion at Princeton University. He is a graduate of Princeton University (A.B.), Oxford University (M.A.), the General Theological Seminary (S.T.B.), and the University of Birmingham (Ph.D.). He was formerly Dean and Professor of New Testament at the Church Divinity School of the Pacific. He is the author of a number of books, including *The Son of Man in Myth and History*, *God's Parable*, and *Power in Weakness*.

WILLIAM P. HAUGAARD is the Diocese of Chicago Professor of Church History at Seabury-Western Theological Seminary. A graduate of Princeton University (A.B.) and the General Theological Seminary (S.T.B. and Th.D.), he was formerly dean of the Seminario Episcopal del Caribe and chancellor of the Caribbean Center for Advanced Studies. Along with a number of scholarly and more popular articles and essays, and presently engaged in preparing a portion of the commentary on the Folger Library Edition of *The Works of Richard Hooker*, he is the author of *Elizabeth and the English Reformation*.

MARION JOSIAH HATCHETT is the Professor of Liturgics and Music at the School of Theology, University of the South,

Sewanee, Tennessee. He is a graduate of Wofford College (A.B.), University of the South (B.D.), and the General Theological Seminary (S.T.M. and Th.D.). For fourteen years he served churches in South Carolina, his native state. He is the author of *Sanctifying Life, Time and Space, The Making of the First American Book of Common Prayer, Commentary on the American Prayer Book*, and a number of other works.

JOHN E. BOOTY is Dean of the School of Theology, University of the South, Sewanee, Tennessee. He is a graduate of Wayne University (B.A.), Virginia Theological Seminary (B.D.), and Princeton University (M.A. and Ph.D.). He was formerly Associate Professor of Church History at Virginia Seminary, and Professor of Church History at the Episcopal Divinity School. He is author of *The Church in History, The Servant Church*, and *Meditations on Four Quartets*, and is editor of *The Godly Kingdom of Tudor England*, and Vol. 4 of the Folger Library Edition of *The Works of Richard Hooker*.

REGINALD H. FULLER is Molly Laird Downs Professor of New Testament at Virginia Theological Seminary in Alexandria, Virginia. He was a scholar of Peterhouse, Cambridge (B.A., first class honors, and M.A.). He also studied at the University of Tübingen and at The Queens College, Birmingham. He has taught at St. David's College, Lampeter, Wales, at Seabury-Western Theological Seminary, and at Union Theological Seminary in New York where he was Baldwin Professor of New Testament. He is the author and translator of several books, including *The Formation of the Resurrection Narratives*.

WILLIAM TAYLOR STEVENSON is Professor of Philosophical Theology at Seabury-Western Theological Seminary. He is a graduate of Princeton University (A.B.), Virginia Theological

Seminary (B.D.), and Durham University (Ph.D.). He was formerly Associate Professor of Theology at Marquette University. He is the author of *History as Myth: The Import for Contemporary Theology*, and he was editor of the *Anglican Theological Review* from 1970 to 1983.